Effective Computer Display Design

William W. Banks
Oxford Research Institute
and
San Jose State University

Jon Weimer, Ph.D.
Oxford Research Institute
and
General Motors Corporation
(Advanced Product
Engineering)

Prentice Hall
Englewood Cliffs, New Jersey 07632

Library of Congress Cataloging-in-Publication Data

Weimer, Jon.
    Effective computer display design / Jon Weimer, William W. Banks.
        p.   cm.
    Includes bibliographical references and index.
    ISBN 0-13-401027-2
    1. Computer terminals. 2. Video display terminals.   I. Banks,
William W. II. Title.
    TK7887.8.T4W45 1992   92-4768
    005.7--dc20   CIP

Editorial/production supervision: *Laura A. Huber*
Production assistant: *Jane Bonnell*
Acquisitions editor: *Michael Hays*
Editorial assistant: *Dana L. Mercure*
Cover design: *Wanda Lubelska*
Pre-press buyer: *Mary Elizabeth McCartney*
Manufacturing buyer: *Susan Brunke*

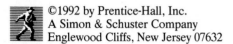 ©1992 by Prentice-Hall, Inc.
A Simon & Schuster Company
Englewood Cliffs, New Jersey 07632

The publisher offers discounts on this book when
ordered in bulk quantities. For more information,
write:

      Special Sales/Professional Marketing
      Prentice Hall
      Professional & Technical Reference Division
      Englewood Cliffs, New Jersey 07632

The opinions expressed in this work are exclusively those of the authors and do not represent the
opinions of General Motors, Lawrence Livermore National Labs, the University of California,
or San Jose State University.

Printed in the United States of America

10 9 8 7 6 5 4 3 2 1

ISBN 0-13-401027-2

Prentice-Hall International (UK) Limited, *London*
Prentice-Hall of Australia Pty. Limited, *Sydney*
Prentice-Hall Canada Inc., *Toronto*
Prentice-Hall Hispanoamericana, S.A., *Mexico*
Prentice-Hall of India Private Limited, *New Delhi*
Prentice-Hall of Japan, Inc., *Tokyo*
Simon & Schuster Asia Pte. Ltd., *Singapore*
Editora Prentice-Hall do Brasil, Ltda., *Rio de Janeiro*

DEDICATION

This book is dedicated to the memory of the following people who have indelibly touched our lives. We miss you.

Mr.   William W. Banks, Sr.
Mr.   William Howard Green
Dr.   Vernon J. Perez
Ms.   Darla Tubbs
Ms.   Gay Tiernan Walton
Ms.   Donna Lee Weimer

TABLE OF CONTENTS

CHAPTER 5   Information Coding

CHAPTER 6   Using Color in Displays

CHAPTER 7   From Screens to Dialog

List of Figures

List of Tables

List of Case Studies

PREFACE
Why Is This Book Different?

This book is about straight talk -- the straight talk of computer display design. There are many books available that profess to show you how to design better computer interfaces. Many of them do just that. Most of them, however, make you wade through long discussions of research and then leave you to draw your own conclusions. This fails you in a number of ways.

First, long descriptions of theoretically interesting research fail the practitioner by not giving them anything they can use on their job, therefore wasting the time of the practitioner. Second, such an approach fails students by giving them a bank of theoretical knowledge that may or may not be applicable in the real world. Some of the newer books have tried to bridge the gap between theory and practice by introducing sample guidelines without tying them to the text, which remains largely theory. Our book is different.

We are not academicians, though we have held academic posts. We are practitioners in the field of the human factors of computer display design. Consequently, our book is a little different than most. Theoretical discussions are kept to a minimum, unless needed to illustrate a particular point. On the other hand, this is not a book of guidelines. This is a book that you can use to help you start doing your job better **TODAY**!

This book is geared to the industry practitioner and for academic programs that are preparing computer interface designers for careers in business rather than academia. It draws upon our years of experience in industry to present you with checklists, worksheets, case studies, and sample guidelines that you can use on the job to be more productive. This book takes a business-oriented approach and presents user interface design as a means of decreasing corporate expense and increasing corporate revenue, rather than a pie-in-the-sky value add. We firmly believe that the principles, if followed as they are outlined in this book, in the long run, will increase corporate profits and decrease corporate losses by creating information systems that result in greater user productivity and fewer user errors.

While each chapter in this book is fairly modular in nature, the arrangement of the chapters is intentional, and we do not advise academic digression from this arrangement. Inasmuch as possible, each chapter corresponds to a specific activity in the design of computer displays. The arrangement of the chapters corresponds, roughly, to the sequence in which each of the activities is performed, keeping in mind that good design is iterative in nature.

Chapter 1 presents you with a corporate context for the design of computing systems. It presents the topic of human error as a major "hidden" source of lost corporate revenue. We present you with a technique that you can use to determine the financial impact of user errors on your corporation, and offer some suggestions as to what can be done to reduce user errors in a computing system. This chapter also contains a valuable checklist for assessing the user error risk of your current system.

Chapter 2 is a rigorous tutorial on performing a task analysis. This chapter is unique in that we have never seen a book on computer display design with a chapter on task analysis. Rather than present you with a historical perspective or the theoretical bases for performing a task analysis, we have opted to explain that task analysis is the next logical step to take once a corporate commitment has been made to reduce user errors and increase user productivity. We outline the basics of the technique and show, through example, how the analysis is performed. We introduce the topic of the User Profile Worksheet and show how it can be used to define the characteristics of the user population. The chapter ends with a collection of blank task analysis worksheets that can be photocopied and used on the job.

Chapter 3 is also unique in that it deals with the topic of designing a system with constraints. More theoretically-oriented books skirt this very important issue, concerning themselves more with lecturing the reader on the "shoulds" of human-computer interface designs. For instance, a $3,000 piece of technology might improve a driver's performance, but it is unlikely that someone who is buying a $10,000 automobile will pay $3,000 for an option. In addition to market constraints, we also discuss political constraints, environmental constraints, hardware constraints, and more. After all, designers in the real world have to deal with constraints every day.

Chapter 4 shows you how to take the results of the task analysis and match those results to numerous types of screen elements to find the best "fit" between the presentation of the information and the task. Types of elements discussed are mimic displays, computer-driven analog displays, windowed displays, and others.

Chapter 5 presents information on the coding of displays and gives you a number of very valuable reference tables that you can use when making a determination as to how to code complex information so that the performance of users is enhanced with increasing levels of information, rather than impaired.

Chapter 6 presents an in-depth discussion of color as a coding scheme. As the cost of color monitors and color graphics cards decrease, more and more designers are starting to use color as a coding strategy. Deceptively simple in its appearance, color is one of the most complex coding strategies. For that reason, and because of the myriad of different impacts that color has on the performance of users, we have devoted an entire chapter to the design of color displays. We have also included a number of useful tables and guidelines to help you choose a strategy when designing color screens.

Chapter 7 deals with integrating the screens together through selection of an appropriate dialog. Computer dialogs can make or break a system and must be closely matched to the needs of the user. Emphasis is placed on matching the results of the task analysis and user profile to the design of a computer dialog that integrates the designed screens. Extensive design advice is offered for each dialog type.

Appendix A provides you with a sample set of computer interface guidelines. This set of guidelines is sufficiently complete to act as a set of corporate guidelines if your company does not have its own set of guidelines.

Appendix B shows you a methodology for evaluating existing training to see if it meets the needs of a newly designed system. This chapter also contains a valuable checklist for assessing the current training system.

Appendix C presents you with a sample set of screen layouts that can be examined and implemented into their designs.

As practitioners, we have tried to make a book that will continue to be invaluable to other practitioners. We have culled information from a number of diverse sources into a reference which we think you will want to keep close at hand. But most of all, on the topics presented in this book, we have tried to talk straight.

William W. Banks   Jon Weimer
Pleasanton, CA   Sterling Heights, MI

March 1992

ACKNOWLEDGEMENTS

We would like to thank the following individuals without whose help this book would not have been possible.

Material Content:

Dr. Harold Blackman, INEL
Capt. Robert Carter, NMRI, USN
Dr. Richard Doolittle, ONT
Dr. David Gertman, INEL
Mr. Walter Gilmore, Westinghouse, Savanah River
Mr. Arlie Hart, Wichita State Univerity
Mr. Stephen Hunter, LLNL
Dr. Jim Jenkins, NASA
Dr. John Loval, Cal. State -- Hayward
Dr. Stewart Miller, Towson State University
Dr. John Obrien, EPRI
Dr. Chuck Overby, FAA
Dr. Jack Paris, EPRI
Dr. Bob Waters, DOE
Ms. Denise Yanko, ARD

Manuscript Review and Editing:

Dr. Charles Halcomb, Wichita State University
Mr. Arlie Hart, Wichita State University
Mr. E.J. Herron
Ms. Laura Huber, Prentice-Hall
Mr. Mike Hays, Prentice-Hall
Dr. John Loval, Cal. State -- Hayward
Dr. Elizabeth Maier, Prodigy Services Company
Ms. Dana Mercure, Prentice-Hall
Mrs. Anna McBride-Weimer

CHAPTER 1
Predicting and Preventing User Errors

Every object designed by engineers is in some way, a direct extension of the human body, mind, or sensory system. For example, an automobile is an extension of your legs, radar is an extension of your vision, clothing is an extension of your skin, and the pencil and paper you use every day is an extension of your mind/memory. Thus, any system design must be congruent with the way people think, sense, and behave. If there is a mismatch between the system design and the way people behave, think, or respond then a human error will occur. Far too often, human error is dismissed as an inevitable fact of life. However, as this chapter points out, human error is one of the largest single costs to companies even though there are many successful approaches to reducing the frequency of human error to an acceptable level. In most instances, user errors are triggered by poorly designed interfaces between people and equipment, poorly validated training programs, poorly developed procedures, and poorly conceived management practices. It is an unfortunate fact that most user errors can be economically prevented through carefully designing a system to take into account the physical and cognitive limitations and capabilities of the human user. This is ironic since management should be oriented to increasing rather than decreasing productivity. As we shall see, political [intra and extra-corporate], budgetary, social, and system constraints result in ineffective interface designs that may decrease user productivity in the best case and may result in the death in the worst case.

1.0 Human Error Is a Major Corporate Problem

These days, systems analysts and data processing professionals seem to be preoccupied with preventing the infestation of their systems with viruses, which can crash or disable them. While this is a very legitimate concern, one of the largest and most serious threats to data integrity is often ignored or dismissed. Human error has the highest probability of occurrence of all computer security threats, yet computer security analysts often overlook the factors that cause human mistakes. In all but a very few instances, the causes of human error can be eliminated or mitigated through the careful application of Human Factors principles to the development of new systems or the redesign of current systems. It is ironic that this high probability, and costly, event (human error) is too often dismissed as being inevitable and unpreventable when it can be controlled using some highly cost-effective techniques and methods.

For example, in the 1970s, a large east coast university computer center reported that human errors, caused by "unfriendly and ambiguous" software and hardware design, were responsible for 60% of the total downtime for their large mainframe system. That's bad enough. But, when one system transmits data to another system, the errors present in the first system are "inherited" by the receiving system thus creating "inherited" errors (Figure 1-1). Inherited errors may represent the largest hidden threat to data integrity in distributed data processing.

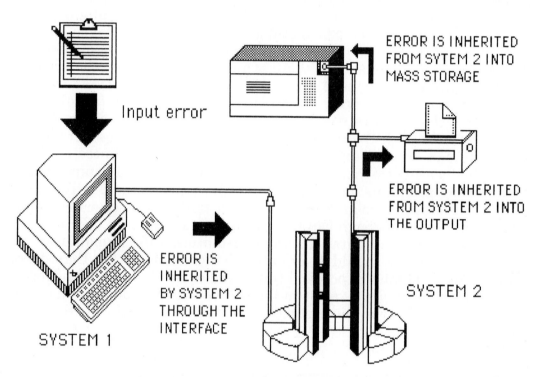

Figure 1-1: Inherited Error

1.1 The High Cost of Human Error

The costs associated with finding and correcting human errors may be one of the largest hidden costs to a company. One communications company found that, at $2.00 per error, they were spending $100 million per year finding and correcting human errors (Bailey, 1983). We believe that today's business world must realize that the costs associated with human error must be reduced in order to remain competitive and to prevent the occurrence of events such as the Chernobyl nuclear accident (NUREG-1251) and Three Mile Island (Kemey, 1979), events caused by faults in equipment, procedures, management and training that led directly to a series of human errors, which in turn propagated into events of severe economic, political, environmental, and societal consequences.

But surely these are isolated incidents. You may think that your company can't be spending that much on human error. Don't be so sure. Let's assume that a typical data entry employee at your company makes $15,000 per year. That $15,000 in salary is only the money, or "unloaded" portion of the salary. Health insurance, retirement plans, and other benefits add to the employee's salary. This "loaded" portion of an employee's salary can be as much as 25-30% of the "unloaded" portion. In other words, you are really paying the employee much more than $15,000 per year. If we assume a salary loading of 25% ($3,750), then you are actually paying that employee $18,750 per year.

Now, let's suppose that it takes this employee 1 minute to find and correct a data entry error. What is the cost of that error to the company? First, we must determine how much the employee earns per minute. This is fairly easy to do. A 250 day work year is fairly standard. So, we take $18,750 (the employee's loaded salary), and divide it by 250 days. This gives us $75 as the salary of that employee per day. If we take that figure and divide it by 8, the number of hours in a work day, then we find that the employee's loaded hourly pay is $9.38 per hour. Finally, if we divide that figure by 60, the number of minutes in an hour, we find that one minute of that employee's time costs the company about 16 cents. Sixteen cents does not seem like a lot of money.

If we assume that an entry clerk can input 100 entries per hour, that the clerk makes 1 error for every hour worked (i.e., 99% accuracy of data input), and that each error takes the clerk 1 minute to find and correct, then the company loses 16 cents per hour due to human error. Over an 8 hour work day, the cost of those errors is $1.28 per clerk. Assuming a 250 day work year, the annual cost of errors for that one employee is $320 per clerk. If we are a large company with 500 data entry clerks, the annual cost of human errors is $160,000. This is for an error that only takes 1 minute to find and correct. In the real world, how many errors occur that ONLY take 1 minute to find and correct, and how often is our data input accuracy 99%? The cost to a company increases dramatically as the amount of time needed to find and correct an error increases . If the above errors are made by 500 employees making only $2,000 a year more, the above estimate increases to $172, 916. If it takes 3 minutes to find and correct each error, these values balloon to $518,748. If these errors are not found and corrected, and if they are inherited into other systems, as in Figure 1-1, the resulting cost could be catastrophic.

1.2 Definitions of Human Error

An antiquated view of human error is that there is nothing one can do to prevent errors from occurring since "to err is human." However, there is ample scientific evidence showing that much can be done to decrease the occurrence of error. Human error rates are effected by a known set of influencing variables that are under the control of the manager or designer. A slight shift in value of any of these causal variables can produce dramatic behavioral changes in error rates.

Human error can be defined as: *a change in a deviation from a desired level of performance which results in an undesired or unplanned system state or outcome.* Human error can also be expressed in terms of the probability of the unsuccessful human performance of specific tasks or task combinations, which -- if uncorrected -- will lead to an undesirable event or situation. These errors may take the form of errors of omission or errors of commission. An error of omission is a situation where the user fails to take the prescribed or required action. An error of commission occurs when the USER executes a prohibited or incorrect action that leads to an undesired state or event.

In reality, human error is usually ascribed as the cause of some event for which there were no other obvious causes. When compared with hardware component failure post mortums, the causes of human error can range from very simple to highly complex.

As a rule, the valid identification of human error and reliable predictive estimation can only be made when a set of multivariate features of the situation (i.e., equipment, procedures, prior training, system norms, and operating experience) are well understood by the analyst.

1.3 Human Errors Unique to Computing Systems

When examining human errors made by the users of computing systems, it helps to identify three types of errors specific to computing:

1. Navigation errors
2. Data input errors
3. Inherited errors

1.3.1 Navigation Errors

By navigation errors, we mean errors made while traversing through the system using commands, pull down menus, hypertext buttons, or function keys. Navigation errors result when the user becomes "lost" within the computer's interface. The best example of this is taking the wrong branch of a menu (i.e., selecting option 1 instead of option 2). Menu-oriented systems and hypertext systems are particularly susceptible to navigation errors if there are more than three layers. As the number of nodes in the hierarchy increases, the probability of a user becoming lost in the depths of the menu or hypertext nodes, resulting from the selection of an incorrect node (i.e., a navigation error) increases. Inexperienced users are more likely to make navigation errors, since more experienced users will have formed a "mental-map" of the systems.

The cause of navigational errors can almost always be traced back to the absence of "land marks" or reference points that novice users need to determine where they are in the system. To avoid the potential for traumatizing novices, you can provide a *safety-net* which novices can use to get back to the root of the menu system. For example, menu-oriented systems should have a safety net manifested as an option which the user can select to return to the root node of the menu.

Navigation errors may result in more than just confusing users. For example, suppose the shutdown system of a process control plant is computer controlled. In the event of a serious breach, serious injury could result to the residents in the surrounding neighborhood if the control room operator cannot navigate from the monitoring system to the shutdown system in time to prevent the breach or if the operator becomes lost in the spider's web of the system's menu structure.

1.3.2 Data Input Errors

Data input errors are much easier to understand than navigational errors. This type of error occurs simply because the data input technician has left out some crucial piece of data (e.g., leaving off a digit when inputting a social security number) or has accidentally input erroneous information. Preventing data input errors will be a major concern in the remainder of this book. While the effective human engineering of a system's interface will reduce data input errors caused by user confusion, it will not reduce errors due to incorrect data stemming from preparation errors (i.e., mistakes on the form that the data input technician uses). Thus, Human Factors principles need to be applied to data recording forms as well.

Data input errors can be substantially reduced through the careful choice of command names, reducing screen clutter, designing the interface to be consistent with the user's expectations of the required task and function (i.e., spreadsheets for bookkeepers), and through iterative construction and testing of prototypes of new designs.

To illustrate some of the points and concepts regarding human error in computing systems we will now present a case study.

CASE STUDY 1-1
User Error

As any information systems manager will attest, data entry personnel tend to make input errors as they update information or create new data files. These errors can degrade the integrity of the data and cost substantial amounts of money in corrections and lost time. There are many inexpensive controls that can be used to minimize these errors. The following case study illustrates this point.

Bob Franklin was a records and billing manager in a medium sized insurance company. The company planned to fully automate their billing procedures and was in the process of transcribing all hard-copy files into a large database. Over 150 key-to-disk users were to work around the clock to make the transition as fast as possible. Low cost equipment was installed and a vendor supplied the data entry format used.

After about two weeks, Bob discovered that many of the data entry employees were complaining of headaches, backaches, watering eyes, and a host of other physical complaints. One week later, there was a large attrition rate (46% turnover) and employee absenteeism increased from 6-18%. The data verification supervisor reported that the keyed in error rate had increased from 4% on the first day to over 13% by the end of the second week. The vendor, concerned that the sale might go sour, hired a Human Factors Engineering consultant to evaluate both the hardware and the data entry tasks.

After only 1 day of examining the work environment, the consultant found several problems related to the VDT workstations, the task activities, and the work flow. Here are the problems he uncovered and how they were corrected:

1. An awkward data entry format, supplied by the vendor, conflicted with the source data format and, in some cases, was reversed. This discrepancy, **alone**, was responsible for inducing **50%** of the data entry errors.

2. CRT flicker existed on virtually all of the workstations. The flicker was correlated with the reported nausea and eye fatigue. Part of the flicker was due to the type of CRT phosphor as it interacted with a 30Hz interlaced display and the overhead fluorescent lighting system. These terminals were replaced with a 60Hz interlaced system which used a different type of phosphor.

3. CRT reflected glare was related to complaints of eyes watering and headaches. Overhead glare on numerous CRT screens was eliminated by reorienting several workstations with respect to the overhead lights and placing antiglare screens on terminals which could not be reoriented.

4. Poor screen resolution of alphanumeric characters was related to certain types of data entry errors. This was corrected by changing the font and increasing the point value of the screen characters.

5. Degraded system response to key commands in the edit mode (if the disk was over 70% full of text) caused the users to wait from 5 to 12 seconds for each correction. This source of irritation and lost time was corrected by requesting that new disks be inserted when the system registered a 65% full capacity.

6. No immediate error feedback was given to users when the disk was full resulting in the loss of large amounts of data. The data then had to be retyped on a new disk. Requirement 5 eliminated this problem.

7. Poor figure-to-ground contrast (yellow text on white background) and a highly stylized font was another factor related to the high incident of data entry error. This was corrected when they changed the CRTs and fonts.

8. The older data entry personnel were equipped with ergonomically adjustable chairs which eliminated virtually all complaints of backaches.

Upon the resolution of *all* of these problems, error rates **decreased** to less than **1.2%**, turnover **decreased** to **10%**, and absenteeism was abated to an acceptable level. The cost to implement these types of changes was more than offset by the dramatic improvement in human productivity as measured by the number of error-free records entered per day.

1.4 Generic Types of Human Error

Generic human errors can be broken down into two categories: errors of omission and errors of commission. Errors of omission occur when the user does not do something (i.e., leaves out a step or steps required to complete a task). Errors of commission occur when the user does something, but it's the wrong something (i.e., performs some action that results in a system error). Many times, the causes of errors of commission and omission can be traced back to an interface design that is out of synch with the mental model of the user (Section 1.6.2).

1.4.1 Errors of Commission

1.4.1.1 Inadvertent Actions

This error of commission occurs when an individual attempts to change the system state from its current state to a new state and inadvertently changes more than they planned. For example, if a user desires to press function key F1 and accidently or unknowingly presses F2, either before or after F1, then the classification of this action would be "inadvertent". Users are particularly prone to inadvertent errors when the system function does not match their mental model (i.e., mental representation) of that function (Section 1.6.2).

1.4.1.2 User Inhibits

This type of error occurs if a user intentionally defeats or overrides a necessary system function, because the user has misdiagnosed the situation, or because the function is annoying or inconvenient. Some examples: a control room operator who covers up the blinking status lights, because the blinking is distracting; the workman who tapes down the "deadman's switch" on a machine, because it's annoying to keep the switch depressed; or the computer user who disables a virus checker because it checks every file on every disk put into the floppy drive.

1.4.1.3 User Selection

This type of error occurs when the user must make a decision between a number of different actions and chooses the wrong one. For example, the user who picks the wrong choice from a menu of functions.

1.4.1.4 Sequence Error

A sequence error occurs when the user performs the actions out of the correct sequence. Suppose that a user wants to copy a file from the hard disk to an external drive and then delete the hard disk file. If the user inadvertently deletes the hard disk file first, they have committed a sequence error.

1.4.1.5 Time Errors

Time errors occur when the user over or underestimates the time required to perform a task. Either way, the result is periods of unproductivity. For example, one of the authors recently down-loaded a file from CompuServe, but underestimated the time required. Not only was his Macintosh and phone line tied up for two hours, but he also spent $20 more in on-line charges than he intended to.

1.4.2 User Omission

This type of error occurs because a user fails to perform a step or steps required to complete the task. For example, if a data input clerk misses a field, saves the record, and then moves on to the next record, they have committed an error of omission, since they omitted a step.

1.5 A Checklist for Detecting Risk from Human Error

The following human error checklist (**HECK!**) will help identify other controls and considerations to keep human error very low during keyed entry and process control activities using VDTs. Items labeled with an (H), are items of high risk of human error, while items labeled (M) and (L) are medium and low risk, respectively. Similarly, items labeled (VH) are very high risk, while those labeled (VL) are very low risk. Items eliciting a "no" response should be given careful consideration as being at risk for human errors, particularly if labeled (H).

Information Quality

1. Is information displayed on the screen correct/accurate? (M)

2. Is the information presented on the screen at an appropriate level of detail so that the user does not become confused and make errors? (M)

3. Is the information presented limited to the specific task needed for the user to make the next decision/command? (M)

4. Are messages and terms consistent with the language and meaning of terms and values found in the operating procedures? (M) [This will minimize the potential of unwanted data entry errors.]

5. Is the information presented in a clear and unambiguous manner? (H)

6. Is the CRT free from perceived flicker or glare? (M)

Data Organization

7. Are displayed data organized logically? (M)

8. Is the organization and separation of information subgroups made apparent to the user through use of blank spaces, lines, or some other form of visible separation? (L)

9. Is the data presented free from human requirements for transposing, computing, interpolating, or mental translation/transformation? (M)

10. Is related information formatted or clustered together? (L)

Labels and Abbreviations

11. Are descriptive titles provided for each group of messages that may be unfamiliar to less experienced system users? (M)

12. Are abbreviations meaningful and understandable to all personnel who will use the system? (M)

13. Are labels free from masking effects by adjacent colors, characters, or objects? (L)

14. Do descriptors appear on or immediately adjacent to the control or display? (L)

15. Are all descriptors located in a consistent manner? (L)

16. Are descriptors oriented horizontally? (L)

17. Are descriptors located either above or to the left of the data or message they describe? (M)

18. Are descriptors essential to comprehending the displayed data highlighted or otherwise accentuated? (H)

19. Is descriptor highlighting free from interference with the scanning of data? (H)

20. Are labels as brief as possible without losing meaning? (H)

Feedback and Cues

21. Do error messages provide specific, concise information to the user regarding required corrective action? (VH)

22. Can the user easily correct individual errors without affecting valid entries? (H)

23. Are feedback messages offered to the user to indicate changes in display system status (e.g., whether the system is still operating or not)? (VH)

24. When a process requires the user to standby, is "periodic feedback" provided to indicate normal system operation and the reason for the delay? (VH)

25. Is a signal presented (either visually or acoustically) when the system is down or inactive? (H)

26. When a process or sequence is completed by the system, is a positive indication presented to the user concerning the outcome of the process? (VH)

27. Is a prompt provided once a process is complete? (VH)

28. Is highlighting used to attract the user's attention to important displayed information? (VH)

29. Does information highlighting, in addition to merely getting attention, have the same meaning in all applications? (M)

30. Is blinking of symbols or messages reserved for emergency conditions or conditions requiring immediate user action? (L)

31. When blinking is used for highlighting, is a maximum of two blink rates used? (L)

32. Is blinking used to attract attention rather than blinking the item to be read? (M)

33. If a single blink rate is used, is the rate approximately 2 to 3 blinks per second, with a minimum of 50 milliseconds between blinks? (L)

34. When two blink rates are used, does the fast blink approximate 4 per second and the slow blink approximate 1 per second? (VL)

35. When two blink rates are used, does the on-off ratio approximate 50%? (L)

36. When two blink rates are used, does the higher rate apply to the most critical information? (L)

37. Is image reversal used primarily for highlighting in dense data fields, such as a word or phrase in a paragraph of text or a set of characters in a table of data? (M)

38. Are graphic coding methods (e.g., symbols, boxes, underlines, colors) used to present standard qualitative information to the user, or to draw the user's attention to a particular portion of the display? (M)

39. Do graphic codes, used separately or in combination, have the same meaning in all applications? (H)

40. Are the number of basic symbols used for coding kept small (upper limit under optimum conditions being 20; upper limit under adverse conditions being 6)? (M)

41. Are colors used on the screens to convey information which is consistent in use and meaning with all other color codes used by the user in performing the tasks that comprise his work? (M)

42. Once a color is assigned a specific use or meaning, are other colors prevented from use for the same meaning? (H)

43. Are visual warning signals clear and properly situated to attract attention? (M)

44. Is feedback (beep) used to reward correct entries rather than simply used to punish (buzz) incorrect entries? (M)

Visual Display Terminal Characters

45. Are alphanumeric and graphic characters easily readable by the user under existing or expected room lighting? (H)

46. Does the CRT have a minimum screen background luminance of 23 foot lambert? (M)

47. Is the contrast between light characters and a dark screen background a minimum of 15:1? (M)

48. Is the contrast between dark characters and a light screen background a minimum of 1:15? (M)

49. Is the width-to-height ratio for alphanumerics between 3:5 and 1:1, respectively? (M)

50. Is the stroke-width to character-height ratio between 1:5 and 1:10? (M)

51. Is horizontal separation between characters or symbols between 10% and 65% of character or symbol height? (H)

52. Are simple character fonts free from stylization (For example, slanted, shifted, or varied in stroke width)? (L)

53. Is the minimum of a 7 x 9 matrix applied when dot-matrix characters are used? (L)

54. Do characters generated by dot matrix merge sufficiently to produce a sharp and well-defined image? (M)

Instrument Characteristics

55. Do circular scales increase in value in a clockwise direction? (M)

56. Do vertical scales increase in value from the bottom to the top? (M)

57. Do horizontal scales increase in value from left to right? (M)

58. Does the coding of qualitative zones (e.g., danger, empty, hot, cool) interfere with the reading of quantitative descriptions (i.e., numeric values)? (H)

59. Are alphanumeric characters on any type of scale printed vertically? (L)

60. If graphic pointer movement is more that 360 degrees, is the zero point located at the 12 o'clock position? (M)

61. Where positive and negative values are displayed around a zero or null position, is the zero or null position located at the 12 o'clock position? (M)

62. When the scale covers less than a full rotation of the graphic pointer, are scale end-points indicated by a break in scale? (VL)

63. Is the break in scale at least one numbered interval in length? (VL)

64. Is the break in scale based on equivalent distances from the 6 o'clock position and centered at the 12 o'clock position? (VL)

Digital Display Characteristics

65. Are digital readouts oriented to be read horizontally from left to right? (M)

66. Do digital readout characters use simple character fonts (not stylized) with no slanted characters or variable stroke widths? (L)

67. Do successive digital readouts progress at a rate less than two per second when the user is expected to read them consecutively? (VH)

68. Do digital readouts change at a rate faster than twice the maximum readable rate? (L)

Column Chart and Graph Characteristics

69. Are bar graph charts constructed with a scaled grid overlay? (VL)

70. Are numbered grids bolder than unnumbered grids? (L)

71. When table columns are long, are numbers separated into groups by providing a space between groups of five? (M)

72. Are all quantitative data, which must be scanned and compared, in either tabular or graphic form? (M)

73. Are displayed trend plot scales (graphs, bar charts) consistent with the intended use of the data? (M)

1.6 Reducing User Error in Your System

Once you have identified areas in your system that have the potential for generating human errors, the next step is to generate a plan for reducing that potential. In the design of fairly simple systems, or systems that will not result in the catastrophic loss in human life, the Human Factors professionals on the design team are usually called on to predict the probability of occurrence of errors, usually through some form of task analysis (Chapter 2), and asked to recommend design changes that will reduce the probability that the predicted errors will occur.

There are two main causes of human errors. The first of these is the influence of performance shaping factors. Performance Shaping Factors (PSFs) are variables that influence the user's behavior such that errors are more or less likely to occur (Table 1-1). The second major cause of human error is the design of a system interface that conceptually at odds with the user's mental model (i.e., mental representation) of how the system functions. Unfortunately, both of these sources of causation come into play in many systems, thereby increasing the likelihood that errors will be made by the user.

1.6.1 Incorporating Performance Shaping Factors in Design

Significant user error is frequently, but not always, effected or caused by the interaction of physiological, psychological, environmental, managerial, equipment/task factors, and precedents. Some of these performance shaping factors are listed in Table 1-1.

Each of these variables may interact in a multivariate fashion either to enhance human reliability or to increase the probability of human error. It is vital that the Human Factors engineer identify the relevant performance shaping factors in a system, and determine how they interact to enhance or degrade performance, so they can make a make changes in the system interface, training, or documentation to obviate the potential impact of these factors. Remember, that performance shaping factors often **interact** to influence behavior. For example, training alone **will not** improve user performance if: operating procedures are defective, documentation is badly written, the interface design is at odds with the user's mental model, or management has no desire to change its operating philosophy. Realize, however, that it is unrealistic to assume that the ideal user will perform a given task under ideal conditions (i.e., with optimally human engineered equipment, a perfect set of procedures, close management supervision, and a training program with perfect content and predictive validity). More often than not, design constraints will dictate that some aspects of the system will be suboptimal.

Table 1-1: Performance Shaping Factors

Physiological	Psychological	Environmental
Work-Rest Cycles	Cognition	Workspace
Strength	Intelligence	Time
Circadian Rhythm	Stress	Noise Levels
Sensory Acuity	Workload	Temperature
Physical Health	Confidence	Ventilation
Reach Envelope	Training	Radiation
Physical Stature	Attitude	Lighting Levels

MANAGERIAL	TASK-EQUIPMENT
Morale	Task Complexity
Motivation	Design
Incentives	Operability
Leadership	Procedures (quality)
Experience	Placement-Location
Staffing	Maintainability
Philosophy	Task Sequencing

In short, you must examine multiple variables in parallel in order to assess human error probabilities, or at the very least, make judgmental assumptions as to which performance shaping variables will impact user performance the most in your system's design. The probability of human error may differ from one system to another because of differences in tasks, equipment, procedures, users, management, and training.

Although human error is an important contributor to system risk and reliability, often there are few fully trained and experienced specialists from the behavioral sciences involved in the design of systems. In fact, very often, little consideration is given to the actual tasks the user will be expected to do to complete the desired tasks. Too often, systems are designed to be technically elegant or efficient rather than designed to be easily used or to be compatible with the tasks the user needs to complete.

> **Note**: In situations where system, budgetary, or other constraints result in a suboptimal design, the Human Factors engineer should work with the design team to cooperatively develop innovative solutions to obviate the effects of the suboptimal design. The field of Human Factors engineering may not be well understood by some members of the design team or, worse yet, perceived as being "common sense". In the worst case, Human Factors engineers may be viewed as a resource drain, overly steadfast, and an impediment to production schedules and to the design process. It is our **opinion** that the Human Factors engineer should strive harder than any other member of the design team to project a cooperative approach at arriving to solutions so that the other members of the team perceive the Human Factors engineer as an invaluable part of the design process.

There are a variety of methods that you can use to estimate the influence of each type of performance shaping factor. These techniques include link analysis, task analysis, human performance modeling, specific evaluation guidelines for performance-shaping factors, and human error quantification. A discussion of all of these techniques would fill its own book. Perhaps the best place for you to start is with an in-depth analysis of the tasks that the user will be performing. Chapter 2 provides a thorough introduction to task analysis and should be studied closely.

However, if a similar system is in place, it may not be necessary, and definitely not productive, for you to "reinvent the wheel." It is necessary for you to be aware of available data that may influence your decisions regarding expected user behavior. For example, if information exists regarding the incidence of prior human errors in a system of similar design, you should try to obtain a standardized data set from which to assess the possible influence of work load, user experience/qualifications, training quality, control placement/layout, CRT screen design and format, procedure adequacy and time/sequence considerations, and so forth.

Regardless of the techniques used to identify performance shaping factors, typical users of the system should be used for periodic "reality" checks in the design process. The potential users can also be helpful by working with the other design specialists to provide first hand information, data, and insights into task action content, time, and priorities. In addition, typical users should always be analyzed as a system element, incorporating the relevant Human Factors such as procedures, training, management, equipment, interfaces, environment, and time dependencies, into an assessment of the probability that the user performs as required.

1.6.2 Incorporating Mental Models in Design

The degree of match between the interface's conceptual presentation and the mental model of the user is probably the most powerful determinant of whether or not the user will make errors when using the system. A mental model is simply the mental representation that a user has of how a given system operates; mental models can be very general and vaguely defined, or they can be extremely specific.

For example, you may have a very general idea as to how your car works. Turning the key somehow makes a connection between the battery, the starter, and the sparkplugs. The spark from the sparkplugs ignites the gas, causing the pistons to move up and down, thereby turning the wheels. This is a mental model shared by most of us who drive. The general, fuzzy, incomplete nature of this model is typical of mental models. As users develop more experience with a system, their models become more focused, and the gaps in the model begin to close as the user develops knowledge or experience with the system and learns how the different components interact (e.g., the rotor makes contact with the sparkplugs as it rotates, the current from the connection causes the sparkplug to spark, igniting the gasoline in the cylinder, the resulting combustion pushes the piston downward, turning the crankshaft, etc.).

1.6.2.1 Users Are Not Passive

The mistake that designers often make -- too often to count -- is to assume that users are active only to the extent that they follow operating procedures. This is in fact a fallacious assumption. Users are extremely active participants in the human-computer dialog. Even the most extremely passive user, is still not passive. Users form goals, expectations, inferences, and intentions about the way the system "should" behave. This tendency to form expectations and goals about the way the system "should" perform is what gets most novices, and sometimes even seasoned professionals into trouble. They automatically assume that the system will behave rationally, not realizing that their frame of reference for rational behavior may be vastly different from that of the system's designers (Hanisch, 1988).

Unless your end user population is extremely computer literate, it is unlikely that they have a good mental representation of the internal workings of the system. The internal workings of the system may be invisible to them (Casner and Lewis, 1987); from the user's perspective, they may simply enter the information into the black box and it does something to the information and gives them something back in the form of output or feedback. It is this very fact, that the full functionality of the system may not be know to the user, combined with the fact that users actively form inferences about the functionality of the system that result in human errors. Mayhew (1992), citing Casner and Lewis (1987), offers an excellent example from UNIX:

> "In the UNIX command language, the command "Cat," followed by a filename, generally displays the file. The command "Chmod," when followed by a filename, makes that file inaccessible (that is, undisplayable) to all users. However, there is no feedback (no immediate, visible effect) when the Chmod is issued. The system simply returns the usual system prompt. Later, however, if the user asks to display the file through the "Cat" command, the file is *not* displayed, and an error message is issued . . . In this example, a single command, the "Cat" command, has two different results in two different instances: in one it displays a file; in the other, it does not display the file and issues an error message instead. . . this inconsistency is a *paradox* that users must resolve in their mental model of the system. To resolve it, they must *hypothesize* what went on in the "black box" when the Chmod command, since they received no immediate, visual feedback from that action." (Mayhew, 1992)

Lack of appropriate feedback is an important concern and major cause of human error. The remainder of this book deals with designing systems to give the user better feedback, a better look inside of the black box. The more "transparent" you can make the "walls" of that interface "black box" the fewer errors the user will make and the less corporate resources will be expended finding and correcting user errors.

Improving the match between the mental models of the user and the conceptual design of the interface will be discussed throughout the rest of this book. Here, however, are some guidelines offered by Mayhew (1992), that you can use to help reduce the possibility of users drawing the wrong inferences:

1. **Whenever possible, the functioning of the system visible to the user rather than invisible**. The success of direct manipulation interfaces such as the Macintosh and Windows is due to the fact that the functions performed by the operating system are presented in a visual format, which is easy for a user to comprehend. After all, placing a piece of paper into a folder is something we do everyday, so dragging a file into a folder with a mouse seems natural and intuitive.

2. **ALWAYS provide the user with feedback**. The main problem with operating systems such as UNIX are that they don't give you any feedback, as shown in the "Cat" example. Whenever you design a system that does not give the user sufficient feedback, you are inviting trouble. For example, a very common problem encountered due to lack of feedback is superstitious behavior. An example of this is the fellow who walks up to an elevator and presses an illuminated up button. Though he undoubtedly knows his

behavior won't get the elevator there any quicker, the behavior persists. A corollary in the computer industry is the type-ahead problem. In systems with slow response times, that buffer keyboard presses, impatient users will typically engage in the superstitious behavior of repeatedly pressing the return key. The buffering of the extra returns will result in a string of carriage returns being sent when the processor is freed up, resulting in an even more unfortunate situation for the user. This behavior can easily be stopped through the use of a "shrinking bar", or a clock with rotating hands, or a percentage count-down meter that provides the user with feedback that in essence says, "sit-tight, and I'll be with you when I finish processing this data."

3. **Make the interface and the functionality appear consistent**. As you saw with the "Cat" command, the appearance of inconsistency can be devastating. If we had to pick the one thing that was most important to the design of an effective computer display system, it would be consistency.

4. **Whenever possible, use a familiar metaphor to present the functionality**. Again, the popularity of direct manipulation interfaces such as the Macintosh computer and MicroSoft Windows, is because they are easy to use. That ease of use is a direct result of their reliance on familiar activities as metaphors for computer functions (e.g., putting papers into manila folders as a metaphor for moving a file from one directory to another).

1.7 What Next?

This chapter is not, by far, the final word on human error prevention. It is intended solely to acquaint the reader with the impact that human error can have on a system and the need for controlling human error through effective design.

Once a commitment has been made to controlling human error through system design and redesign, the next step is to conduct an in-depth task analysis to identify which parts of the system are most likely to be at risk for human error. The task analysis will break down the job into an elemental set of tasks. Analyzing these tasks will help you to identify which areas of your system are most prone to human errors, and help to target the system components that need design changes.

1.8 References

Bailey, R.W. (1983) *Human Error in Computing Systems*. Englewood Cliffs, NJ: Prentice-Hall.

Banks,W.W. and Schurman, D.L. (1984) *Review of Human Error Assessment Methods and Models.* Idaho National Engineering Lab, EG&G Report No. SCE-NTPD-84-003.

Casner, S., and Lewis, C. (1987) Learning about hidden events in system interactions. *CHI '87 Proceedings*, pgs. 197-204.

Hanisch, K., A., and others. (1988) Novice-expert differences in the cognitive representation of system features: Mental models and verbalizable knowledge. *Proceedings of the Human Factors Society's 32nd Annual Meeting*, pgs. 219-223.

Hannaman, G.W., and Spergin, A.J. *Systematic Human Action Reliability Procedure (SHARP).* Electric Power Research Institute, Palo Alto, CA, Report No. NP-3583, June 1984.

Kemey, J. C. (Chairman), (1979) *Report of the President's Commission on the Accident at Three Mile Island,* Washington, D.C.: U.S. Government Printing Office.

Mayhew, D.J. (1992) *Principles and Guidelines in Software User Interface Design.* Englewood Cliffs, NJ: Prentice-Hall.

Swain, A. D., and Guttmann, H. E. (1980) *Handbook of Human Reliability Analysis with Emphasis on Nuclear Power Plant Applications*, NUREG/CR-1278, Washington, D.C.: U.S. Nuclear Regulatory Commission.

Siegel, A. I., Bartter, W.D., Knee, H. E., and Haas, P.M. (1983) *Front-End Analysis for the Nuclear Power Plant Maintenance Personnel Reliability Model.* , NUREG/CR-2669, Washington, D.C.: U.S. Nuclear Regulatory Commission.

U.S. Nuclear Regulatory Commission. (1989) *Severe Accident Risk: An Assessment for Five U.S. Nuclear Power Plants* (2nd Draft Report for Peer Review, Vol. 1), NUREG-1150, Washington, D.C.: U.S. Nuclear Regulatory Commission.

U.S. Nuclear Regulatory Commission (1988) *Implications of the Accident at Chernobyl for Safety Regulation of Commercial Nuclear Power Plants in the United States,* NUREG-1251, Washington, D.C.: U.S. Nuclear Regulatory Commission.

U.S. Nuclear Regulatory Commission. (1975) *Reactor Safety Study—An Assessment of Accident Risks in U.S. Commercial Nuclear Power Plants,* NUREG-75-014/WASH-1400, Washington, D.C.: U.S. Nuclear Regulatory Commission.

Wells, J.E., Banks, W.W., Ryan,T., Potash, L. (1990) *Task Analysis Linked Evaluation Technique (TALENT):A Method For Integrating Human Factors Expertise into The Probabilistic Risk Assessment Process.* Lawrence Livermore National Laboratory.

CHAPTER 2
Task Analysis

After a commitment has been made to improve human performance, the next step in the design process should be the construction of a profile of the proposed users of the system and a systematic evaluation of the job those users will be performing. Breaking down a job into its elemental components, called *tasks*, gives you a better understanding of the contribution made by each task to the completion of the job, the information needs of the users, potential for user error, and the demands placed on the users at each task step.

Once the tasks and their requirements for successful completion are identified, you can improve job performance by carefully assigning tasks to either the user or the system. Computers are better at some tasks than humans (e.g. rapid calculations), and the contrary is true as well (e.g., humans are much better at recognizing human speech and making decisions based on incomplete information). Performance is optimized when the tasks are assigned to the system component (human or computer) that can best perform the task. The user profile provides you with information on the strengths and weaknesses of your user population. This profile helps you to match the needs and strengths of the user population with the needs of the task by determining which tasks should be allocated to the human user and which should be automated. The system is then designed so that tasks are allocated to maximize the strengths of man and machine.

2.0 What Is the Purpose of Task Analysis?

Making a commitment to improve human performance and reduce user error is the hard part. Once that initial hurdle has been cleared, the next step is to take a rigorously analytical look at the work that the users/workers are performing. Before substantial strides can be made to increase the performance of users, the work itself has to be understood. What separates good performance from bad performance? To understand human performance as it relates to the completion of a job, you must break that job down into its elemental components, called *tasks*, which are combined in some sequence to form a process that we refer to as work or a job. This evaluation is called *task analysis*. There are many variations in the way the analysis can be performed; however, all of the methods involve breaking down the job into its elemental components, or steps. These steps are called tasks. It is important to note that task analysis is not the same as job analysis. Job analysis is a global description of the tasks assigned to one worker (e.g., input data from forms), rather than the specific task descriptions developed through a task analysis (e.g., read the number from line 8 of the form, type the value into the field labeled SKU code, press enter).

By breaking a job down into a set of elemental steps or tasks that are *necessary* and *sufficient* to successfully complete a specific job, you obtain a better understanding of how each of the tasks contributes to the completion of the job. It also affords you a better understanding of the information needs of the user, potential sources of user error, and the demands placed on the user at each task step. Some additional benefits gained from performing a task analysis are:

1. Reduction in total development and maintenance costs by defining the task environment and interface technology prior to development.

2. A reduction of life cycle costs.

3. A reduction in the probability of human and system errors.

4. An increase in total system reliability.

5. Early identification of potential limits and constraints placed on the system's users.

6. Early identification of potential Human Factors design deficiencies that may cause user problems and complaints later.

7. A first-order set (outline) of operating procedures can be defined, and documented as an output of the task analysis.

8. Human performance and safety can be improved by insuring a better integration of control-display systems.

9. Risk management can be enhanced by pinpointing human error risks and safety hazards early in the design phase.

10. Levels of responsibility and supervision can be specified by grouping tasks into jobs.

11. The definition of tasks helps identify jobs requiring additional training programs and suggests efficient ways of training workers for particularly difficult tasks.

Once a job has been broken down into tasks, you can use this information to allocate job functions. When performing a function allocation, you assign a task or function to either human or machine control. This step is vital. Humans don't multiply eight digit numbers very well and computers cannot do employee performance appraisals. Computing systems and humans have their own unique set of capabilities. The closer a task matches the computer or human's capabilities, the better the performance of the task will be. A user profile (Section 2.3), constructed at the beginning of the task analysis interview, provides you with information on the strengths and weaknesses of your user population (e.g., reading level, computer literacy, color blindness, etc). The user profile helps you match the needs and strengths of the users with the needs of the task to determine which attributes a particular task should be allocated to the human user or automated. The system is then designed accordingly. Some additional criteria used to determine whether a system function should be allocated to a human or machine are:

1. frequency with which the task is to be executed per unit time,

2. level of user work load,

3. life cycle cost to automate the task versus providing manual control,

4. probability of human or machine failure (reliability),

5. severity of the consequence of human or machine failure,

6. degree of availability required for the specific function.

Schaich, Banks, and Van Ness (1987) have successfully used the output of task analysis, in a process control setting, to do the following:

1. prepare first order operating procedures,

2. make time estimates of task execution,

3. improve man/machine interfaces for better operability,

4. identify critical process failure points,

5. identify and assess potential risks and hazards,

6. identify functions as candidates for automation (function analysis),

7. establish and verify system design requirements,

8. define jobs and tasks for operations and maintenance,

9. plan and design plant control software,

10. specify requirements for training requirements and support equipment,

11. identify where system lockouts should be placed to inhibit human error.

By performing an in-depth task analysis and using the outcome to guide the design of the system, you can save corporate resources by reducing the need to retrofit the system to reduce user errors and increase user satisfaction.

2.1 What Are Tasks?

A task is: *a unit of work (human performance) that prepares, changes, or verifies system status, and contributes to the achievement of a specific functional objective*. More simply put, tasks are the discrete steps that must be performed to complete a desired job. Removing the lugs from your car's wheel is a task that is performed in the job of changing a tire. Tasks performed by humans may be cognitive or physical. The level of detail of your task descriptions will depend on your purpose for doing the task analysis.

For example, getting money is not a narrow enough definition to allow you to delineate a set of objectives and associated tasks. A better example might be using an automatic teller machine (ATM) to make a withdrawal. This description is narrow enough to clearly define a set of tasks. To define a set of tasks that accomplish a particular work objective, all that you have to do is to take a large, nebulous job (Use an ATM to make a withdrawal), and break it down into smaller, more specific parts (insert bank card, use keys to input ID number, press the withdrawal key, etc.). Each of the tasks in the previous sentence have a unique set of objectives that lead to the completion of the larger job (getting money). Those discrete steps **are** the tasks. When defining tasks, **always** be sure that all of the tasks are about the same size or scope. This will ensure that a constant level of human performance requirements is maintained (Drury et al., 1987). Table 2-1 shows a listing of the tasks associated with the simple job of using the ATM to make a withdrawal.

2.1.1 Task Characteristics

As mentioned, it is extremely important that the size and the scope of the tasks be controlled. Drury, et al.(1987) has listed 5 characteristics for defining and controlling the size of tasks. These characteristics are as follows:

1. A task is an action usually performed by a single worker or user.

2. Cues to begin a task and feedback can be provided by displays, instrumentation, other workers, a manager, or sensory perception.

3. Two tasks are related to each other by sharing a common goal(s), their occurrence in time, and their sequence of performance.

4. The starting point of a task is a stimulus or cue. That cue is often an accumulation of information rather than a single discrete stimulus. (e.g., monitoring disk space to determine when to switch disks: Case Study 1-1).

5. Each task has a unique stopping point that occurs when the user receives feedback indicating the task has been completed.

Table 2-1: Task Analysis of an ATM Withdrawal

Task Description	Task Purpose	Initiating Event	Number of Repetitions	Risk
1. Input card	Gain access	Need money	1	Card rejected (Inserted backwards)
2. Input your personal ID number using keypad	Gain access	Message: "Input Your PIN"	6 (1 input per each digit of a 6 digit PIN)	Card kept by ATM due to input of an incorrect PIN
3. Press blue "Cash From Checking" button	Indicate user intention to ATM's computer	Message: "Please Input Desired Transaction"	1	Incorrect transaction initiated.
4. Input $60.00 using keypad	Indicate the amount to withdrawal from checking	Message: "Please input amount of withdrawal."	4 (4 digits in $60.00)	Withdrawal too much (e.g., $6000)
5. Lift lid and remove cash from drawer.	Retrieve money	Message: "Please take your cash."	1	Leave money in cash drawer
6. Press NO	Indicate to the ATM's CPU that you don't want another transaction	Message: "Another transaction?"	1	Routed back to the prompt to input a transaction type
7. Press YES	Indicate to the ATM's CPU that you want a receipt	Message: "Would you like a receipt?"	1	No record of transaction
8. Take receipt	Obtain a record of transaction	Receipt is ejected from ATM	1	No record of transaction
9. Remove card from ATM	Retrieve card	ATM beeping and screen message	1	Lose your ATM card and hence your ability to make withdrawals

2.1.2 Three Types of Tasks

Drury et al. (1987) identifies three types of tasks: discrete or procedural, continuous or tracking, and branching. The tasks shown in Table 2-1 are examples of discrete tasks. Discrete tasks are initiated by a single event and each task is fairly independent. Each task, while dependent on the completion of some other task as its initiating event, is self-contained and does not overlap with any of the other tasks. Each of the tasks are also executed in a linear or procedural fashion.

Continuous tasks are quite different from discrete tasks. A continuous task requires constant monitoring to maintain the system's values within some specified range. In this type of task, the user must continuously sample the values of the system and make adjustments. The best example is monitoring your speed during driving. The driver must check the speedometer to verify that their speed is not in excess of 55 miles per hour. The cyclic nature of continuous tasks makes it difficult to specify when one cycle ends and the next begins. However, it is crucial that the originating point, the terminating point, and the time interval of the sampling cycle be specified since these three values define the task's beginning and end.

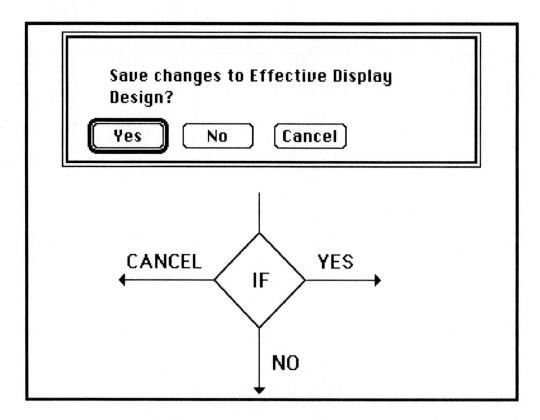

Figure 2-1:   Branching   Task

Branching tasks may either be discrete or continuous, though they are more often discrete. Branching tasks require the user or the system to make a decision. The course of action taken depends on the outcome of that decision. Those decision tasks are of the form If X then Y. Consider Figure 2-1, a dialog box taken from MicroSoft Word IV when one of the authors attempted to quit without saving his work. The author is asked to make a decision, the outcome of which will have profoundly different effects on the system. A selection of Yes will cause the file to be saved to disk, a selection of No will not save the file and his work will be lost, and the selection of Cancel will return the system to its edit state.

2.2 Performing a Task Analysis

A task analysis may be performed in many different ways. The approach taken depends, primarily, on the type of work being performed and the perspective of the analyst. For example, a systems analyst might identify tasks through an analysis of the system's functions and processes, while an analyst from OSHA (Occupational Safety and Health Administration) might analyze the tasks to determine if the users have to make frequent, repetitive movements, hold their bodies in postures inducing static loading of their muscles, be exposed to harmful levels of radiation from the CRT, or any other types of interactions that could adversely affect the health of the user.

Whatever method is used, you should begin with the construction of a user profile (Section 2.3) and use it to re-examine design and equipment options from a human performance perspective as you identify the task, performance, and risk implications in progressively greater detail during the analysis. Generally speaking, an integrated, top-down task analysis may be the best means of conducting a task analysis of a computing system. This approach is very compatible with computing systems since computer programs are very often constructed in a top-down fashion by software and systems engineers.

2.2.1 The Top-Down Task Analysis Method

Top-Down analysis begins with the assumption that the flow of work functions are error free and normal. Complicating factors such as system crashes, fatal errors, equipment failure, restart after down time for normal maintenance, and continuation after emergencies are addressed in later iterations. The analysis, therefore, focuses on aggregate functions (i.e., the mission of the system) rather than maintenance functions (administrative/support).

Decisions and tasks provide the basis for beginning the analysis. A generic, top-down task analysis can be outlined as follows:

Step 1:   Establish the purpose or objective for the task analysis.

Step 2:   Identify potential users and/or subject matter experts.

Step 3:   Determine whether or not one-on-one interviews or consensual interviews are warranted.

Step 4:   Interview the individual users, construct user profiles (See User Profile Worksheet, Section 2.3), assemble the experts, or walkthrough the activities.

Step 5:   Use the answers to the questions asked during the interview to establish a rough framework of task categories (See Data Form 1, Section 2.4.1).

Step 6:   Break the job down into discrete steps to define functional task sequences.

Step 7:   Identify sequential tasks through videotape recordings, walk-throughs, or planning and state the purpose for each task step.

Step 8:   Specify the tasks in behavioral and system terms.

Step 9:   Input the data into a PC database package such as DBase, Paradox, FoxPro for future analysis.

Step 10:   Analyze or synthesize the data for each purpose originally stated.

Step 11:   Prepare an analytic report.

It sometimes helps, from an organizational standpoint, to condense these steps into a preparation phase, a task analysis phase, and a report generation phase (Table 2-2).

2.2.1.1 Preparation Phase (Steps 1 thru 5)

Step 1:   Organize a management meeting to establish objectives and scope of the task analysis.

You should schedule an initial meeting that includes members from the departments that will be affected by your task analysis. For example, if the analysis concerns the job impacts of the design of a control console for the control room of a nuclear power plant, the typical attenders would include representatives from Systems Development and Operations, Process Engineering, Safety, Procedures, Training, and Industrial Engineering. Your list may differ somewhat from this one.

The purpose of this meeting is to discuss the project with management and agree on the project's objectives. The value of getting support from all of the departments involved cannot be underestimated. Without interdepartmental support, political turf battles can arise which could threaten your entire project.

Table 2-2: Phases of Task Analysis

Preparation phase	1. Establish task analysis objectives and scope 2. Establish management support and commitment of personnel 3. Familiarize participants with objectives, work plan, and method 4. Establish data collection model
Task analysis phase	5. Construct a user profile by completing the User Profile Worksheet in Section 2.3 6. Define process/system functions 7. Analyze process/system functions to develop a task list 8. Review the task list, or obtain agreement from experts if a panel of experts is used 9. Analyze tasks, and complete task analysis forms
Report writing phase	10. Review task analysis data forms and revise if necessary 11. Enter data into a computer data base 12. Match data to project objectives and prepare a written report

You should bring to the meeting a brief demonstration, like the one in Table 2-1, and you should give a **brief** explanation of task analysis as a tool for integrating system development, reducing costs, increasing user performance, and managing risk.

This meeting will determine what the members of the team wish to obtain from the analysis, for example:

1. a delineation of the job functions, broken down into tasks and analyzed;

2. a first order set of operating procedures;

3. human-computer or man-machine interface requirements;

4. a list of job functions which may contain tasks suitable for partial or full automation based on criteria of risk, human error, task difficulty, consequence of error, and frequency of task execution;

5. identification of areas where design improvements could be incorporated into operations and maintenance activities;

6. production of a preliminary set of training requirements based on the the user profile, and a breakdown of job functions into tasks, and a categorization of the training requirements into system academic, and administrative knowledge/skill requirements;

7. provision of a operational job requirements for management;

8. provision of risk management tracking tools for management based on the actual operational job requirements.

Step 2:   Establish management support and commitment of personnel.

Individuals at the preliminary meeting should each obtain the support of their management so they can have access to, and the cooperation of, subject matter experts or expert users. This is a **key** preparation step. A pool of resource personnel needs to be identified from which subject matter experts or select users can be identified for interviews.

Step 3:   Locate subject matter experts and potential users.

Locating subject matter experts is often overlooked. The system that you are going to analyze may be too complex for you to be an expert in all of the aspects of the system. Some systems will require extensive "hand-holding" in order for you to understand and analyze all of the steps involved in the performance of the component tasks. Other systems will only involve checking with the experts in order to verify some task, or to have them review the task analysis to verify its completeness and fidelity to the functioning of the proposed or redesigned system.

Table 2-3 shows some of the subject matter experts who might be needed in the construction of one type of computing system. In any case, you will want to identify the potential users to complete the User Profile Worksheet (Section 2.3).

Table 2-3: Subject Matter Experts (Computerized Process Control)

Type of Expert	Contribution
Operations	Explain functions Delineation of task requirements Identify potential hazards Identify potential sources of error
Process engineers Systems analysts	Identify facility/equipment design options Identify operational sequences and timing
Industrial health Industrial safety Radiation protection Radiation engineering	Contribute to the identification of hazard sources Delineation of task requirements Consequences of error potentials Means of mitigating errors and hazards
Human factors	Verify logical sequence of tasks Verify task-human performance compatibility Verify task-display/control design compatibility Verify task-operations compatibility Identify human error prone tasks

You must not forget, nor underestimate, the importance of completing the User Profile Worksheet and having the potential users involved **early** in the task analysis. If the potential users have used some previous version of the system, they can provide an invaluable wealth of information about the good and -- more often -- the bad aspects of the old system. This user input can not only help you closely map the proposed system to the users' mental representation of the tasks, but it will also prevent you from discarding the good aspects of the old system and retaining the bad aspects.

Once you have identified the subject matter experts and potential users, the next step is to extensively interview about the nature of the operations to be performed and the ramifications involved with each task.

Step 4:   Familiarize participants with objectives, work plan, and method

A kickoff meeting should be conducted for experts and users who will be the participants in the data development and review. Objectives and scope should be reviewed at this meeting. Provide the participants with an orientation to task analysis. The experts or users will have a great deal of knowledge in a given technical area, but they will probably have no knowledge of task analysis. Review the steps of the work plan and discuss scheduling issues. Keep in mind that participants have other job responsibilities besides working with you on the task analysis, and they are likely to feel that this is just one more burden. It is extremely important to be diplomatic at this point, and to couch the discussion of the analysis in terms of how the outcome of the analysis will improve their job. The final item on the agenda of the kickoff meeting should be an agreement on the types of data about a task that should be developed in the analysis.

Step 5:   Establish the data collection model

A data collection model used in previous task analyses conducted in other departments or facilities, if available, can be used as a starting point. Data categories and category definitions should be added, deleted, and modified to suit the system under analysis and the objectives of the management. Certain data items may be identified as questionable in terms of their applicability to the present system under analysis, but these should not be excluded until they can be tested as the analysis progresses. They may ultimately be omitted during the course of the analysis. Additional modifications will be made to clarify data category definitions as questions arise during the analysis.

The data collection model is embodied in the task analysis Data Form 1 (Section 2.4.1) and a corresponding set of task analysis category definitions, that will be used to create an analytic report.

2.2.1.2 Task Analysis Phase (Steps 6 thru 10)

Step 6:   Define job functions

Job functions will be defined in the form of brief narrative statements that specify:

1. starting conditions,

2. major activities resulting in changes in system status,

3. end conditions.

The job function descriptions serve to bound the tasks to be included in each job activity and to indicate major task groupings. Modifications are made as the task list is developed. When filling in the detailed steps of a job activity, task groupings that may initially be overlooked are identified, and better ways of bounding job activities or ordering activities with the job will emerge.

Step 7:   Analyze job functions to develop a task list[1].

The initial task list will be developed in several interview sessions with either a typical user of the proposed system or with a development team composed of subject matter experts. Generally speaking, if the proposed system is an enhancement to, or is based on an existing system, then interviews with typical users will provide information for eliminating the inadequacies of the old system and retaining the useful aspects of the existing systems. On the other hand, if no design precedent exists, because the system is novel or revolutionary, then a panel of design experts should be assembled. This group will define the specific steps that would need to be performed by the proposed users of the new system.

In either case, job function descriptions provide a framework for the ensuing interview. These interviews will provide the information needed to guide design changes or to create initial designs. If the interviewee is technically oriented, use proposed screen, control, display or plant layouts, anticipated equipment, control requirements, and schematics to stimulate the discussions.

Step 7A: Interviewing subject matter experts

In this step, you will interview subject matter experts, rather than users, in order to derive a list of the elemental steps which represent the tasks comprising the operation which the user will be performing. Due to the cost and extremely limited nature of an expert's time, this step is conducted when a new system is being put into place and no typical users exist, or when the input of an expert will give the analysis a depth or dimension not available from a typical user (e.g., in systems that are linked via a network, it would be important to have an expert's input to help chart the flow of information between the linked systems in order to assess the potential for inherited error. The overall view, or "big picture", may not be known by any single user, but will be known by the network manager or the systems analyst in charge of the network).

Prior to the actual interview, you should carefully familiarize yourself with operations manuals, documentation, common jargon, and so on. This is done in order to establish a common ground between the interviewer and the subject matter expert. Since subject matter experts' time is usually limited, this also reduces the amount of time needed for the interview by reducing the need for the expert to bring you "up-to-speed" on information that can be obtained through reference material.

Most task analytic interviews are conducted on a one-to-one basis. While the potential for distractions during the interview should be reduced as much as possible, it is absolutely essential to analyze the interaction between the user and their workplace; the interaction between user and system cannot be fully understood unless it is directly observed. For example, if the task to be analyzed is going to involve interaction between a portable CRT unit, a portable computer, or some type of heavy machinery on the floor of a shop or plant, then that portion of the interview should be conducted at the job site.

Step 7B: Interviewing individual users and completing the User Profile Worksheet:

Individual users will give you the greatest insight into user-system performance issues. These are the people who do the job on a day-to-day basis. While their so-called "gripes" about the system may be written off by management as whining or typical employee "sour grapes", *you should keep a keen ear for such complaints, because they are likely to signal an underlying problem with the existing system that may be resulting in user errors and costing the company resources*. Also take this opportunity to gather information about the users' strengths and weaknesses by filling out the User Profile Worksheet (Section 2.3.1). The information gathered using the User Profile Worksheet will be used later for allocating the tasks to user or system, which will determine the design of the interface.

The Institute for Nuclear Power Operations (INPO) (1985) lists the following suggestions for conducting the actual task analysis interview. The following interviewing suggestions have been adapted and expanded from that material.

○ An analysis of the task sequence is much easier to perform if the interview is conducted so that the steps involved in the job are discussed in the sequence in which the worker/user performs them. This will make the analysis of the task sequence much easier to perform.

○ Ask neutral, rather than leading questions (i.e., the answer is implied in the question).

○ Frequently stop, summarize, and confirm the accuracy of your recorded information.

○ Ask only one question at a time to keep from tiring the interviewee.

○ If the interviewee is verbose, and the verbosity does not add useful information, then narrow the scope of your questions. If the interviewee is reticent or reserved, then broaden the scope with open-ended questions.

○ Always use simple words and sentences to reduce the potential for confusion.

○ Never be condescending, patronizing, superior, or authoritarian with the interviewee. Strive to make them feel like your equal.

○ Avoid interrupting the interviewee unless you need to clarify something that is unclear.

○ Make sure the recorded information about each step is complete. If not, ask for clarification.

○ Follow up leads that may be pertinent to the current topic, but avoid getting side-tracked.

○ If the interviewee has a tendency to stray from the topic, gently and politely steer them back to the topic.

○ Use the Data Forms in Sections 2.4.1 and 2.4.2 to facilitate the quick, legible, and accurate recording of data. These forms should also be used in the preliminary analysis of the tasks during the interview so that you and the interviewee can check the flow and accuracy of the tasks.

○ As the end of the interview approaches, **always** summarize and check the recorded tasks with the interviewee, paying careful attention to the reported order of each task sequencing and the accuracy of the recordings.

Step 7C: Consensual task analysis

A consensual meeting assembles the subject matter experts for the purpose of discussing design alternatives and arriving at a collective agreement (consensus) on the construction of each task. Consensus meetings are used instead of one-on-one interviews when a new system is being designed and no design precedents exist for the type of system being designed.

For example, suppose that the current project is the design of a virtual reality control system for repairing satellites using remotely piloted vehicles launched from an orbital, space platform. In a situation such as this one, at the time of this book's writing, no precedent exists for using virtual reality as a means for controlling remotely piloted vehicles. In this case, a number of subject matter experts in human performance in virtual reality systems as well as experts in aerospace engineering, mechanical engineering, electrical engineers, software engineers, and human factors engineers with experience in the control of remotely piloted vehicles, would be required to define the types of activities which would be undertaken by the user of this system.

What follows are suggestions for conducting a consensual task analysis adapted and augmented from INPO 85-006 (1985).

○ Specify the goal of the meeting (i.e., create a list of tasks using a remotely piloted vehicle).

○ Have the subject matter experts create a list of tasks within their specialty.

○ State the group leader's role (e.g., moderator, facilitator, and clarifier of problems).

○ Don't permit any one individual to dominate the discussion. Ensure that the discussion includes all of the experts as equally as possible.

○ Discuss only one job area at a time. Do not move on to another area until all tasks in that particular job area have been clearly defined and all conflicts between experts have been resolved.

○ Resolve **all** conflicts. In the infrequent event that a conflict cannot be resolved, use the majority opinion or the option that provides the least amount of hazard to the user or to system integrity.

○ Collate the tasks, given by the experts, into a unified list outside of the meeting.

○ Give the list to the experts and have them verify its accuracy.

○ Have the experts rate each task in terms of its potential for human error, and the relative hazard associated with human error to the user and to system integrity.

○ Take each rating and determine the mean, median, or mode of each expert rating, whichever makes the most sense under the circumstances.

○ Summarize the results and the ratings.

○ Take the finished task list and give it to additional subject matter experts for review in each area of expertise.

Step 8:   Conduct a review of the task list.

Distribute the completed task list to all members of both the data development and review groups for review and comment. Arrange a meeting where changes can be discussed and agreed on by the data development and the review groups. The resulting task list will serve as the starting point for completing task analysis Data Form 1 (Section 2.4.1).

The completion of the data forms will identify any need for additional information or changes in the task list. Another iteration of task list development sessions should be conducted involving **all** participants, to resolve issues identified in the detailed analysis, incorporate additional information, and establish a final task list.

Step 8A: Typical questions to ask once the task list has been completed

The type of questions asked during the task analytic interview are extremely critical. **Never** ask leading questions. What follows is a group of questions, based on Danchak (1981), which should be asked once the task list is completed to provide a structure for defining information requirements. The answers to these questions provide the basis for design decisions and should be used to analyze each task. The answers to these questions should be recorded on a Data Form 2, (Section 2.4.2). This form can then be used to select screen elements (Chapter 4) appropriate for displaying the required information.

○ **Upon how many dimensions of information does this task depend?**

Examples of dimensions are temperature, pressure, flow, time, switch position, social security numbers, account numbers, credit card numbers, and so forth. For example, if a task depends only on temperature, then it is unidimensional; if the task depends upon temperature and pressure, it is duodimensional; if it depends upon more than two dimensions, then it is a multidimensional task. Using a different example, if budget reconciliation depends upon the input of a single budget estimate, then the task is unidimensional; if it depends upon a budget estimate and a project number then it is duodimensional, and so on.

○ **Upon how many variables and with what precision does the task depend?**

A single variable is a single value (e.g., a single temperature measurement, social security number) or a particular combination interpreted as a single entity, for example, a combination of water temperature and pressure (i.e. single variable, duodimensional). Tasks with more than one, but less than six, variables are classified as limited multivariate. For example, a display showing market share, profit-loss, and corporate growth based on a "what if" business risk analysis would be a limited multivariate (Figure 2-2).

○ **How many visual samples does the user need for this task, and is the sampling rate adequate for accurate user control and decision making?**

In the simplest case, only a single, discrete value of a given variable is needed. However, often multiple samples will be taken over a period of time. Two to 15 samples constitutes a limited series, and more than 15 constitutes a series. The number of information samples to be displayed to the user may depend upon how rapidly the information changes, is updated, or is the source sampled . However, at this point, you only need to identify the number of samplings the user would need to perform under the worst case scenarios.

○ **Is the displayed information derived directly from measured data, or is it derived from a formula or model; will the deviation affect the user's confidence in the data?**

You may wish to distinguish between measured and derived data, since the quality of the derivation may affect the user's confidence or provide insight into the cause of conflicting or ambiguous information.

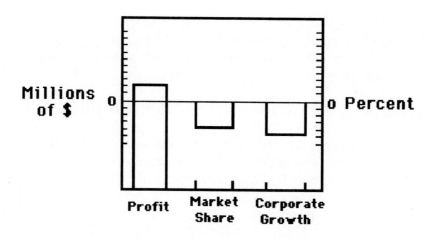

Figure 2-2: Limited Multivariate Display

○ **For what purpose is the information made available?**

The purpose is to alert, alarm, call attention, or otherwise make known to the user that some noteworthy event has happened. Such displays allow the user to answer the question "What happened?"

Examples include:

- a technical specification is about to be violated,

- a circuit breaker has been tripped,

- a CPU has failed,

- an emergency safety system has been self-activated,

- a system error has been encountered,

- important data has been updated.

A secondary purpose is to inform or supply detailed information about specific state variables and system configuration. Such displays allow the user to obtain qualitative or quantitative values for a variable or variables. Examples include displays of:

- a qualitative value such as temperature or pressure,

- some relative information such as "X" is greater than "Y",

- a status such as "On" or "Off," "Normal" or "Abnormal."

○ **How quickly will this information change in response to control actions so that the user obtains fast confirmation?**

Some variables change value very rapidly in response to control actions made by the user, while others do not. Both rapidly and extremely slow changing variables may require certain display enhancements. With extremely slow reacting variables, the system may have to predict the future impact of current control actions. The user may use different scales or completely different screen elements when controlling rather than monitoring a variable.

○ **Does this task require displays of quantitative or qualitative information for cognitive processing?**

If numeric values or percentages are required, the task requires quantitative information displays, while status indicators and warning signals are examples of qualitative information displays. Often, a user is supplied with quantitative information that must be converted into qualitative terms, such as "high," "low," "on," "off," or "danger." Whenever possible, anticipate how users will use the displayed information and avoid display designs that require users to convert quantitative information into qualitative information.

○ **What is the realistic usable range of this variable?**

Before selecting the screen elements (Chapter 4), you must consider the normal operating range of the variable and its highest and lowest meaningful values.

○ **What is the required accuracy level of the variable?[2]**

The required level of accuracy may depend on the current range of the variable. Different tasks require different levels, accuracy, and/or different ranges for the same variable.

○ **What is the signal-to-noise ratio of the incoming data?[2]**

Data such as plant or vehicle system data will inherently have some noise. This noise often results from sensing raw data or transmitting the signals from sensors to the computer. Noise may even occur in the channel from the computer to the monitor. Identify the signal-to-noise ratios of all information channels to determine how information can best be displayed. A very noisy signal may require preprocessing to smooth out unwanted noise. Alternatively, display scales insensitive to inherent noise may be chosen.

○   **Is the information to be used in an absolute or relative manner?**[2]

Most quantitative information is presented in absolute terms (e.g., 911° F or 14 psig or 95 gpm). However, often the absolute value is not as important as is the relationship between one value and another. For example, in a nuclear power plant, the prevention of thermal shock depends on the relative difference between the temperature of the crucible vessel and the temperature of the incoming coolant. In cases such as this, the display must convey the values in a manner amenable to comparison.

Although answering this set of questions may not completely define the information to be displayed, the answers provide an adequate start for the design process. Additional significant characteristics of the information to be displayed may be identified when answering these questions. The purpose of this design step is to identify the information needs of the user in terms of the attributes of the data to be displayed and the intended use of the information. As mentioned previously, the use of a data forms such as those included in sections 2.4.1 and 2.4.2, is suggested when assembling the required information.

Step 9:   Analyze tasks, complete the task analysis data forms.

A series of group interview/discussion sessions should be conducted to complete the task analysis data in accordance with the task category definitions.

Step 10:   Review task analysis data forms and compare them with the User Profile Worksheet.

Conduct a review with those who participated in the detailed analysis and completion forms. The comments made during this review will be incorporated in the on-line data base.

2.2.1.3 Report Generation Phase (Steps 11 thru 12).

Step 11:   Enter data into a data base management system.

A system for task data management should be developed in a data base package such as DBase, FoxPro, or Paradox. The system should allow keyword searching and rapid sorting and retrieval of selected data. The system should also include routines for calculation and plotting of risk indicators and/or other quantifiable parameters of tasks.

Step 12:   Synthesize/analyze data and prepare report.

The final treatment of the data is straightforward. The method of analysis should be designed so that the task descriptions will constitute a set of first-order procedures. Training requirements should be consolidated into a list of unique items that identify all of the tasks and subtasks to which each training item is applicable. In addition, lists of the types of errors and hazards intrinsic to task requirements should be generated. The descriptive lists of types of error and hazards may be used to identify tasks that should be given particular attention in procedures, training, and supervision. Human factors engineering evaluation of high-risk tasks may also be warranted to reducing risk through facility or system design and/or equipment enhancement.

2.3 Constructing a User Profile

While performing the task analysis interviews, you should construct a profile of each of the users, in order to gain a better understanding of their strengths and weaknesses. The user profile is a psychological and occupational sketch of the system users that will help determine how closely the tasks are matched to the abilities of the users.

Mayhew (1992; pg 60-76) presents an excellent method of creating a user profile with checklists. This method is both time-saving and an easy way to construct a "snap shot" of the "typical" user. The User Profile Worksheet that is presented here is a modification and extension of the Mayhew method. While Mayhew's checklist is an excellent way for formulating profiles of users of small systems, it is not sufficiently detailed. Some of the sections of her checklist have been streamlined, while others have been greatly expanded to make it more compatible with larger, inter-corporate systems. The motivation and attitude measures have been eliminated in our worksheet. While these measures are very important and very relevant to performance, we would argue that, for large corporations (e.g., General Motors, IBM, AT&T, and so on), these perceptions are an outcome of the corporate environment. Motivation, for instance, may determine the degree to which a person is willing to learn to use a new system; however, motivation is largely a product of management style and not of the interface. If management style is paternalistic and authoritarian, and users must learn to use a system or be fired, motivation to use the system will be high, albeit satisfaction will be low. While interfaces should be designed to be as non-threatening as possible, often there is little that a system designer can do to change a threatening and hostile work environment that is the result of an over-authoritarian management style.

In keeping with the tone of this book, we have tried to keep our approach to profile construction generic. However, we strongly encourage you to also review Mayhew's approach to determine if her approach better suits your needs.

2.3.1 User Profile Worksheet

Inasmuch as a road map serves as a guide for a long trip, the user profile serves as a guide for mapping the needs of the user (user profile) to the needs of the job (task analysis). The completed task analysis will show the elemental components of the job (tasks). It is your job, or whoever is actually performing the analysis, to determine where the abilities of the user match and do not match the job's needs. For example, if the job requires the user to be able to type at a rate of

100 words per minute (wpm) and the user can only type 40 wpm, then a mismatch exists between the abilities of the user to perform the task and the requirements for completion of the task. When a mismatch occurs, user error rates rise and user satisfaction falls. To reduce any mismatches, carefully analyze the abilities of the user and the requirements of the job/task to determine what changes can be made (e.g., automation of some tasks) to reduce this gap, thereby reducing user errors (increasing performance) and increasing user satisfaction.

The first step is to complete the User Profile Worksheet, included at the end of this section. This worksheet will give a thorough profile of what the user's abilities are. This worksheet is geared to computer-based systems, since that is the topic of this work. However, you can copy this worksheet or easily modify it to suit non-computer (e.g., manual labor) jobs.

What follows is a description of the categories that appear on the worksheet and a discussion of their relevance to computer system design. The worksheets follow this section.

2.3.2 Constructing the Profile

The User Profile Worksheet is divided into 5 sections: Physical Characteristics, Education, Work-related Experience, Computer Experience, and Job/Task Characteristics. Each of these sections describe different characteristics of the user that will influence design decisions. The answers in some of the sections may suggest interface designs that may be at odds with interfaces suggested by other sections. That's okay. Every user is unique, and thus each profile will be unique. The results from **ALL** of the user profiles should be weighed so that informed design trade-offs can be made.

2.3.2.1 Physical Characteristics

Physical Characteristics describe the overall physical condition of the user and outlines any physical limitations that could influence their ability to complete the task.

Age is important for a number of reasons. First, visual acuity begins to decline around age 50, as does hearing. In addition, research has shown that the ability of individuals to divide their attention between two competing tasks (e.g., monitoring oncoming traffic and changing the radio station) also begins to decline with advancing age. Finally, certain motor and information processing illnesses, such as Parkinson's Disease and Alzheimer's Disease , have their onset with increasing age.

Sample User Profile

User Identification Number: 167-54-3437   Date: 1/30/92
System or Subsystem: Remote Sales System   Job: Field Ordering
Interviewer: Jon Weimer, Ph.D.

Physical Characteristics:

Age: 41-50   Gender: Female   Color Blindness: No

Visual Acuity: 20/20 Corrected (Bifocals)   Hearing: Normal

Physically Challenged: No

Education:

Reading Level: 9th to 12th grade   Education: College Graduate

Mathematical Level: Algebra   Native Language: Spanish

Work-related Experience:

Job Category: Sales (Pharmaceutical Sales)   Typing Skill: "Hunt and Peck"

Experience With Targeted Task/Job: Expert (in sales)

Computer Experience:

General Computer Experience: Novice   Years Using Computers: 0-1

Computer Literacy: Low

Specific Computer Activities: Data Entry & Manipulation

Applications Used: Spreadsheet

Operating Systems Used: GUI Operating System (e.g. Macintosh, Windows)

Hardware Used: Personal Computers

Sample User Profile (Page 2)

User Identification Number: 167-54-3437   Date: 1/30/92
System or Subsystem: Remote Sales System   Job: Field Ordering
Interviewer: Jon Weimer, Ph.D.

Job Characteristics:

Target Job Category: Sales   Typing Skill Required: None

Computer Experience Required by Job/Task: Expert

Computer Literacy Required by Task/Job: Intermediate

Specific Job/Task Activities: On-line Order Placement, Inventory Monitoring

Type of Application: On-line, Field Ordering System

Type of Operating Systems Used: Graphical User Interface (GUI)

Frequency of Computer Use Required to Perform Task/Job: High

Turnover Rate on Job/Task: High

Job/Task Structure: High (Ordering task is rigidly defined)

Job/Task Importance: High

Type of Job/Task Training Provided: Manual only

Design Recommendations:

A remote, notebook pc-based system, with a fax/modem and a GUI based
operating system. The language employed in the system should be Spanish, and
the system should include a GUI shell that will enable the user to maintain the
GUI interface while logged onto the mainframe via a modem connection.
Training should be required to increase the literacy of the user, while the system
should concomitantly be redesigned to require less literacy on the part of future
users.

Gender <u>does</u> play a role in the design of interfaces. For example, color blindness is a sex-linked trait resulting in a greater percentage of males who are color blind than females, and anthropometric differences may limit the type of hardware (e.g., size of trackball) you choose if the entire population of users is female (Mayhew, 1992, pg 71).

Color blindness, **visual acuity**, and **hearing** ability will influence the type of display that can be implemented. Color blindness will limit the colors that can be used; visual acuity will determine font size, stroke width of characters, and viewing distance and angle; hearing will determine the volume and pitch of auditory signals. In most cases, you can simply ask the user what their vision is. Most people don't know what their hearing abilities are, but many big companies require routine physicals and that information can be obtained from those records with the permission of the user.

Color blindness is interesting in that some individuals can go through most of their lives without any knowledge that they are color blind. One of the authors was recently showing a group of executives a touchscreen display that used yellow-green squares to simulate active buttons and darker green to simulate inactive buttons. One of the executives replied that he couldn't tell the difference between the active and inactive buttons!

The **physically challenged** pose particularly challenging design problems. With increasing numbers of the physically challenged in the workplace, it is more important than ever before that the needs of the physically challenged be considered during the design process.

2.3.2.2 Education

The **education** of the user is very important, since not all computer applications are equal in their complexity. The computer system that is used by high school kids to checkout movies at your local video rental store requires much less educational background than SYSTAT, which assumes a high level of statistical sophistication on the part of the user.

Reading Level refers to the **highest** grade level at which a person is capable of reading. Reading level is often inferred by education level, because a correlation is assumed, even if it is not always a correct assumption. Even a Ph.D. degree cannot help you decipher computer manuals that are hard to read due to poor writing, poor grammar, or poor organization. Reading level refers to the grammatical construction of the sentences (grammar is assumed to be accurate) and the number, size and familiarity of the words used.

> **NOTE:** To determine the reading level of on-line instructions and user manuals, use the Automated Readability Index (Kincaid, 1975). First, select five or more 100-150 word samples. Determine the average letters per word and average number of words per sentence for each sample. Then apply the following formula, where L = average number of letters per word and W = average number of words per sentence:
>
> $$\textbf{Reading Grade Level} = 4.71L + 0.5W - 21.43$$

The user's **Mathematical** abilities are important to know -- particularly when the task requires calculations to be performed. If the users are weak, mathematically, then perhaps the bulk of the calculations can be automated to relieve the user of the burden of performing the calculations themselves. In addition, mathematical ability is also often correlated with spatial ability, and good spatial reasoning is helpful when navigating through complex menu hierarchies and hypertext.

The **Native Language** of the user is extremely important. If a company is thinking of exporting a successful system abroad, it may not be as simple as translating the instructions from English. Subtleties exist in every language that can be lost during translation. Whenever possible, try to work with an individual whose native language is the same as the target system so that subtleties can be exploited to make the system easier to understand. In addition, the native language could effect screen layout (e.g., Hebrew is read from right to left and English is read from left to right).

2.3.2.3 Work-related Experience

The **Job Category** of the user is very important for determining the user's level of technical sophistication. For example, a system that was designed for a traveling salesman (see the sample user profile) would be very different from the one that you would design for a user who has been a computer data-entry clerk for 15 years. Similarly, **Experience With Targeted Task/Job** shows whether the system is meant to augment the user's current abilities, or if it must also include some imbedded training to train the person on the task as well as the system.

The **Typing Skill** of the user is a very important concern. If all of the users have no typing experience or are of the "Hunt and Peck" variety, and if the system does not rely on verbal inputs (e.g., a control panel in a nuclear power plant) then you might consider using a graphical interface with a pointing device (e.g., touchscreen, light pen, mouse, trackball) instead of a keyboard for input.

2.3.2.4 Computer Experience

General Computer Experience refers to the amount of experience that the user has working with computers, in general. General computer experience is a qualitative measure that is related to the quantitative measure of **Years Using**

Computers. For example, a user could spend 5 years doing data entry, using the same program, and have less computer experience that an individual who has only used computers for a year, but who has had intensive experience using 5 different applications.

Computer Literacy, which is related to general computer experience and years using computers, refers to how much the user actually knows about computers. Do they know jargon? Do they know the difference between hardware and software? Could they install software upgrades if they had to? This characteristic is particularly important to interface designers, since all too often system designers and programmers use a great deal of computer jargon (e.g., queue, buffer, saving, function keys, memory, and so on) when they design an interface. That jargon, while clear and parsimonious to them, may confuse and frustrate less literate users.

The more **Specific Computer Activities** the user has engaged in the higher their computer literacy probably is, and the more experienced they probably are. Similarly, the more **Applications Used**, the more **Operating Systems Used**, and the more **Hardware Used**, the more experienced and literate the users are likely to be. This information is invaluable when making design decisions. If the choice is between designing a system with a graphical user interface (e.g., Windows) and designing it with a command line interface (e.g., DOS), and if all of the users have experience using graphical user interface systems, it is probably a wise choice to stay with a graphical user interface.

2.3.2.5 Job Characteristics

This section outlines the defining characteristics of the job, rather than the user. This is done on the same form to facilitate the comparison of the user's needs with those required to perform the task.

When designing an interface, the **Target Job Category** must be considered. An on-line ordering and inventory system would not meet the needs of a physician, but they are well suited to the needs of a traveling salesman with a laptop computer and a modem. The interface must serve as an easy-to-traverse bridge between the user and the job/task.

Typing Skill Required here refers to whether or not typing is necessary to complete the task rather than the abilities of the user. Similarly, **Computer Experience Required by Job/Task** refers to the experience required to operate the system and complete the task. The experience required must match the needs of the user, otherwise errors will occur. While the users can be trained to use the new system, training and manuals should never be relied upon to bring users "up-to-speed." The system should fit to the user rather than expecting training to fit the user to the system. Too many systems are designed that expect the user to fit themselves to it. Those systems are the ones that waste corporate resources by generating a large number of user errors, user absenteeism, and large training costs. A system in which the interface closely matches the expectations and abilities of the users will be fairly self-explanatory (e.g., consider the Macintosh delete procedure of dragging the target file's icon to the trash, which bulges when the file icon is superimposed over the trashcan icon). The more self-explanatory the interface, the less training will be required, thus saving the corporation valuable resources that would have been spent on training.

Similarly, how much **Computer Literacy Required by Task/Job** is an often overlooked issue. Too often, designers assume that users have more computer savvy than they do, thus resulting in interfaces that are cryptic and frustrating to the users.

Often, the **Specific Job/Task Activities** (placing orders) will determine the **Type of Application** (On-line, Field Ordering System).

The **Type of Operating Systems Used** (e.g., Graphical User Interface) should be determined by the amount of computer experience and computer literacy of the target user population, and the type of task to be performed. If the users are novices, a graphical user interface will better suit their needs than a command language interface, because a graphical user interface uses pictures of familiar objects (icons) to represent functions, with the purpose of making the underlying functions more intuitive to novice users (e.g., throwing an old file into the trash), who might be inexperienced with remembering a large lexicon of command names.

Frequency of Computer Use Required to Perform Task/Job is important for two reasons. If the task is to be performed infrequently, then a command language interface might not be the best choice, because the users might forget the commands between each usage. Second, if the task requires a number of repetitive actions, such as those occurring in calculations and in doing "what if" modeling of business scenarios, then you should try to automate the repetitious actions to reduce the burden of the user.

High **Turnover Rate on Job/Task** is often a clear signal that something is wrong with the design of the existing job or the immediate management structure. While high turnover is often the result of poor management or an overly hostile management style, it may also be caused by frustration with the existing interface. In any event, high turnover means that something is wrong and further attention is required.

If the **Job/Task Structure** is high (e.g., if engine temperature = X degrees then increase the level of coolant flow by Y number of gallons per minute) then consider automating this task/job, since highly structured tasks lend themselves to automation.

Job/Task Importance determines the severity of the consequences resulting from failing to successfully complete the task. If the user fails to successfully use an ATM, the only consequence is that they may be given their card back and told to try again (or at worst have their card eaten). However, in the case where a user is monitoring the core of a nuclear reactor, the situation changes. There can be no doubt that the individual monitoring the reactor core places somewhat greater emphasis on making sure that their job is done correctly than does the person using an ATM. The person monitoring the reactor core has the responsibility for not only protecting their own life, but also the lives of their family, all of the other workers at the plant , and the lives of the thousands of people who live in the surrounding communities. Thus, job importance has the side effect of increasing the motivation of the user to perform the task more accurately. It will also determine how seriously users take their training.

Type of Job/Task Training Provided must be carefully matched to the characteristics of the user and the needs of the task. There are very few instances, in our opinion, in which a manual-only format is sufficient, since most users don't read their manuals. Have you read the manuals that came with your car? Your VCR or stereo? Most users who have some computer experience prefer to learn about the system through guided exploration (Carroll, Mack, Lewis, Grischkowksy, Robertson, 1985; Carroll, Smith-Kerker, Ford, and Mazur-Rimetz, 1987-1988). In fact, some recent research has suggested that guided exploration may be the best way to learn to use a system (Carroll, Smith-Kerker, Ford, and Mazur-Rimetz, 1987-1988). The training that will be provided must be judiciously chosen, just like the method of interface, so as to meet both the needs of the task and the needs of the user.

User errors are decreased and user satisfaction increased when the needs of the interface and the capabilities of the user are closely matched. By "knowing" what the user can and cannot do, the designer can make an informed decision as to which functions to allocate to the user and which functions to allocate to the system. The User Profile Worksheet, which begins on the next page, gives the designer a fairly comprehensive description of the limitations of the user. The old phrase "A man has to know his limitations" is never more appropriate than in the field of system design, where a designer must "know their users' limitations." The information gathered using the User Profile Worksheet should be studied in conjunction with the information gleaned from the task analysis data sheets that appear in sections 2.4.1 and 2.4.2. The information obtained from the task analysis data sheets describe the needs of the task. We have found that the allocation of functions is easiest when the information from these three worksheets are studied together.

The User Profile Worksheet offers additional benefits. It is a useful document for training and documentation designers, since training and documentation must also be designed around the capabilities of the user population. Also, the User Profile Worksheet is helpful when tradeoffs must be made. Since it is a rare system that is designed in the absence of constraints, the User Profile Worksheet acts as a useful guide when prioritizing system functions. For example, GUI systems require terminals with graphics capabilities. If the current hardware does not support graphics, the change-over of all of the existing hardware could be a very costly one. The User Profile Worksheet can help determine if a GUI interface is needed, or if it is simply desirable.

User Profile Worksheet

User Identification Number: _____   Date: ____
System or Subsystem: _____   Job: _____
Interviewer: _____

Physical Characteristics: (Check all that apply)

Age: Gender: Color Blindness:

❑ 18-30   ❑ Male   ❑ No
❑ 31-40   ❑ Female   ❑ Protanope (Red Insensitive)
❑ 41-50   ❑ Deuteranope (Green Insensitive)
❑ > 50

Visual Acuity: Hearing:

❑ 20/20   ❑ Normal
❑ 20/20 Corrected   ❑ Impaired _____
    ❑ Monofocals   ❑ Corrected _____
    ❑ Bifocals
    ❑ Other _____
❑ Legally Blind

Physically Challenged:

❑ No
❑ Yes _____
_____

Education: (Check all that apply)

Reading Level: Education:

❑ Less that 5th grade   ❑ Didn't graduate high school
❑ 5th to 9th grade   ❑ High School Graduate
❑ 9th to 12th grade   ❑ Technical Degree
❑ Collegiate   ❑ College Graduate

Mathematical Level: Native Language:

❑ Arithmetic   ❑ English
❑ Geometry/Trigonometry   ❑ Spanish
❑ Algebra   ❑ Japanese
❑ Calculus   ❑ Other _____

User Profile Worksheet (Page 2)

User Identification Number: _ _ _ _ _ _ _   Date: _ _ _ _
System or Subsystem: _ _ _ _ _ _ _ _ _ _ _   Job: _ _ _ _ _
Interviewer: _ _ _ _ _ _ _ _ _ _ _ _ _ _ _ _

Work-related Experience: (Check all that apply)

Job Category: Typing Skill:

❑ Skilled Laborer   ❑ None
❑ Clerical   ❑ "Hunt and Peck" (< 40 wpm)
❑ Sales   ❑ Average Touch Typist (40-54 wpm)
❑ Professional/Technical   ❑ Good Touch Typist (55-89 wpm)
❑ Manager   ❑ Skilled Touch Typist (90-134 wpm)
❑ Executive   ❑ Expert Touch Typist (>135 wpm)

Experience With Targeted Task/Job:

❑ None
❑ Novice (requires supervised help to complete)
❑ Intermediate (occasionally requires help on more difficult parts)
❑ Expert (self-reliant, resource for others)

Computer Experience: (Check all that apply)

General Computer Experience: Years Using Computers:

❑ None   ❑ 0-1
❑ Novice (requires supervised help)   ❑ 1-3
❑ Intermediate (occasionally requires help)   ❑ 3-5
❑ Expert (self-reliant, resource for others)   ❑ > 5

Computer Literacy:

❑ None (never used a computer and has no computer knowledge)
❑ Low (little or no knowledge of jargon, low level activities only, e.g., data entry)
❑ Intermediate (some knowledge of jargon and hardware components, moderate
    activities such as advanced word-processing and basic software installation)
❑ Advanced (proficiency with jargon, adept at learning new software and
    hardware, can perform most software and hardware installation tasks, could
    be a resource for others.

User Profile Worksheet (Page 3)

User Identification Number: _ _ _ _ _ _ _ _   Date: _ _ _ _
System or Subsystem: _ _ _ _ _ _ _ _ _ _ _   Job: _ _ _ _ _
Interviewer: _ _ _ _ _ _ _ _ _ _ _ _ _ _ _ _

Computer Experience: (Continued)

Specific Computer Activities:

❑ Data Entry   ❑ Data Manipulation   ❑ System Monitoring
❑ Programming   ❑ Word-processing   ❑ Other _ _ _ _ _ _ _ _ _ _ _ _

Applications Used:

❑ Graphics System   ❑ Databases   ❑ CAD/CAM
❑ Spreadsheet   ❑ Word-processing   ❑ Programming Language
❑ Other _

Operating Systems Used:

❑ Command Language Operating System (e.g., DOS, UNIX, VM/CMS)
❑ Natural Language Operating System (e.g., SQL)
❑ GUI Operating System (e.g., Macintosh, Windows)

Hardware Used:

❑ Personal Computers   ❑ Workstations   ❑ Minicomputers
❑ Mainframes

Job Characteristics: (Check all that apply)

Target Job Category: Typing Skill Required By Task/Job:

❑ Skilled Laborer   ❑ None
❑ Clerical   ❑ "Hunt and Peck" (< 40 wpm)
❑ Sales   ❑ Average Touch Typist (40-54 wpm)
❑ Professional/Technical   ❑ Good Touch Typist (55-89 wpm)
❑ Manager   ❑ Skilled Touch Typist (90-134 wpm)
❑ Executive   ❑ Expert Touch Typist (>135 wpm)

User Profile Worksheet (Page 4)

User Identification Number: _ _ _ _ _ _ _ _   Date: _ _ _ _
System or Subsystem: _ _ _ _ _ _ _ _ _ _ _   Job: _ _ _ _ _
Interviewer: _ _ _ _ _ _ _ _ _ _ _ _ _ _ _ _ _

Job Characteristics: (Check all that apply)

Computer Experience Required by Job/Task:

❏ None
❏ Novice (requires supervised help)
❏ Intermediate (occasionally requires help)
❏ Expert (self-reliant, resource for others)

Computer Literacy Required by Task/Job:

❏ None (never used a computer and has no computer knowledge)
❏ Low (little or no knowledge of jargon, low level activities only, e.g., data entry)
❏ Intermediate (some knowledge of jargon and hardware components, moderate
    activities such as advanced word-processing and basic software installation)
❏ Advanced (proficiency with jargon, adept at learning new software and
    hardware, can perform most installation tasks, can be a resource for others.

Specific Job/Task Activities:

❏ Data Entry   ❏ Data Manipulation   ❏ System Monitoring
❏ Programming   ❏ Word-processing   ❏ Other _ _ _ _ _ _ _ _ _ _ _ _

Type of Application:

❏ Graphics System   ❏ Databases   ❏ CAD/CAM
❏ Spreadsheet   ❏ Word-processing   ❏ Programming Language
❏ Other _

Type of Operating Systems Used:

❏ Command Language Operating System (e.g., DOS, UNIX, VM/CMS)
❏ Natural Language Operating System (e.g., SQL)
❏ GUI Operating System (e.g., Macintosh, Windows)

Frequency of Computer Use Required to Perform Task/Job:

❏ None
❏ Low (Computer occasionally needed to perform infrequent tasks)
❏ Moderate (Computer used to perform infrequent to moderately frequent tasks)
❏ High (Computer required to perform the entire job)

User Profile Worksheet (Page 5)

User Identification Number: _____   Date: ____
System or Subsystem: _____   Job: _____
Interviewer: _____

Job Characteristics: (Check all that apply)

Turnover Rate on Job/Task:

❑ None
❑ Low (< 10% within the last year)
❑ Medium (10%-20% within the last year)
❑ High (> 20% within the last year)

Job/Task Structure:

❑ None (Worker-defined structure)
❑ Low (Job is basically unstructured with a few structured component tasks)
❑ Moderate (Part of the job is structured and part is unstructured)
❑ High (Entire job is rigidly defined, e.g., by operating procedures)

Job/Task Importance:

❑ Low (Optional, small un-required component of overall job productivity)
❑ Moderate (Required as part of overall job productivity)
❑ High (Failure to perform task would result in financial loss or loss of life, e.g., monitoring a nuclear reactor, pilot monitoring altitude, etc.)

Type of Job/Task Training Provided:

❑ None (Optional, small un-required component of overall job productivity)
❑ Manual only
❑ Elective Formal (i.e., classroom lecture)
❑ Mandatory Formal
❑ Manual-based Tutorial
❑ Computer-based Tutorial
❑ Interactive-Video Tutorial

2.4 Task Analysis Data Forms

The data forms that follow are examples of the types of forms that should be used when conducting the task analysis. Copy these forms or modify them to suit your needs. The particular forms shown have been useful in task analyses conducted at the Lawrence Livermore National Lab's Laser Isotope Separation Facility (Schaich, Banks, and Van Ness, 1987). Since they were developed for use in the nuclear power industry, you may have to modify them somewhat to fit your unique needs. You should also complete the user profile (Section 2.3) at this time.

2.4.1 Data Form 1

Task Analysis Data Form 1 is used to collect information during the task analysis. The items of information to be recorded on Data Form 1 are explained later. The item numbers correspond to the column numbers on the form. These numbers should be matched to fields in the on-line task analysis data file. In the event this information will be loaded into a database, a practice we strongly recommend, we have recommended sizes for each field in parentheses after the explanation of each item. There may be times when no information may be appropriate for some items (e.g., no "support equipment" needed to perform task).

The first three fields are used for identification purposes.

1. Facility   (20 Characters)
2. Position   (30 Characters)
3. Subposition   (10 Characters)
4. Task Number   (20 Characters)

Each task and subtask must be assigned a number. This number identifies the process in which the task/subtask occurs, and its position relative to other tasks/subtasks in the process. In the following example, the process is "4.0 Copy File":

4.1   Make a New Directory
4.1.1 Type "MKDIR <New Directory Name>" and press return
4.2   Copy the file CONTROL.DAT into the new directory
4.2.1 Type "CD <New Directory Name>" and press return to move into the directory
4.2.2 Type "Copy C:\<Old Directory Name>\CONTROL.DAT C:\<New Directory Name>\CONTROL.DAT" and press return

The task analysis number is repeated in the first column of each page of the data form. This is done to provide easy reference to the task across the separate pages.

5.   Task Description (160 characters)

This column describes what must be done to complete each task or subtask. The task description column should be filled out first since all other columns refer to it. Each task should begin with a verb or verb-adverb combination that makes the worker behavior clear. Verbs should be chosen from a standard verb list for procedures. Here are some typical verbs:

Acknowledge	Delete	Look up
Activate	Direct	Link
Adjust	Download	Make
Approve	Edit	Move
Break-out	Enlarge	Open
Break-up	Evaluate	Print
Calculate	Increase	Remove
Change	Inform	Resize
Check	Insert	Rotate
Close	Initiate	Select
Copy	Load	Set

6.   Task Purpose (420 Characters)

The purpose should be a brief statement of what is to be accomplished by performing the task. The task description defines the behavior; the purpose defines the reason for the behavior, an operating objective. Please do not make statements such as the purpose for starting a tool is to make it run.

7.   Initiating Event (210 Characters)

This statement explains why a particular task is undertaken at a specific time. Precursor events and situations that provide justification for performing the task should be detailed here. For example, if the task description were "inserting a new disk," the initiating event might be the following warning: "Current disk is 80% full." The initiating event may also be a supervisor's order or a procedural requirement.

8.   Systems Effected (350 Characters)

This column is applicable only to tasks which involve multiple computing systems or plants. Here you detail all of the systems which are affected by the completion of a given task. This is also one of the **most important,** since this field will be where errors will be passed onto other systems thus creating **inherited** errors.

9.   Support Equipment (240 Characters)

Support equipment is any nonstationary item which is required to perform the task identified in column 4. Examples include gloves, goggles, mouse, light-pen, touch screen, laptop/notebook computer, or a checklist.

10.   User Time (30 Characters).

User time is the elapsed time that it takes the usual user or users to perform the task. The number of users involved is indicated in column 19. Man-hours/man-minutes can be estimated from columns 10 and 19. This is estimated, average time, assuming no interruptions or unusual occurrences. Personnel should be assumed to be fully trained on the job.

11.   System Time (30 Characters)

This is the time it takes for the system or equipment to respond to the task action performed by the user (this time is often reflected in system response time or system refresh). For example, if the task description were to "download usage files," the difference between system time and user time could be significant. It may take the user two seconds to issue the appropriate set of commands. This is user time. However, depending on the system, it may take several minutes to several hours to download the requested files. This is system time.

12.   Task Difficulty (1 Character only)

Task difficulty refers to a combination of both physical and mental effort, so please rate task accordingly. Task difficulty is a judgment made by subject matter experts. Task difficulty is supported relative to all other tasks performed in the job. The most difficult task or tasks will be rated 5. The least difficult task will be rated a 1. All other tasks will be rated between 1 and 5 in whole number values only.

13.   Task Frequency (1 Character only)

In this column, the frequency of task performance should be ranked from 1 to 5 according to the following scale:

    1 = 1-2 times per day
    2 = 3-4 times per day
    3 = 5-6 times per day
    4 = 7-10 times per day
    5 = Continuous or intermittent throughout process

14.   Feedback (350 Characters)

This column is applicable to tasks which involve systems in which the user makes a change and the system responds by providing the user with feedback regarding the change in the system as a result of the user's action. This column is used to identify the form and source of information about system response to task actions.

15.   Most Likely Human Errors (120 Characters)

This column requires documentation of the most serious human errors that could be made during the performance of the task being analyzed. For example: inappropriate timing (delay in beginning or completing task, or introduction of the task when it is inappropriate), omission of the task, and/or improper performance.

The seriousness of an error depends on the potential consequence. Sometimes the consequence of the error depends on system conditions or other situational factors when the error occurs. For example, it may be that users will forget to backup their work onto external media. Most of the time this error of omission would not matter because the system is highly reliable. The omission could be highly serious in the event of a system failure. Months of work could be lost. For example, if the text of this book were kept solely on the hard disk of one of the authors, and that hard disk failed, over a year's worth of both author's work would be lost. Multiple, redundant, backups on external media reduce the probability of this consequence. Thus, in defining an error, it may be necessary to define the specific conditions under which the error is serious.

16.   Consequences of Human Error (280 Characters)

In this column, a statement that describes the effects of committing the error(s) stated in column 15 should be indicated. Using the previous backup example, the consequence of failing to backup work on external media is "unrecoverable loss of data."

17.   Error Probability Rating (1 Character only)

This is also a judgment to be made by the subject matter experts. The procedure for this rating scale is to rank the probability relative to all other Human Errors in column 15. The rating scale ranges from 1 to 5. Nominal values are assigned to the scale definitions as a guide.

1 = Almost no probability of occurrence, 10^{-5}
2 = Very low probability of occurrence, 10^{-4}
3 = Low probability of occurrence, 10^{-3}
4 = Medium probability of occurrence, 10^{-2}
5 = High probability of occurrence, 10^{-1}

Probability ratings should not be viewed as a prediction of error/consequence occurrence. The use of this rating and the others on this form is to identify tasks that may require special attention in design engineering, procedures, training, or supervision.

18. Severity of Consequence (1 Character only)

In this column, you should rank the severity of the consequences of each error described in Column 15. The rating scale is:

1 = No consequence to personnel safety or system security or data
2 = Very minor severity
    - Deletion of a backed-up file
    - Shutdown of a noncritical back-up operation
3 = Minor severity
    - Shutdown of noncritical operation
    - Reformating/erasure of backed-up hard disk
    - Non-intrusive injury (broken bone, bruise, abrasion)
4 = Severe
    - Deletion of non-backed-up files
    - Robot activation resulting in injury requiring surgery
    - Injury resulting in long-term disability
    - Controllable environmental release of radiation (<= 1,000 dpm)
5 = Very Severe
    - Fatality
    - Deletion/loss of non-recoverable data
    - Erasure of a non-backed-up hard disk
    - Large or uncontrollable environmental radiation release

19. Others Involved in Task (120 Characters)

This column is used to identify other personnel directly involved in performing the task. Involvement of others is defined as the actual assistance the person receives. The person may need information or directions from a supervisor to accomplish a task, or a supervisor may verify that the task has been performed to a satisfactory level.

20. How Are Others Involved (210 Characters)

This column is used to indicate the roles of other personnel identified in column 19.

21-24 Ways to Lessen Risk (70 Characters/ Subcolumn)

These columns are used to indicate how the potential for human errors and their consequences can be minimized. There are four categories to choose from: (21) Equipment (referring to equipment selection/design, and workspace design), (22) Procedures, (23) Training, and (24) Supervision. One or more may be chosen. The choices indicate where provisions can be made most effectively to assure safe and successful performance of the task. Check marks may be placed in the columns to identify the preferred means. If a specific provision can be suggested, it should be written in the column.

25-30   Preferred Mode(s) of Training (50 Characters)

These columns are used to suggest the mode(s) of training considered most effective for the task. There are six categories: (25) Drill, (26) Classroom, (27) On-the-Job (OTJ), (28) Manuals, (29) Video, and (30) Simulation. More than one may be chosen, and choices should be indicated with check marks.

Manuals, in this analysis, refer to manuals which are geared to user self-instruction or include tutorials. Simulation includes not only simulation proper, but also physical mock-ups and on-line tutorials. Drill is distinguished from simulation in that drill is a repeated practice activity that does not require a simulation or mock-up. Video, in this case, not only refers to video presentation of training, but also interactive video, interactive laser disk/CD-ROM, and multi-media that uses video segments, whether from tape or laser disk/CD-ROM.

31-33   Knowledge Required to Perform This Task

In this section, subject matter experts are requested to determine the elements of knowledge essential to perform each task effectively. Knowledge requirements are broadly defined here to include knowing how to do something (i.e., skill mastery) as well as knowing information and concepts. This section is composed of three columns (31-33). Each column identifies a specific category of knowledge. The three categories are summarized as follows:

31. Academic Knowledge (400 Characters)

This category defines the knowledge of the kind generally acquired in formal education prior to job entry, or in instructional programs (generally in a classroom setting) provided by the employer. For example, the user may need to have a familiarity with aspects of computer systems, or environmental safety, or finance, or may need to know certain mathematical relationships and procedures. Basic requirements such as ability to read and understand technical documents/ manuals may be also specified in the category of academic knowledge.

32. Administrative Knowledge (160 Characters)

This category refers to standard practices, procedures, organizational relationships, resources, and constraints. For example, knowledge of chain-of-command gives the user the information needed to obtain permission to remove or transfer files or document problems that occur when using the system.

33. Systems/Equipment Knowledge (240 Characters)

This category refers to the types of knowledge needed to operate system components and tools, or to use other equipment necessary for the task. For example, knowledge of the specialized software may be needed to complete the task.

34. Level of Supervision (1 Character)

This is a rating reflecting the hazards involved in task performance and the potential consequences to personnel and the organization if the task is omitted or performed improperly. The rating scale includes five choices.

1 = No supervision required
2 = Another worker should verify the completion of the task
3 = Satisfactory completion of the task should be formally self-verified (e.g., by checklist, worker sign-off, etc.)
4 = Supervisor should verify satisfactory completion of task
5 = Supervisor should monitor performance of the task

35. Hazards (300 Characters)

This column is used to specify hazards other than worker error that may be associated with performance of the task. An example would be flying debris or sparks during the operation of an automated cutting tool.

36. Performance Standards (300 Characters)

This column is used to identify the criteria for satisfactory performance. Performance standards should be objective and verifiable, and they also may be quantitative. A quantitative standard might specify, for example, task completion within a certain time period or task completion within a certain degree of accuracy. An example of categorical standards would be: "follows procedural steps correctly."

Task Analysis Data Form

Process:

1. Facility	2. Position	3. Subposition	4. Task Number	5. Task Description	6. Task Purpose	7. Initiating Event

Task Analysis Data Form (Page 2)

Task Number	8. Systems Effected	9. Support Equipment	10. User Time	11. System Time	12. Task Difficulty	13. Task Frequency	14. Feedback	15. Most Likely, Serious Human Errors

Task Analysis Data Form (Page 3)

Task Number	16. Consequences of Human Errors	17. Error P Rating	18. Error Severity Rating	19. Others Involved in Task	20. How Are Others Involved

Task Analysis Data Form (Page 4)

Task Number	21-24. Ways to Lessen Risk				25-30. Preferred Modes of Training					
	Equipment	Procedures	Training	Supervision	Drill	Class	OTJ	Manuals	Video	Simulation

Task Analysis Data Form (Page 5)

Task Number	31-33 Knowledge Required to Perform Task			34. Level of Supervision	35. Hazards	36. Performance Standards
	Academic	Administrative	System/Equip.			

2.4.2 Task Analysis Data Form 2

Task Data Form 2 should be completed during Step 8A of the task analysis. The answers to the questions asked in Step 8A should be entered into this form. This form is used along with the User Profile Worksheet to aid you in deciding what types of screen elements best suit the user's needs.

Function:	
Task:	
Information Required:	
1. How many dimensions of data are there?	
2. How many variables are used for the display?	
3. How many information samples are used for the display?	
4. Does the display alert or inform user of status changes?	
5. What is the response to control actions?	
6. Is the displayed information measured or derived?	
7. Is the displayed information qualitative or quantitative?	
8. What are the range and units of the display?	
9. What is the required information accuracy?	
10. What is the Signal-to-Noise Ratio?	
11. Is the information relative or absolute?	
12. Does the display require sustained attention (Vigilance)?	
13. Is the display used in emergency situations?	
14. What is the highest cost of an error (e.g., Death)?	
15. What are the worst case viewing conditions?	
16. How often is the display updated?	
Recommended Display Element	
Alternative Recommendation	

2.5 Estimating Human Error Probabilities

Once you have completed the task analysis and the user profile, you can estimate the impact that human error is likely to have on your system by estimating the probability that certain types of errors will occur and assigning a risk value to each error. In order to do this, however, you must first have some measure of how often users make errors within a given computer system.

At this point, you will have identified the tasks that need to be completed, and documented the system and human performance requirements necessary for their completion. The next step is to determine which tasks are most likely to generate errors (least reliable). This is done by going back to the expert panel or the users and having them identify the types of errors that occur during each task and having them estimate the frequency with which each type of error occurs in each of the given tasks. By identifying the errors that can occur in each task, and estimates of the frequency of error occurrence for each type of error, you can identify tasks that are prone to errors and tag them for close examination. It is the error prone tasks that are likely to cost the company large sums over the life cycle of the system. Also, pay careful attention to the tasks that have high consequences (loss of life) associated with them.

The probability of a human error occurring (HEP) is expressed in the form of an equation:

$$\text{HEP} = \frac{\textbf{Number of Errors}}{\textbf{Number of Opportunities For Error}}$$

Note: "The denominator . . . is often difficult to determine since the opportunities may be covert", (Miller and Swain, 1987; pg. 221).

Human error probabilities cannot always be estimated accurately, however, because failure data is not available for humans, particularly in cases of new systems, forcing you to rely on expert predictions. This inability to accurately estimate error probabilities will propagate throughout your estimations, lowering their effectiveness.

2.6 Notes

1. Remember there are many different ways to perform a task analysis and additional variables could be included which are not displayed in Table 2-1. A list of other variables which could be collected follows:

    1. Task description
    2. Purpose of the task
    3. System effected by the task action
    4. Event which initiates the execution of the task
    5. Frequency of task execution per unit time
    6. Time it takes to execute the task
    7. Time it takes the system to respond to the task action
    8. Level of difficulty
    9. Type of human error most likely to occur during the task
    10. Support equipment necessary for task execution
    11. Type of feedback provided to user (visual, auditory, tactile, or kinesthetic)
    12. Level of supervision required for task completion

2. These questions may not be applicable to qualitative information displays.

2.7 References

Banks,W.W. and Paramore, B. (1982) *Integrated Systems Management: A Pilot Task Analysis of the DOE Size Reduction Facility, 243-5Z Plutonium Finishing Plant.* EG&G Idaho Report SD-T-82-001, Idaho Falls, ID

Banks, W.W., Paramore, B.A., Buys, J.R. (1984) *Task Analysis: A Detailed Example of Stepping Up From JSA.* Presented at the 1984 National Safety Congress, UCRL-91596, Lawrence Livermore National Laboratory.

Carroll, J.M., Mack, R.L., Lewis, C.H., Grischkowsky, and Robertson, S.R. (1985) Exploring exploring a word processor. *Human Computer Interaction*, 1 (3), 283-307.

Carroll, J.M., Smith-Kirker, P.L., Ford, J.R., Mazur-Rimetz, S.A. (1987-88) The minimal manual. *Human Computer Interaction*, 3 (2), 123-154.

Danchak, M.M. (1981) *Techniques for Displaying Multivariate Data on Cathode Ray Tubes with Applications to Nuclear Process Control.* Hartford, Ct: The Hartford Graduate Center.

Drury, C.G., Paramore,B., Van Cott, H.P., Grey, S.M., and Corlett, E. N. (1987) Task Analysis. In *Handbook of Human Factors*, Gavriel Salvendy (Eds.), New York: Wiley-Interscience.

Embry, D.E. (1976) *Human Reliability in Complex Systems: An Overview* (NCSR.R10). Warrington, England: National Centre of System Reliability, United Kingdom Atom Energy Authority.

Institute for Nuclear Power (1985) *Principles of Training System Development* (INPO 85-006). Pgs. 2-3-11 through 2-3-15.

Kincaid, J.P., Fishburne, R.P., Rogers, R.L., and Chissom, B.S., (1975) *Derrivation of New Readability Formulas (Automated Readability Index, Fog Count, and Flesch Reading Ease Formula) for Navy Enlisted Personnel.* Navy Training Command Research Branch Report 8-75.

Laughery, K.R, and Laughery, K.R. (1987) Analytic techniques for function analysis. In *Handbook of Human Factors*, Gavriel Salvendy (Ed.). New York: John Wiley and Sons.

Mayhew, D.J., (1992) *Principles and Guidelines in Software User Interface Design.* Englewood Cliffs: Prentice-Hall.

Meister, D. (1984) Human reliability. In F.A. Mucker, Ed., *Human Factors Review: 1984.* Santa Monica, Ca: Human Factors Society.

Miller, D.P., and Swain, A.D. (1987) Human Error and Human Reliability. In *Handbook of Human Factors*, Gavriel Salvendy (Ed.). New York: John Wiley and Sons.

Pew, R.W., Feehrer, C.E., Baron, S., and Miller, D.C. (1977) *Critical Review and Analysis of Performance Models Applicable to Man-Machine Evaluation*. (AFOSR-TR-77-0520). Washington, DC: Air Force Office of Scientific Research, Bolling Air Force Base.

Schaich, P.C, Banks, W.W., Van Ness, H. (1987) *Objectives for Performing SIS Task Analysis*. Unpublished Lawrence Livermore National Labs Technical Report.

CHAPTER 3
Designing With Constraints

There always will be factors which limit the type of system that can be designed, developed, and implemented. These limiting factors must be taken into consideration when designing the system. Before the design process can proceed, these constraints must be identified and taken into account. These constraints narrow the set of acceptable design solutions (i.e., the type of screen elements to be presented and the hardware used to display them). Nevertheless, the system designer must strike a balance between the impinging constraints and the needs of the user so that the interface designed is within the scope of the constraints but not at the expense of the user. Too often, design teams focus too closely on the impinging constraints, such as budget or time limitations, and not on the larger picture of designing a system that is easy and satisfying to use. The result is often a system that was brought in on time and on budget, but has interface deficiencies that spawn user errors and dissatisfaction. The real loser in these situations is the corporation which suffers long-term losses due to user errors that could have been prevented, had the schedule or budget been increased. Not only do corporations end up suffering losses due to user errors, but they also incur the added expenses associated with future retrofitting of the system.

3.0 What Are System Constraints?

Constraints are any factors that service to limit or narrow design alternatives. The primary types of constraints are:

1. Hardware
2. Software
3. Requirements
4. Budgetary
5. Political
6. Market
7. Manpower

The important thing to remember about constraints is that they do not occur in a vacuum. Every constraint has the potential for affecting, and even constraining, every other constraint. For example, budgetary constraints may prevent you from adding additional hardware and adding additional designers. Similarly, market constraints and political constraints can influence the size of your project's budget.

3.1 Primary Constraints

Primary constraints are the project killers. That is, these are the type of constraints that have the greatest impact on the scope of your project. These are the constraints that determine whether or not your project gets implemented or shelved. These are the kinds of constraints that not only determine whether or not your project will go into production, but also determines whether or not you will be employed next year.

3.1.1. Hardware Constraints

Hardware constraints result from the existing architecture and components of the system. For example, in the 1980s, it was virtually impossible to use the same software on an IBM personal computer that you were using on an Apple Macintosh. The two hardware configurations were not compatible. Thus, if you bought an Apple Macintosh, it was often very difficult to find specialized software, because most specialized software was being written for the IBMs since they already had well established corporate markets.

Hardware constraints are often the most easily identified and remedied constraints. If your software requires 3 megabytes of RAM, but your PCs only have 512K of RAM, then the solution to this constraint may be as easily solved as simply buying extra memory. Likewise, if your software requires personal computers to link to mainframes, then it's obvious that each PC will either need a communications card such as an IRMA board or a modem.

3.1.2 Software Constraints

Due to the plasticity of software, this is probably the easiest of the constraints to overcome given sufficient budgetary and manpower resources. Most software problems stem from compatibility issues. A typical software constraint is the corporate-wide use of an operating system. Suppose that your corporation is dedicated to the exclusive use of the UNIX operating system. Any software that you design is thus constrained by the requirement that it must be compatible with the UNIX operating system. This constraint can be particularly troublesome if the job to be done requires a specialized, off-the-shelf, piece of software (e.g., a medical diagnostic program) and is unavailable to run under your operating system, in this case UNIX.

3.1.3 Requirements as Constraints

Requirements can also be constraints. For example, suppose the goal or requirement of a given display system is that it can withstand a safe shutdown of a Laser Isotope Separation facility during an earthquake. This requirement limits the selection of the display-hardware vendors to those who can supply a narrow range of MILSPEC or "hardened systems."

Another type of requirement could be legal. Suppose your company has a binding contract with a particular supplier. If you wanted to obtain software consulting from another supplier, you might be prohibited from doing so due to the terms of the contract with the other contract that requires you to purchase your software consulting from them.

3.1.4 Budgetary Constraints

Your company might be able to do some incredibly accurate market analysis and prediction with a Cray supercomputer, but if you only have enough money in your budget for a single copy of Lotus or EXCEL, then you have to set your sights somewhat lower. Similarly, there are often many changes which we would like to make to improve human performance. But we also have to be realistic. You can't suggest a change that will cost the company 4 million dollars to make in order to save five dollars in lost productivity (unless of course the change will prevent loss of life).

Budgetary constraints are often the most difficult to overcome. In today's increasingly tight marketplace, it's often very hard to convince upper management of the need to allocate large sums to make seemingly (to them) trivial changes. This is why it is so important to do an in-depth task analysis to determine the types of human errors that are likely to be made. Once the potential errors are identified, you can assign a cost estimate to them and use that information as leverage to convince management of the need to allocate additional budgetary and manpower resources for redesigning the system.

3.1.5 Political Constraints

Often the most insidious and likely to kill a project, political constraints are rarely addressed in textbooks and technical books. There could be many reasons for this, not the least of which is that we would like to believe that projects are killed for appropriate technical or business reasons. However, there are cases in which viable projects that were sound from both a technical and business standpoint were killed because they were not "politically correct" projects.

For example, suppose that your company makes laptop computers. Your new line of notebook computers are designed to include a color LCD display and a full-travel, electro-mechanical keyboard. Your market research has shown that your market segment prefers large, brightly lit displays rather than smaller displays. However, your company is relying on a display company for a piece of a large avionic contract. The other company has just landed this contract and has offered to subcontract the microprocessor component design to your company, however this other company has traditionally supplied your company with their displays. Another company is offering you cheaper displays with a brighter backlight and better resolution. Staying with your existing supplier would mean that you would have to go with a display with a dimmer backlight and lower resolution. Who do you risk alienating? Your customer base or the company with a multimillion dollar subcontracting deal?

3.1.6 Market Constraints

Most of us would hope that market considerations, rather than political, drive design. Such is the case with CD-ROM. It has taken a long time, in computer years, for CD-ROM technology to catch on. No one can doubt its usefulness, but at the time of this book's writing, CD-ROM had not yet found a consumer niche. Looking at it a different way, if market research has indicated that your software is too highly priced for the marketplace, then reducing the cost of future versions becomes a major consideration. If producers get too far out of touch with their market, competitors can sneak in and steal away your customer base. Such was the case with FoxPro, which started out as a third party enhancement to DBase but ended up being its biggest rival.

One of the best ways to stay in touch with your consumers is through getting the engineers and designers involved with the market research. Most market research involves telephone interviews, market clinics, or focus groups.

Telephone interviewing involves calling people who would be typical users of your system. Market research companies usually purchase lists of people's names who fit certain demographic types (i.e., personal computer owner). These people's names find their way onto these lists when they fill out those questionnaire cards that are attached to their warranty registration. That company in turn sells the people's names to market research companies who use the lists to recruit for focus groups or to conduct phone interviews. There is not much that engineers can be involved with during phone interviews, other than to suggest the addition of design relevant questions to the questionnaire the interviewer will be using. Focus groups and clinics are different.

Focus groups are usually smaller than clinics. In focus groups, a small number (10 to 20) of representative customers are recruited by a local market research company. The customers usually come after work to the market research company where they are served refreshments and sit around a large conference table where they are asked questions about products by a moderator who is very similar to a talk show host, who follows a rigidly defined script of questions and who must remain objective. Often, prototypes, called properties, are available for the participants to inspect or to interact with. The sessions are frequently videotaped or able to be viewed from an observation room, through two-way mirrors. The engineers and designers can impact the focus groups by asking market research if they can add certain design relevant questions to the script of questions asked by the moderator.

Clinics are similar to focus groups, only with more people. Clinics involve several hundred to several thousand potential customers. They are often held in convention centers and last several days. The participants of clinics are recruited in the same way as focus groups and telephone interviewing. The participants, upon arriving at the convention center or auditorium are given a battery of preference questionnaires. When they have finished, they are taken and shown the company's product line mixed with the product line of competitors. The participants are given questionnaires with questions related to the different design aspects of the products, and asked to make on-site comparisons of the different products. Sometimes, the responses of the questionnaires are scored on-site, and the responses of a participant will result in him or her being placed into a specialized follow-up group for more specialized, in-depth, perhaps one-on-one interviewing. As with focus groups, designers and engineers can obtain a wealth of information by working closely with market research to make sure that market research addresses their needs.

However, politics may serve to constrain the input that engineers can have on the script if the departments within your company have a strong territorial imperative, thus your offer of input may be viewed as a major encroachment and a major breech of corporate etiquette. This should not dissuade you though. Much useful information can be gleaned from these groups, and there is no better time to get in touch with the potential users of your product or interface. If you don't become involved personally, then you are at the mercy of the information gathered by others which may or may not meet your needs. It is important to gain as much market information as early as possible so that any potential market constraints can be dealt with through design meetings.

3.1.7 Manpower Constraints

There are two primary ways in which manpower can constrain design. First, you may have to scale down your design. If you don't have enough programmers to write all the code necessary to perform the necessary functions, then rewriting the existing code to introduce a GUI (graphical user interface: like the Macintosh or Windows) is going to be a hard item to sell to management. Second, manpower can constrain the amount of work needed to be done. If your task analysis reveals that the current job design requires workers with five arms, seven eyes, and the ability to multiply eight digit numbers while humming Dixie, then the job might be a good candidate for automation, or -- at the very least -- the addition of more manpower. If the current budgetary constraints have led to the imposition of a hiring freeze, and rumors of a layoff, it would be ill-advised to propose the addition of an interface that would necessitate hiring additional employees. When budgetary constraints impose manpower constraints, look to automation of job duties.

For example, consider replacing fill-in-the-blank forms, which have to be typed into the computer, with fill-in-the-circle forms that can be read into the computer by an optical character reader. The redesign of the forms and the additional cost of buying or leasing an optical character reader would be much less costly, financially and politically, than adding additional headcount (remember salary loading from Chapter 1?).

3.2 Secondary Constraints

Primary system constraints can also impose secondary constraints. For example, all commercially available display systems designed to withstand a safe shutdown during an earthquake may have a maximum pixel resolution of, let's say 256 X 256 pixels on a 13 inch monitor. This secondary constraint may limit the possible types of images that can be displayed and could eliminate color entirely, if a plasma display is used. Secondary constraints occur as the result of interactions between primary constraints. Frequently occurring secondary constraints are:

1. location of the equipment,
2. electrical power for the equipment,
3. operating environment for the equipment,
4. availability of signals,
5. system feedback,
6. dynamic display characteristics,
7. use of a specific software language,
8. machine independence of software,
9. existing software,
10. future upgrades to the system,
11. impact on the operator's tasks,
12. maintenance requirements,
13. industry standards, guidelines, and regulations.

> **Note:** Although data archiving and data security **are not** explicitly discussed in this chapter, these issues **must** be resolved too.

3.2.1 Space and Location Constraints

A critical issue arises when you attempt to resolve the following questions: (1) Where does the user need the information to be displayed? and (2) Where is space available for the equipment? Based on the study of the tasks (Chapter 2) that are to be supported by the system, you should identify several candidate locations and measure and record them for later use. When identifying the candidate locations, consider the control locations, the location of other instrumentation which the user must see, and the location of procedures or other printed material (e.g., operating manuals), which the user will need at hand for reference. Ensure that the proposed locations do not obstruct the user's view of important controls or instrumentation and do not interfere with the user's movement (i.e., reduce the user's reach envelope) when performing other tasks. Space around equipment for regular and emergency maintenance (including complete and partial removal of equipment for testing and installation) should be considered as well. You also need to consider the availability of space for installation of equipment outside of the user's workspace.

3.2.2 Available Power Constraints

The ready availability of electrical power for the monitors, input devices, and other equipment should be determined for each location identified. The characteristics of the power (e.g., requirements for an uninterrupted power supply and for filtered power) and available capacity should also be determined.

3.2.3 Operating Environment Constraints

You need to consider the operating environment, including temperature and humidity ranges, dust, and electromagnetic interference, at each potential equipment location. Typically, vendors will be able to quote permissible operating temperature and humidity ranges in terms such as "+10 to + 40° C with 95% relative humidity, noncondensing." However, most maintenance people agree that equipment operating at extremes will have increased failure rates. For example, excessively dusty environments will increase the need for preventative maintenance (e.g., cleaning filter fans) for mass-storage devices. Electromagnetic emanations from mechanical relays, larger power apparatus, and portable two-way radios can interfere with high-speed logic signals and magnetic storage media. Remember to evaluate each candidate location carefully for the potential of being a troublesome environment. You can never be too careful. One of the authors remembers a computer facility being built beneath a men's room. The frequent leaks from the urinals would short out the mass storage devices.

3.2.4 Signal Access Constraints

If you are dealing with a system that uses sensors to generate the information that will be displayed to the user via the computer's display, start to compile a list of the different sensor signals needed to produce the display screens. The availability of these signals must also be determined and listed. Alternative information channels and displays must be provided in the event that the required display-generating signals become unavailable. The preferred method is to provide within the display system all necessary interconnections and instrumentation to produce all of the information needed to support the user's tasks. If the information cannot be provided within the display system, then the user will be forced to look at other instruments for that information or interrupt his or her work, resulting in lost productivity. Frequent losses in productivity result in losses of corporate resources and are the hallmark of a poorly designed display system.

In addition to ensuring the accessibility of the sensor signals, you must also understand the signals' meanings. For example, for sensor signals indicating valve status, does the signal indicate a command to the valve, the actual position of the valve (e.g., limit switches on the valve stem), or the functional performance of the valve (e.g., differential pressure across the valve)? Can (or must) any signals be verified prior to display to the user? (See also Screen Update Time.)

You also need to determine the accessibility of each sensor signal that is required to generate the necessary information. Questions about the meaning of the signals should be listed and resolved at this point. If any signals remain unavailable, you need to resolve the issue before working any further on developing the display screens or defining constraints.

3.2.5 System Feedback Constraints

Feedback is critical in person-to-person, machine-to-machine, or person-to-machine communication. Feedback is particularly important in real-time situations where the rate of display updating is important and the lag time in presenting critical information should be minimized. If the system is updated infrequently, consider using display status indicators (e.g., SYSTEM OK AT 3:00 P.M.) to inform the user that the system is still working.

3.2.5.1 Display Update Rate

The term "update rate," also known as screen refresh rate, is defined as the frequency of CRT updates per unit time, or the delay between the change of a system parameter and its graphical or numerical update on a CRT screen. For example, if the temperature changes in a system but the CRT display update lags this change by 5 seconds, the update rate or screen refresh rate is said to be 5 seconds. Numerous factors will significantly influence the update rate of displayed parameters as users interact with a computer system. Some of these variables are:

- ○ sampling rate,
- ○ available memory,
- ○ I/O overhead,
- ○ cable length,
- ○ type of CRT terminal,
- ○ computer architecture,
- ○ complexity of the averaging algorithm,
- ○ number and type of sensing transducers,
- ○ port configuration.

While this list is not exhaustive, it does indicate that any optimally prescribed update rate may be constrained by any one or combination of these limiting factors. Because of these constraints, it's more realistic to identify the update rates only for the critical tasks (e.g., those tasks where a delay of information will lead to the crash of a 747). Continuous, real-time control tracking tasks (e.g., controlling a remotely piloted vehicle or robot) will be seriously impeded when the update of visual information feedback exceeds 0.5 seconds. In situations where the margin for safety must be high (control of a 747 or nuclear power plant) or where immediate user response may be required, update rates should be less than 0.5 seconds if the parameter or display is crucial. The update rate for a system that involves a human operator or user should be analytically determined by systematically examining:

○   type of tasks performed by the user,
○   margin of safety required,
○   safety critical values of controlled parameters,
○   consequences of a delayed value on a worst case basis,
○   temporal response requirements of the system.

Figure 3-1 shows a hypothetical comparison of update rates for data as a function of control task importance. Note that as the controlling task becomes more important, the update rate must become faster.

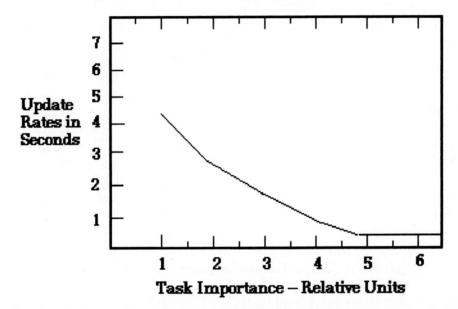

Figure 3-1: Hypothetical Update Rates as a Function of Task Importance

For example, in an informal research conducted at the Loss of Fluids Test Reactor (LOFT), using interactive graphic displays and LOFT operators, one of the authors found that update rates of 3 seconds were acceptable to the operators. These observations were made, however, under conditions in which all operating personnel were **expecting** adverse situations to occur. Because of this expectancy effect, and because the control task was not randomly ordered, the observations are more directed at preference rather than performance.

Some user tasks, such as clock monitoring and other tasks of relatively low importance, might have a less stringent update rate (e.g., greater than 5 seconds) with no appreciable decrement in performance. However, usability studies must be conducted in order to accurately determine minimum acceptable update rates for different categories of tasks.

3.2.5.2 Display Status Indication

Display status indication is used to describe a method, technique, or signaling device (usually auditory or visual) that permits the user of a CRT to easily, accurately, and rapidly detect whether the computer and the terminal are functioning normally.

To understand why this variable is necessary, consider a real scenario. Three operators were monitoring fluid flow on a CRT graphic display. At the lower left portion of the screen, a digital, real-time clock was the only device on the screen that provided an indication as to the status of the computer system or of the terminal. The operators were unaware that the clock had stopped and that the system had "crashed" 5 or 6 minutes earlier; the operators continued to examine the display looking at information that was 5 or 6 minutes old. In a nuclear power plant, a situation such as this one could have grave implications. For this reason, it is essential that each computer system be equipped in such a manner that failure of either the terminal or the computer system can be detected rapidly. This would allow the operator to query alternate information devices as needed.

An example with less dire consequences comes from the consumer products realm. Have you ever been in the situation of installing software, but the installation program provides you with no feedback? One of the authors worked for a software company that provided a product with an installation program such as this. Early versions of the software drew the wrath of customers because the installation program would churn away and provide the user with nothing more than the message "Please Wait." The users had no way of knowing if the system had crashed or was still working. The problem was solved by using a simple completion meter like the one in Figure 3-2. The graphical bar increases as the system completes a step in the installation process, thus providing the user with immediate feedback as to the system's status. The provision of this simple display dramatically increased user satisfaction with the installation program, which only shows that system changes do not have to always be big to increase performance and satisfaction.

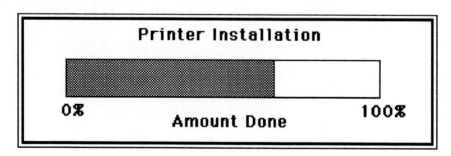

Figure 3-2: Completion Meter

Even though it is often very simple to provide users with the feedback they need, there are still many instances in which the only way to detect a terminal or computer system failure is through a passive technique (e.g., the screen does not update or the clock stops). One recommended way of dealing with this is to continuously display a sweeping vector, like the sweeping second hand of a watch, located in the upper right quadrant of the screen. It would be obvious to the user that a problem exists when the sweeping vector ceases or disappears. Another approach would be to place a 0.5 inch square or a circle, 0.5 inches in diameter, for a viewing distance of approximately 28 inches, that pulses from black to white at a rate of one pulse per second while the system is operating normally. If the computer system fails, the pulsing would stop and be detected rapidly by the user.

Note: These suggestions of including a sweeping vector or pulsing square should only be used in systems which **do not** use flashing or blinking displays to indicate an abnormal system state. In such situations, the sweeping vector or the pulsing square could serve to mask the flashing emergency signal.

To the best of our knowledge, no explicit guidelines exist for passive failure detection with CRT displays. This area needs the input of electrical engineers and computer scientists for the development of an active failure-alert system that could be incorporated into a CRT display. For example, if a self-powered circuit was installed to emit a periodic beeping tone when the system, or any of its peripheral systems, **failed**, then this active device would have more attention-getting power than a passive stimulus.

3.2.6 Dynamic Display Characteristics

Many CRT displays are dynamic in nature. That is, they are continuously driven by various data inputs to update or change the condition of the displayed parameters. The rate of these changes before user overload or loss of comprehension is an area that is not clearly understood and is in need of further research.

Display motion refers to the degree of movement or animation present in a dynamic display (e.g., water moving through a pipe that is dynamically and graphically presented, control rods moving up and down, or a valve changing position from open to closed). All of these examples indicate some type of dynamic movement or change that could be presented graphically to users.

One of the important questions associated with animated display motion is how quickly or slowly the apparent motion of the graphic representation should be projected to the user. The display motion should be of sufficient magnitude to be easily detected and recognized by the operators. If the rate of pixel excitation is too high, the user will not readily perceive progressive or incremental movement; instead a "zipping" effect will be produced. If you were to prescribe an animated fluid-flow rate linearly in terms of pixels per second, such a definition would be unsatisfactory since pixel size and dimension are not standardized with the computer industry. A better definition, one that would enable the easy establishment of guidelines and would be applicable to virtually all types of CRTs, would be to state motion rate in terms of millimeters per second.

3.2.7 Use of a Specific Software Language as a Constraint

Vendor supplied graphics software packages typically are collections of C-Language or FORTRAN callable subroutines. If the software is to be developed in another language (e.g., PASCAL), you need to determine whether links can be made to the code that has been written in the primary language. Alternatively, you may choose to specify that vendor-supplied graphics software packages must be callable from the chosen language, although this decision would limit the field of prospective vendors.

3.2.8 Machine Independence of Software as a Constraint

Businesses with long lifetimes will likely use several generations of data systems and display hardware. As technology advances, improved products are developed, and in some cases, the old devices become difficult or costly to maintain. These days, with software development costs beginning to overshadow hardware costs, an increasing demand is being seen for software that can be reused with new hardware and minimal changes. However, this type of software cannot be developed without extensive planning. Even though industry standards for computer graphics hardware and software are not yet fully developed, they offer the best option from what is currently available. The Association for Computing Machinery is a good source of information on computing standards, graphics, and others. You should determine whether machine-independent software is required.

3.2.9 Existing Software Constraints

Sometimes hardware must be used that will support existing software, due to the high costs associated with replacing the old software and retraining the users on a new package. Determine if the need to transport, compile, load, and run existing software constrains the selection of hardware.

3.2.10 Flexibility to Upgrade as a Constraint

Upgrading of a display system can occur in many ways: enhancing existing displays (software), enhancing existing display devices (hardware), replacing existing hardware, and adding new software and/or hardware. Consideration should be given to identifying and quantifying requirements for future upgrades from project requirements, other projects, or long-range plans. For example, how many more displays or display devices will be required? Where will the new display devices be located? These requirements will all be highly situation dependent.

3.2.11 Demands on the User as a Constraint

The configuration of the display system will affect the user's mental workload. Regular dialogs between the user and and the display system during normal operation are a necessary addition to the user's workload; periodic use of the system is essential to building the user's confidence and acceptance of the system. In addition, other tasks that may be explicitly or implicitly added to the user's workload include periodic testing of the system, data-base updates, data backup, detection and diagnosis of display-system problems, data verification, and the restart of a failed system. The user's involvement in these added tasks may not directly affect the displays or the hardware; however, user involvement will affect software development. Determine the possible extent of user involvement with the tasks previously listed (See Chapter 2, Task Analysis). Possible sources for this information are the users themselves or the operating-system managers.

3.2.12 Maintenance Constraints

Equipment budgets permitting, acquire new equipment that minimizes demands on the maintenance organization. Limit the diversity of equipment to be maintained; that is, use equipment that is similar or identical to the equipment already in use, unless the equipment change is due to the obsolescence of the older equipment. Also set a minimum mean-time between equipment failures and a maximum mean-time to repair for equipment being purchased. Additionally, you should strive to provide a hardware environment that requires minimum preventative maintenance. Please note that these considerations may constrain the selection of hardware. Also, software maintenance will be greatly lessened if a well-structured, high-level programming language is used.

3.2.13 Industry Standards, Guidelines, and Regulations as Constraints

Regulations, standards, and guidelines constitute another source of constraints for you to consider. The documents containing guidelines, standards, and regulatory requirements related to computer-generated displays are too numerous to be outlined here, though some suggested ones appear below. Additionally, each industry has its own separate set of requirements, standards, and guidelines. In fact, larger companies such as AT&T and IBM maintain their own internal standards and requirements that could serve to constrain your display design. If you don't know if your company has their own guidelines, consult senior level designers, who will be familiar with the requirement of your particular industry or business. Industry standards and guidelines are also often available from related professional societies such as the Association for Computing Machinery (ACM) and the Institute for Electricians and Electrical Engineers (IEEE) can be consulted. A sample set of guidelines appear in Appendix A for your convenience.

3.3 Suggested Guidelines

Banks, W., Gilmore, A.E., Blackman, H.S., and Gertman, D.I. (1983) *Human Engineering Design Considerations for Cathode Ray Tube Generated Displays: Volumes I & II.* NUREG/CR 3003, U.S. Nuclear Regulatory Commission, Washington, DC.

Smith, S.L., and Mosier, J.N. (1984) *Design Guidelines For User Interface Software*. Technical Report TR 00.2720, IBM Poughkeepsie, NY.

Smith, S.L., and Mosier, J.N. (1986) *Guidelines For Designing Man/Display Interfaces*. NTIS Document AD A177 198. National Technical Information Service, 5285 Port Royal Road, Springfield, VA 22161.

Human Factors of Workstations With Display Terminals. (1979) IBM Document G320-6102-1, San Jose, CA.

Human Factors Criterion For Information Processing Systems. (1982) Lockheed Missile and Space Company, Inc., Sunnyvale, CA.

CHAPTER 4
Selecting Screen Elements

Having defined the user's information requirements (Chapter 2) and the constraints that impinge on the system's design (Chapter 3), you must carefully select the items that appear on the screen so that the information needed to complete the task is communicated to the user. These screen items, called elements, may be letters, numbers, shapes, colors, symbols, or combinations of all five. Some screen elements are better than others for communicating certain types of information. The characteristics of the information and its intended use determine, in part, the type of display elements to be used. Whenever the characteristics of the information are incongruous with the intended use, an increase in the probability of human error may occur (Chapter 1). Therefore, it is necessary that you select screen elements that increase user performance on the given task.

This chapter will guide you in selecting and combining individual screen elements into displays that increase user performance. This chapter will also show you how to enhance the intelligibility of displays and how to evaluate the content and organization of displays to increase user performance.

4.0 Matching Screen Elements to Your Needs

The process of designing any display begins with the selection of the screen elements that best convey the information to the user. That selection is based on the characteristics of the data, its intended use (taken from Data Form 2), and characteristics of the user (User Profile Worksheet). By carefully matching screen elements to the task, and by carefully organizing those elements, dramatic increases in user productivity can be achieved, which directly translates into corporate savings. For example, Tullis (1988; 1981), through careful system redesign, was able to show a savings of 79 man years for every year (a reduction usage time by 40%) the system was in use!

Screen elements suitable for conveying information in **most** situations fall into one of the 11 types described in Tables 4-1 through 4-5. These tables will help you determine the types of screen elements that best represent the information you are attempting to display. In order to use these tables, you should use the information in Data Form 2 to determine:

Table 4-1: Dimensionality

| Display Element | Dimensions | | |
	Uni-dimensional (1)	Duo-dimensional (2)	Multi-dimensional (>2)
Analog display	1	3	3
Digital display	1	3	3
Binary display	1	3	3
Bar chart	1	2	3
Column chart	1	2	3
Band chart	1	3	3
Pattern display	1	1	1
Trend plot	1	2	3
Mimic display	3	2	1
Narrative text	1	2	2
Parameter versus parameter display	3	1	3

1 = Optimum   2 = Workable but suboptimum   3= Not recommended

Table 4-2: Types of Variables

Display Element	Univariate (1)	Limited Multivariate (2-6)	Multivariate (>6)
Analog display	1	2	3
Digital display	1	3	3
Binary display	1	3	3
Bar chart	2	2	1
Column chart	1	2	3
Band chart	2	1	3
Pattern display	1	1	1
Trend plot	1	2	3
Mimic display	3	2	1
Narrative text	1	2	2
Parameter v.s parameter display	1	2	3

1 = Optimum   2 = Workable but suboptimum   3= Not recommended

Table 4-3: Types of Data Sampling

Display Element	Samples		
	Discrete (1)	Limited Series (2-15)	Multivariate (>15)
Analog display	1	3	3
Digital display	1	3	3
Binary display	1	3	3
Bar chart	1	3	3
Column chart	2	3	3
Band chart	3	2	1
Pattern display	1	3	3
Trend plot	2	1	1
Mimic display	1	3	3
Narrative text	1	2	2
Parameter v.s parameter display	2	1	1

1 = Optimum   2 = Workable but suboptimum   3= Not recommended

Table 4-4: Quantitative Representation

Display Element	Type of Representation		
	Exact Value	Approximated Value	Deviation From Normal
Analog display	2	1	2
Digital display	1	2	2
Binary display	3	3	2
Bar chart	2	1	1
Column chart	2	1	1
Band chart	2	1	2
Pattern display	2	2	1
Trend plot	2	1	1
Mimic display	2	2	2
Narrative text	2	2	3
Parameter v.s parameter display	2	1	2

1 = Optimum   2 = Workable but suboptimum   3= Not recommended

Table 4-5: Qualitative Representation

Display Element	Type of Representation		
	Status And Warning	Value Prediction	Pattern Recognition
Analog display	2	2	2
Digital display	2	3	2
Binary display	1	3	1
Bar chart	2	3	2
Column chart	2	3	2
Band chart	3	2	2
Pattern display	2	3	1
Trend plot	2	1	2
Mimic display	2	2	1
Narrative text	2	3	3
Parameter versus parameter display	2	2	2

1 = Optimum   2 = Workable but suboptimum   3= Not recommended

1. number of dimensions of information (Step 8A from Task Analysis),

2. types of variables (univariate, limited multivariate, multivariate),

3. types of data sampling (univariate, limited multivariate, multivariate),

4. types of data representation (qualitative or quantitative).

Compare your data needs with tables 4-1 through 4-5 and record your findings on Data Form 2.

4.1 Types of Screen Elements

4.1.1 Digital Displays

Digital displays are most often used as counters and are without a doubt the best means for displaying an **EXACT** numeric value (See Color Plate 16). Digital displays are best suited to the presentation of one dimensional, quantitative information, where one variable represents a single value. In the case of Color Plate 16, each of the numeric values represents one dimension of quantitative information.

Digital displays, while unidimensional, may be clustered together to show multiple dimensions or variables, as seen in Color Plates 3 and 16. When using digital displays, each display must have a unique label to identify its meaning (e.g., is it displaying pressure? temperature? stress level?). Color Plate 16 shows a display composed of multiple digital screen elements, which are clustered together to provide the user with all the information they need to perform the given task. Cyan is used to create an outline in the shape of a pressure vessel to indicate, pictorially, the context of the information. This border is extremely important since it reinforces the task context of the displays for the user. The outline also serves to group together all of the information necessary for the performance of
the task.

Multiple digital displays often appear in tables, but this format should be avoided on CRTs, because tables of numbers, when displayed on a CRT, can often appear too dense or cluttered for the user to easily read the correct row or column. Furthermore, placing a straight edge next to a row or column on a CRT display is much more difficult than on printed material, due to the curvature of the cathode ray tube.

The following rules are often used when designing digital displays for CRTs:

1. Include the appropriate number of significant digits for the required level of accuracy. **Never more**.

2. Accommodate the full range of the variable (i.e., highest and lowest value).

3. Ensure that the data will not change so rapidly as to be unreadable.

4. Provide arrows to indicate the direction of change, if needed.

Generally speaking, digital displays are superior to analog displays in terms of speed and accuracy of reading when precise numerical values are required and if the value remains stable long enough to be read (Sinclair, 1971; Zeff, 1965). However, there are situations in which analog displays have a distinct advantage. Analog displays are superior to digital displays when the values of the variable change frequently or when the direction and/or rate of change in the variable is of importance to the user.

4.1.2 Analog Displays

Analog displays are so named because they use moving pointers, needles, scales, or arrowheads to point to a position on a scale which is "analogous" to the value of the variable which it represents. The pointer may move vertically, horizontally, or around the scale. Alternately, the pointer may be fixed while the scale moves. In either case, the relative positions of the scale and the pointer are set to correspond to the value of the variable they represent. The scales may also be circular or linear. Figure 4-1 shows several, typical quantitative displays. Scaled quantitative displays either have a fixed scale and a moving pointer, a fixed pointer and a moving scale, or a moving scale and a moving pointer.

Each analog display generally shows a single discrete value and the rate of change of one variable in one dimension, which is the main reason why non-CRT display panels are so large. Because the user must estimate where the pointer is on the scale, these displays are most appropriate for displaying approximate values or values which are in transition. Users take 2 to 3 times longer to accurately read analog displays than digital displays. A notable exception occurs when analog displays are used to convey qualitative or status information. In addition, analog displays are superior to digital displays when rate and direction of change information is required.

McCormick and Sanders (1982, pg. 71), citing Heglin (1973), offer these rules of thumb for designing systems using analog displays to show quantitative information.

1. A moving pointer against a fixed scale is preferred.

2. If increases and decreases in value are related to more or less or up or down, then a fixed, vertical scale (see "d" in Figure 4-1) with a moving pointer should be used to take advantage of the mental model that users have of thermometers (i.e., mercury rises in the tube with increasing temperature).

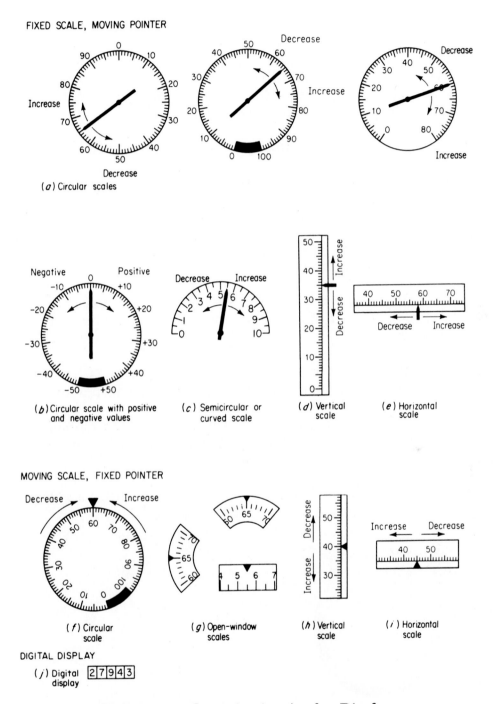

Figure 4-1: Quantitative Analog Displays
(From McCormick and Sanders, 1982, pg. 70)

3. If multiple scales are going to be used for similar functions, scale reading errors can be reduced by keeping the type of analog scales constant across related displays. For example, if a group of displays all show increases and decreases in values, then they should all use vertical displays with ascending values and pointers that move up the scales with increasing values and down the scales with decreasing values.

4. Controls should move the pointer rather than the scale.

5. Small changes are more easily noticed with a moving pointer, as compared to a moving scale.

6. Numeric values are more quickly read if the display uses a fixed pointer and a scale that moves through a window. (See "g" of Figure 4-1) This type of display is simply an analog version of a digital display.

Qualitative analog displays are used when the primary goal is to convey gross values of some variable or rate of change to the user. Qualitative screen elements should be used when:

1. rate of change information is to be conveyed (e.g., rate of flow of water from a tank; rate of climb of an aircraft; or voltage drop across a coil);

2. the user need only maintain the system within some range of values (e.g. maintaining driving speed between 50 and 55 mph) or know how close a task is to being completed (Figure 4-3);

3. the user must determine the status of the system within a given set of ranges (i.e., safe, caution, danger) (See Figure 4-2).

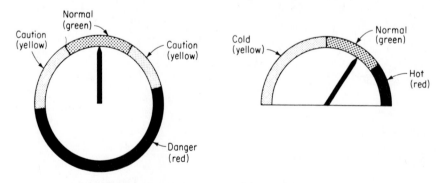

Figure 4-2: Qualitative Analog Display
(From McCormick and Sanders, 1982, pg. 77)

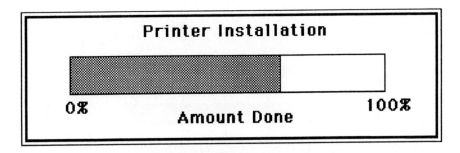

Figure 4-3: Completion Meter

Task analysis Data Form 2 should be used to determine whether the display should be quantitative or qualitative. McCormick and Sanders (1982, pg. 77) suggest:

> "The optimum designs of displays for qualitative reading . . . depend on *how* they are to be used, that is, the particular type of qualitative reading. If the entire continuum of values can be sliced up into a limited number of ranges -- each of which represents some general "level" -- the optimum design would be the one in which each range of values is separately coded, such as by color, [See Figure 4-2]." (McCormick and Sanders, 1982)

In general, analog formats may not transfer very well to computer displays. However, you may choose to use this format either because the nature of the task dictates its use on a computer display (e.g., rate of change information is needed by the user), or because of its familiarity (automotive dashboard gauges).

4.1.3 Bar Charts

A bar chart is a special type of analog display in which horizontal bars of different lengths are used to indicate values (Figure 4-4 and Color Plate 18). The most common use is for one-dimensional, limited multivariate, and/or discrete samples. This would allow, for example, a comparison of water pressure (one-dimension) across four separator cooling blocks (multivariate) at some discrete point in time (one sample). Bar charts permit very clear comparisons, and markers may be added to show deviations from the norm. Bar charts, conventionally, show values increasing from left to right. In the case of Color Plate 18, percentage of power increases from left to right. Note how the colors green and white are used to call attention to the important information. Figure 4-3 uses a bar chart.

4.1.4 Column Charts

Column charts are similar to bar charts, except that the columns are vertical. This seemingly trivial difference leads to subtle differences in how the presented information is perceived. Because the column heights move vertically, there is a natural compatibility between a rise in the value of the variable and a rise in the height of a column. Second, because the scale of the variable is on the Y axis, the

X axis is used to denote time or some other variable. (a bar chart would denote time on the Y axis, which runs counter to conventional displays of time). Column chart values increase from the bottom of the chart to the top (Figure 4-5).

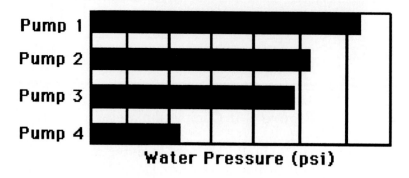

Figure 4-4: Bar Chart

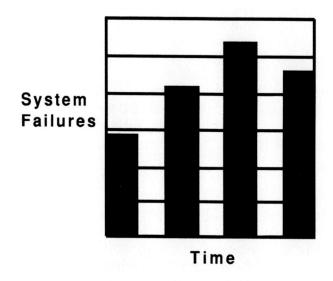

Figure 4-5: Column Chart

4.1.5 Band Chart

A band chart is plotted on X-Y axes, with time on the X axis, and contains bands or strata depicting the various components of a total. The values of the strata are added together so that the top band represents the sum of all bands (Figure 4-6).

For example, this type of chart can be used to show how much each of several turbines contributes to the total electrical output. This format is most useful when all of the elements of the system contribute equally to the total system output, under normal circumstances. However, the displayed data must be unidimensional.

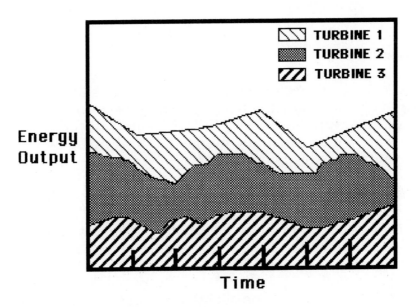

Figure 4-6: Band Chart

4.1.6 Status Indicators

Status indicators are most often used on conventional display panels. A light, flag, or switch that only can assume two or three discrete positions is a status indicator. Status indicators should be used when the message to be conveyed is a discrete condition of some system. The most common type of status indicator is an illuminated light which indicates whether a particular system is ON or OFF. The so-called "idiot lights" (the more accurate term is "tell tales") in your car that illuminate when something is wrong are status indicators, because they notify you of a change, for the worse, in the status of your car.

A similar use of status indicators is as an emergency or warning indicator, where OFF generally means that the system is operating normally and ON indicates some abnormal occurrence. Alternatively, three colors may be used to indicate three possible states. The common traffic signal is a good example of this, where red means danger, yellow means caution, and green means go. In fact, the strong cultural stereotype which results from exposure to traffic lights since childhood makes this coding strategy an extremely powerful one. However, this coding scheme is so strongly ingrained in people's cognition that the use of these colors for other coding may result in severely impaired performance, particularly if the coding scheme is reversed.

It is critical, however, that the status indicators be clearly labeled and understood. Misinterpretation, using this type of display, could cause the user to interpret the message as being opposite of the message which was intended.

Finally, status indicators can be used in place of quantitative displays when the display is **only** used for **check reading**. McCormick and Sanders (1982; pg 79) define check reading as looking at a display to simply determine if a condition is normal or not.

4.1.7 Pattern Displays

The human perceptual system is exceptionally well-suited to recognizing patterns. There is a natural economy in perceiving patterns over a number of independent, nonintegrating features. In fact, users will find and use familiar patterns which were not intentionally designed into the display. You can and should take advantage of this phenomenon.

If much of the user's time will be spent monitoring for changes in some larger system, then the user could benefit from having one type of display for detection and one type for subsequent diagnosis of the system change. Pattern displays are very useful for detecting changes in a system but not for making a diagnosis of the change.

If the task to be performed is one of check reading, patterns can be created by aligning groups of simplified gauges so that the pointers all point in the same direction under normal operating conditions. Figure 4-7 shows four examples of this use of patterns. Markings between pointers can be used to accentuate the pattern. As one pointer begins to deviate from the common orientation, it will break up the pattern and command the user's attention. Dashevsky (1964) has shown that grouped displays, which all indicate null by pointers at the 9 o'clock or 12 o'clock position, are read more accurately and quickly than displays that use some other null configuration.

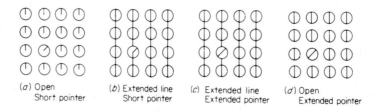

Figure 4-7: Pattern Displays
(From McCormick and Sanders, 1982; pg. 80)

McCormick and Sanders (1982, pg. 81) present a collection of rules to be followed when designing "dial" type pattern displays:

1. Arrange dials with the pointers oriented toward 12 o'clock to indicate a null condition.

2. Make the pointers extend across the face of the dial.

3. Draw lines between the null position of the dials.

Another alternative is to display some familiar shape or pattern and to assign a meaning to the feature of the pattern. This technique is discussed under "intelligibility."

4.1.8 Mimic Displays

A mimic display or schematic profile (Figure 4-8 and Color Plate 17) is usually a combination of graphic or alphanumeric elements. It is a stylized or symbolic/graphical representation that associates data with the pertinent system elements. A mimic may be simple or detailed, and the symbols may range from abstract to pictorial. In general, one should supply the minimum amount of detail to yield a meaningful pictorial representation. Abstract symbols should conform to common symbolic conventions whenever possible (i.e., conventional electrical symbols when the user is an electrician or electrical engineer).

For example, Color Plate 17 is a mimic display that shows the relationship between different pumps, tanks, flow paths, and holding tanks. The color green indicates the pump that is currently available and running, while red is used to indicate the pump that is inactive. Note that the stereotypes of green for "go" and red for "stop" are exploited in this display to decrease user workload. Also note that the flow rates (in gallons per minute) are presented below each pump to reinforce the pump status information. Also note that the symbols presented in this display are standard schematic symbols used in this type of task.

Care must be taken when designing mimics. Extraneous detail will create a cluttered mimic (compare Color Plate 17 with Figure 4-8). In the less severe instance this will distract the users attention from meaningful information, while it may confuse the user in the most severe case. For example, bends in pipes should not be displayed just because there are bends in the actual pipes, unless that fact conveys some important piece of information. Remember, the mimic is meant to be a *symbolic* model of the system. System elements located close together, physically should be located close together on the mimic. However, for the sake of clarity, displayed elements can be moved around. In this case, lines of demarcation should be used to indicate the elements that belong together. In the event that display space is limited, one should attempt to use overlays to designate values, which the user can display on command.

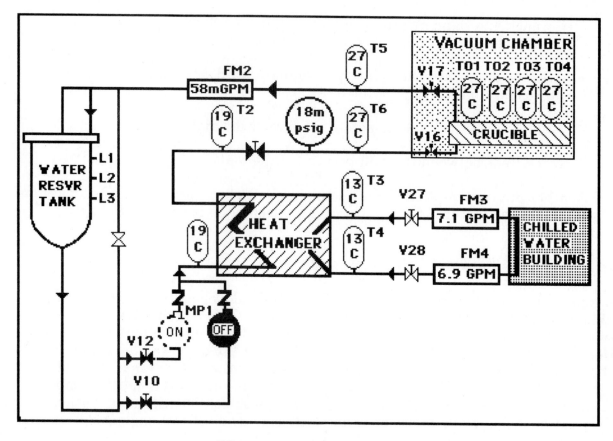

Figure 4-8: Mimic Display

The schematic nature of the mimic display serves two purposes. First, off-normal situations can be shape- and color-coded and are easily detected as departures from normal system functioning. Second, schematic-type displays can help show the interrelations between system components (i.e., pumps, valves, etc.). This type of functionality cannot be easily duplicated with bar or column charts.

As the user becomes more experienced with the schematic profile of the system, abnormal system conditions should become more evident. Research with this type of display element has shown promise but may require more attention to format detail than other types of screen elements.

4.1.9 Parameter Versus Parameter Displays

Parameter versus parameter displays are best used when the task to be performed involves detecting deviations from normal if a target area can be defined. By plotting a brief time history, the user can predict where the displayed values are headed. Care should be taken to distinguish current values from past values, especially when the values change slowly. This can be done by simply placing an X, an arrow, or some other marking at the current value (Figure 4-9).

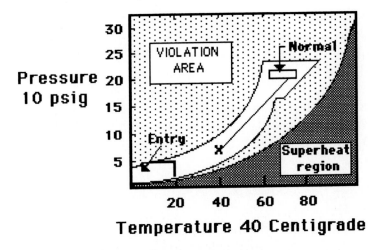

Figure 4-9: Parameter Versus Parameter Display

In order to avoid cluttering the display, the old data points should be removed after some fixed period of time. Ideally, as the newest point is plotted, the oldest point is removed, thereby maintaining a constant number of displayed points. Hardware limitations, however, may force you to plot an entire series of points, clear the screen, and begin plotting over again, an option much less desirable.

4.1.10 Trend Displays

A trend display is simply a specialized form of the parameter versus parameter display that shows how one or more variables and/or one or more dimensions vary over time (Figure 4-10). In trend displays, time is usually plotted on the X axis and shown increasing from left to right.

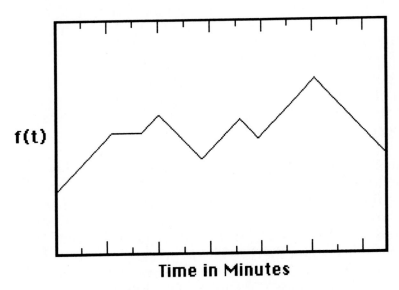

Figure 4-10: Trend Display

If the signals are fairly steady, several signals can be monitored on the same screen, making deviations easy to detect. However, if the signals vary quite a bit over time, or if values of more than one dimension must be read, then no more than two curves should be plotted on a display.

Research has shown that, if time is plotted on the X axis, the most recently displayed data should be presented on the right (Chernoff, 1973). However, if time is plotted on the Y axis, the most recently produced data should be displayed toward the origin.

4.1.11 Narrative Text

Plain English text is probably the most flexible and the least desirable of the techniques mentioned. Almost any information can be conveyed through text (Color Plate 3), but text is slow to read and interpret. Whenever possible, text should be limited to labels, help messages, and brief messages pertaining to infrequent events.

When narrative text **must** be presented, several rules should be followed.

1. For labels and titles, use uppercase only; for narrative text, use upper and lower case letters (Color Plate 3).

2. Use no more than 40 to 60 characters per line.

3. Avoid abbreviations whenever possible. If abbreviations must be used (e.g., limited screen space), they should be consistent with abbreviations used elsewhere in the workplace.

4. Do not scroll automatically. Allow the user to control the scrolling process.

4.1.12 Form Fill-In

Thus far, only output displays have been presented. However, there will be times when it will be necessary to facilitate input by the user. If the type of information is of relatively the same type for each input (e.g , name, address, social security number), the best alternative is a form fill display.

Form fill displays consist of a series of **labeled** input fields, and resemble paper and pencil forms. The algorithm driving the display should jump the cursor from one field to the next when the tab key is pressed or when a field has been filled (Figure 4-11). The cursor movement algorithm is based on the analysis of the task. Consider Figure 4-11. If the cursor is in the Last Name field, where should the cursor move when the Tab key is pressed? It should move to the First Name field, since most times we are asked to give last name, first name, and middle initial, in that sequence. Due to the familiarity of that sequence, the interface should follow that sequence to exploit the existing mental model of the user.

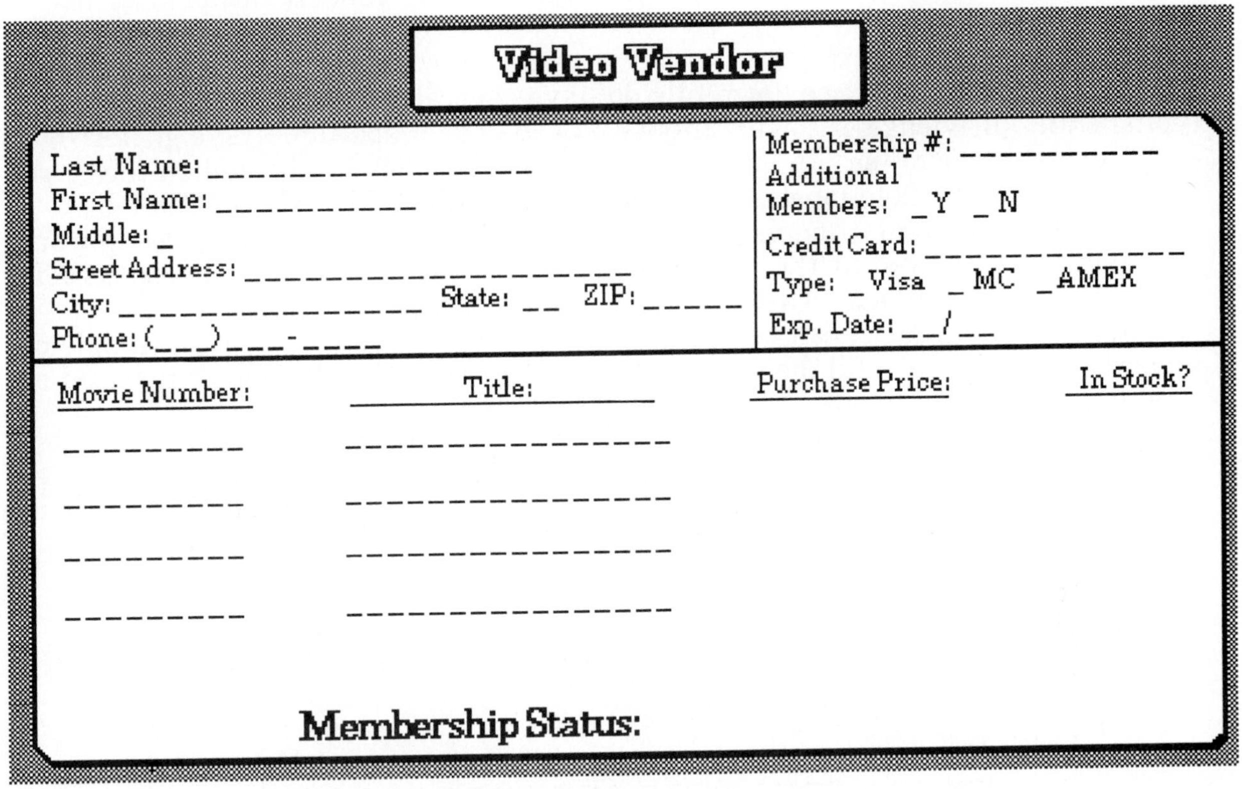

Figure 4-11: Form Fill Display

The form fill in Figure 4-11 has a design that merits further discussion. Note that some of the fields do not have underscores (e.g., In Stock, Purchase Price, and Membership Status). These fields are output only. When a movie number is entered, the title of the film appears along with the purchase price and the words "YES" or "NO" to indicate if the film is in stock. There is no need to show underscores for Purchase Price, In Stock, and Membership Status, since the user will never be using them for input. This also gives a subtle clue to the user that fields with underscores are input fields. Film title is an input and output field. The presence of the underscores indicate that the field can take inputs. A task analysis of most video stores would show the need to query the database as to whether a movie is in stock or not. Most times, customers will simply come to the counter and say, "Do you have Raiders of the Lost Ark?", rather than looking on the shelves. Allowing the user to input a movie title, in addition to the movie number, accommodates this need. The Membership Status field is a binary field that shows one of two messages: current or delinquent. This field will be automatically filled when the user enters the membership number. If the membership is delinquent, an additional window will open to tell the user the specifics of the problem.

Form fill displays continue to be one of the most commonly used means of input because of their ease of use. That ease of use stems from the fact that the captioned fields make form fills self-explanatory and prompt the user's memory for the required input (e.g., Last Name). Form fills also provide the user with "the big picture," since the fields appear within a given context rather than in isolation.

For all their ease of use, form fills do have several drawbacks. They assume typing skill, knowledge of correct inputs, knowledge of special keys (e.g., TAB), and they are error prone. In addition, ease input is solely predicated on the intuitiveness of the field labels, as perceived by the user. The labels **MUST** be **meaningful** and **easily** understood by the user. Labels should come directly from the language employed by the users in doing their jobs. We have all seen screens with unintelligible labels. Obscure labels result in human errors that, as mentioned in Chapter 1, can be translated into wasted resources. An example of a poorly designed form fill display appears in Figure 4-12. This figure is based on a real screen which one of the authors worked on.

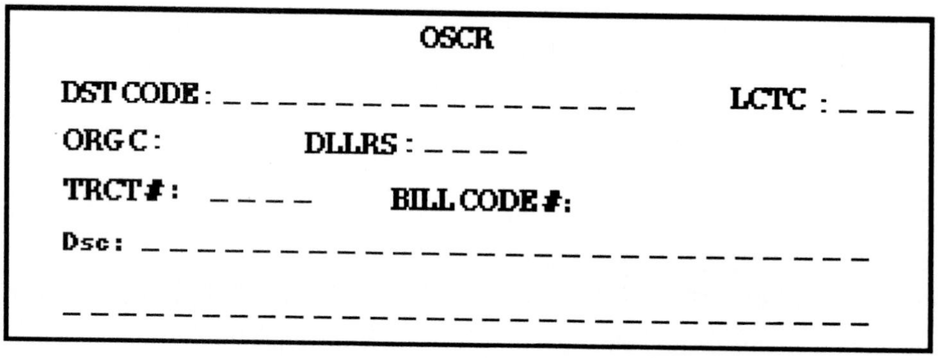

```
                                OSCR

   DST CODE : _ _ _ _ _ _ _ _ _ _ _ _ _        LCTC : _ _ _

   ORG C :          DLLRS : _ _ _ _

   TRCT# :    _ _ _ _      BILL CODE #:

   Dsc : _ _ _ _ _ _ _ _ _ _ _ _ _ _ _ _ _ _ _ _ _ _ _ _


          _ _ _ _ _ _ _ _ _ _ _ _ _ _ _ _ _ _ _ _ _ _ _ _
```

Figure 4-12: Poorly Designed Form Fill

Let's examine what is wrong with this screen. First, what do the codes represent?

OSCR:	Order Screen
LCTC:	Location Code
ORG C:	Ordering Code
DLLRS:	Dollars, in thousands
TRCT #:	Transaction number
BILL CODE #:	Billing code
Dsc:	Description of the order

So, what is wrong with the above screen? First, the labeling of the field names is not consistent. LCTC, ORG C, and BILL CODE are all codes, yet all three are conveyed differently. If abbreviations must be used, then **consistency** in abbreviating must be maintained at all cost. Inconsistency will simply confuse the user and lead to increased errors, which in turn will lead to an unnecessary loss in revenue.

Another problem comes from the inconsistent use of the # symbol. In the TRCT # field, the symbol is used instead of the word "number,". However, the transaction number, in this particular instance, very often contains alphanumeric characters in addition to numbers. In the case of BILL CODE #, however, the # character means that the field is for numeric codes only.

While the problems with this screen may seem overly exaggerated, it is important that you remember that this example was taken from an **actual** system, which users interact with every day. You also might be tempted to conclude that this screen is a fluke, however this screen is representative of the nearly 100 screens which composed this particular application. This screen, like all of those in the system, interfaced with other screens and **migrated** its information to the other system thereby creating the potential for inherited errors.

The reaction of the users to this particular system ranged from frustration to refusal to use it. The company's response was to send the users to a two-day course on how to use the system rather than simply relabeling the fields. This occurrence is all too typical in the software industry. Rather than allocate sufficient resources to design the system adequately in the first place or to redesign the system to be intuitive and consistent, companies will spend millions to educate users in how to "adapt" to the inadequacies of the system. In the long run, this strategy will cost the company an indeterminable amount in lost resources and productivity resulting from inherited errors, human errors, employee attrition, and the costs of educating hundreds of employees to "adapt" to the idiosyncrasies of a poorly designed system. Anything that you can do to reduce the need for training will reduce training costs, thereby, netting larger profits downstream.

In spite of their drawbacks, form fills do one big advantage. If the labels are intuitive, the highly structured format of form fill interfaces make them very easy learn and use. In addition, since information is often entered into form fills from paper forms, there is often a close match between the interface and the mental model of the user, provided the input fields are arranged in the same ordering as the fields on the company's paper forms.

While form fills may seem deceptively simple, they are one of the richest forms of interface available. They are so rich, in fact, that Mayhew (1992) devotes an entire chapter to form fill interfaces. A discussion of this depth is beyond the scope of this book, however, the reader is strongly encouraged to review Mayhew's chapter for additional information if they are considering using a form fill format. In that chapter, Mayhew provides a list of guidelines for constructing form fill displays. Here is a list of the guidelines adapted from Mayhew that will affect the design of nearly every form fill display.

1. Base the form fill design on the outcome of the task analysis (Chapter 2).

2. Group the fields conceptually, sequentially, by frequency of use, or relative importance. Again the organization chose should be based on the outcome of the task analysis.

3. Separate groups of fields using lines, white space, color, or other visual cues.

4. If designing a multiscreen system, keep related fields on the same screen.

5. Unless there is a good reason not to, always left justify the field labels. Right justification of field labels is usually reserved for instances in which labels vary greatly in their length and it is not possible to reduce the length of the field labels and maintain clarity.

6. When using left justified field labels, separate the longest label from its field by no more than 2 characters.

7. Use **bold** versus plain text, UPPERCASE versus lowercase, or different colors to set the field label apart, visually, from the field. In addition, use a colon as a label delimiter.

8. When designing a complex form, group-related fields together beneath a visually distinct group heading. For example:

```
┌──────────────────────────────────────────────────────────────┐
│                        VIDEO VENDOR                            │
│               (Membership Information Screen)                  │
│                                                                │
│  PRIMARY MEMBER                    MEMBERSHIP RECORD           │
│                                                                │
│     Name:     _ _ _ _ _ _ _ _ _       Member #:    _ _ _ _ _   │
│     Street:   _ _ _ _ _ _ _ _ _       Expires:     _ _ _ _ _   │
│     City:     _ _ _ _ _ _ _ _ _       Rentals/mo:  _ _ _ _ _   │
│     Phone:    _ _ _ _ _ _ _ _ _       Overdue/mo:  _ _ _       │
│                                                                │
│  SECONDARY MEMBERS                                             │
│                                                                │
│     Name:     _ _ _ _ _ _ _ _ _                               │
│     Name:     _ _ _ _ _ _ _ _ _                               │
│     Name:     _ _ _ _ _ _ _ _ _                               │
│     Name:     _ _ _ _ _ _ _ _ _                               │
└──────────────────────────────────────────────────────────────┘
```

9. Keep field labels brief, familiar, and descriptive. If data will be transcribed from a paper form, use the same labels used on the paper form, in the same arrangement.

10. Indicate the maximum number of characters per input field. An underscore separated by spaces provides an excellent visual cue.

11. Indicate which fields are optional by labelling them with the word optional, placing an asterisk in front of the label, or by showing the field in a different color than the other fields.

12. Whenever possible, have the system automatically fill fields to prevent input errors and speed the entry of information. For example, some systems contain a list of ZIP codes which the system can access and use to fill in the state and city.

13. If a complex relationship exists between two or more fields, then make the relationship clear. If possible, don't show a conditional field unless its precursor conditions have been satisfied.

14. Whenever possible, allow the system to default an input when a user skips a field. These defaults should be the most likely or most common input. For example, the system could default the current year into the year portion of the date, unless the user enters a different year.

15. Minimize keystrokes in high frequency inputs. For example, allow the input of "Y" or "N" in lieu of Yes or No.

16. Input should be case insensitive unless case is important.

17. Whenever possible, do not combine letter and numeric input into the same field.

18. Do not require leading zeros.

19. When use of the system will be infrequent, provide the user with brief and unambiguous prompts to remind them as to the correct format, content, and syntax of input.

20. Provide the user with the capability of turning of the prompts if they become intrusive and annoying.

21. Offset the prompts from the rest of the form by making them a different color.

22. Place prompts in a **reserved** line at the bottom or top of the screen.

23. Provide unambiguous navigation and form help upon request by the user. **Do Not** make the help intrusive. The best way to avoid being intrusive is to provide help in pop-up windows that can be invoked by the user.

24. Be consistent in locating help and messages, in grammatical style and abbreviations, and in format of input.

25. When a form fill screen is invoked, default the cursor to the top left input field, unless there is a task-related or conceptual reason not to.

26. If the system's cursoring algorithm is fixed (e.g., some systems only allow left to right cursoring) arrange the fields to match the cursoring strategy. For example, if the cursoring algorithm is left to right, then use:

```
                          Instead Of

   a. _ _ _      b. _ _ _              a. _ _ _   c. _ _ _
   c. _ _ _      d. _ _ _              b. _ _ _   d. _ _ _

                          Instead Of

   1. _ _ _      2. _ _ _              1. _ _ _   3. _ _ _
   3. _ _ _      4. _ _ _              2. _ _ _   4. _ _ _
```

27. Permit forward and backward movement within and between fields.

28. Protected areas should be completely **INACCESSIBLE** to the cursor. The cursor should only fall on input fields.

29. Each screen in a multiple screen system should have a title and a screen number.

30. **Always** place the cursor into the error field after an error has been detected in order to speed error correction.

31. Provide unambiguous and nonhostile error messages. For example, Illegal Input is ambiguous and needlessly hostile. One cannot imagine what purpose a designer can serve with a message like this, yet all too often these are the types of messages given. A better message might be: Numeric input only.

32. Suggest fixes rather than just showing an error message. For example:

Numeric input only
ex. 11/15/92

4.1.13 Windows

Windows are special types of screen elements since, unlike the other screen elements, they are not actually displays, but rather vehicles for displaying information. The term window is given to an area on the screen, usually rectangular, for the display of information (Billingsley, 1988; Card, Pavel, Farrell, 1984). The different brain images in Color Plates 6 and 7 are displayed in windows.

Billingsley (1988) suggests that screen elements (e.g., pull-down menus, dialog boxes, etc.) that segment information from the main application fall within the definition of windows. Since windows segment information from the main application, they are often used to present the user with ancillary information during the execution of the main task (e.g., many modern compilers use a debugger window, and application window, and a trace window to help support the programming task). Windows attempt to increase user productivity by allowing users to view different parts of the task simultaneously. This book is an example of how windows can increase productivity.

This book was created using a Macintosh computer and MicroSoft Word IV and Silicon Beach's SuperPaint, running under Multifinder. The Multifinder operating system allowed different applications to appear in different windows simultaneously. The body of the text appeared in the Word IV window, while figures appeared in the SuperPaint window. We could refer to the figures in the SuperPaint window while writing the text, and they could refer to the text when editing the figures. Multifinder also allowed us to switch between applications as simply as using a mouse to select the other window. When a figure was ready to be included in the body of the text, the figure was selected using a mouse, copied to the system's clipboard (an application independent memory buffer), and then pasted into the proper place within the Word IV window. In order to see how much time we saved due to windowing, consider that without windows we would have had to close the paint program, opened Word IV, opened the text file, found the proper area in the text, referred to the passage, closed Word IV, opened SuperPaint, and opened the figure file.

Two main types of windows can be distinguished: tiling and overlapping (Billingsley, 1988). A system with tiling windows divides the screen into discrete, nonoverlapping mini-screens. Color Plate 4 shows an example of a display with tiled windows, where each window shows a different view of a CAD rendering. Most tiling systems allow the user to change the height and width of the windows. Color Plate 4, for example, shows the side view in a larger window to allow the user greater detail. Unlike overlapping windows, tiling windows all lie in the same plane and do not overlap.

Overlapping windows are a product of the desktop metaphor. The desktop metaphor tries to make the interface intuitive to the user by making it appear more like something they use everyday: a desk. The best example of this is the Macintosh interface which uses a grey background to simulate a desk. Overlapping windows appear "on top" of the desk and can overlap with each other to simulate 3 dimensions (Figure 4-13). As you can see from Figure 4-13, in overlapping window systems, the active window, usually selected with a pointing device, is rendered differently than the other windows. The active window is always the top window and the border is usually drawn differently to set it apart from the other windows. In overlapping window systems, the user can resize the active window by selecting a "handle" or a "control" like the one in the bottom right corner of the **DISPLAY BOOK** window in Figure 4-13 (the two overlapping boxes). Controllers such as this allow the user to click on the window and pull it down and to the right to "stretch" it like a piece of elastic or up and to the left to shrink it. In overlapping window systems, the user simply has to click on a nonactive window to make it the active window, just like moving papers around on your desk.

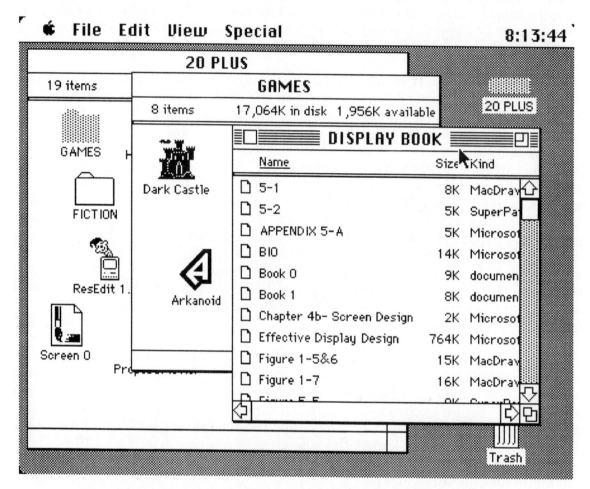

Figure 4-13: Macintosh Desktop With Overlapping Windows

Both tiling and overlapping windows provide the user with the ability of moving, resizing, opening, and closing windows. However, tiling systems limit the number of active windows to the size of the screen. Overlapping windowing systems only limit the number of windows to the computing capacity of the system. Overlapping windows require the system to redraw the window each time a function is performed, which can put demands on the system if too many windows are open, simultaneously. Overlapping windows, within system constraints, do not normally limit the number of displays that the user can have open simultaneously, and allow the user to move the windows about the desk to better suit their needs.

Figure 4-14 shows a typical overlapping window. If the user places the cursor over the close box (upper left), the window will close. The resize box in the lower right is used to "stretch" or "shrink" the size of the window.   The user can select the scroll box and move it up or down to scroll through the information in the window, or can click at different locations on the scroll bar to accelerate through the list, since the scroll bar locations attempt to proportionally approximate positions in the window. The arrows at the ends of the scroll bar are used to scroll through the window one screen at a time in the direction of the arrow.

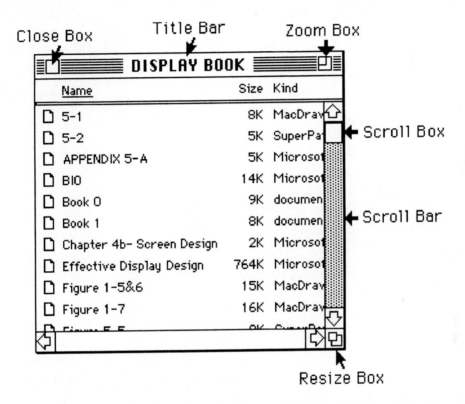

Figure 4-14: Components of an Overlapping Graphical User Interface Window

The following designer's rules of thumb are offered based on Billingsley's (1988) excellent article on windowing.

○   allow users to move and resize system-defaulted/configured windows.

○   provide the user with animation as feedback when they perform open/close operations (this helps because it reinforces the connections between actions and results, windows and icons).

○   When performing window operations, the cursor should behave as though it is "glued" or anchored (Figure 4-15) to the selected window (i.e., window moves with the cursor).

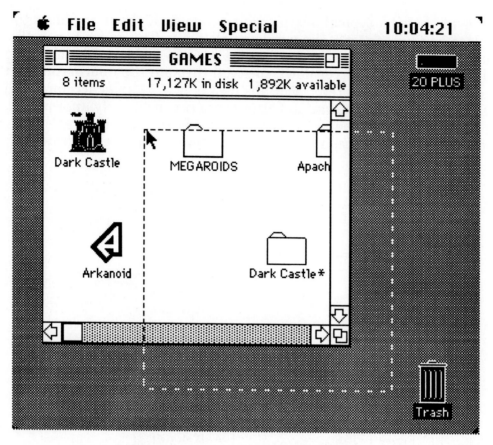

Figure 4-15: Moving a Window

○ If your system does not have the power to animate the movement of windows, leave the window at its original location and provide the user with an outline that moves, showing the final location of the window (Figure 4-15).

○ When designing a tiling system with moveable windows, if possible, provide the user with a brief menu (preferably pull-down) of potential coordinates for the positions of the windows.

○ Windows must have a stable anchor point against which the user can stretch them during resizing (Figure 4-16).

○ Allow the user to see the entire window during the resizing process.

○ Get user input to determine if the text should scroll beneath the window or if the window should move over the text.

○ The scroll box's movement should be proportional to the length of the file. The location of the scroll box should correspond to the location of the window's current view in the file. This gives the user navigational feedback regarding their location in the file.

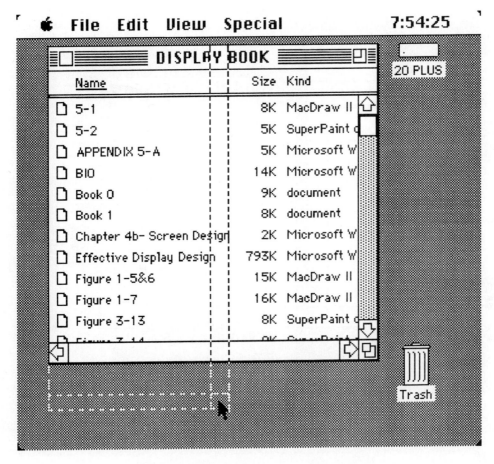

Figure 4-16: Resizing a Window

○ Allow users to move windows without activating them.

○ If the system uses overlapping windows, provide the user with a pull-down menu of available windows, since windows can often be obscured from view by other windows. **Note**: Neither Macintosh nor Microsoft Windows provide this feature.

○ Windows should be activated by a pointer selection in the interior of the window or anywhere on the window's border.

○ Make the active window obvious to the user by changing its border and/or other visual aspects of the window (e.g., scroll bars), see Figure 4-17. **DO NOT** rely solely on the presence of a blinking cursor to inform the user of the active window.

○ Visual cues for window activation should not be so powerful that they distract attention from the primary task, thereby reducing performance.

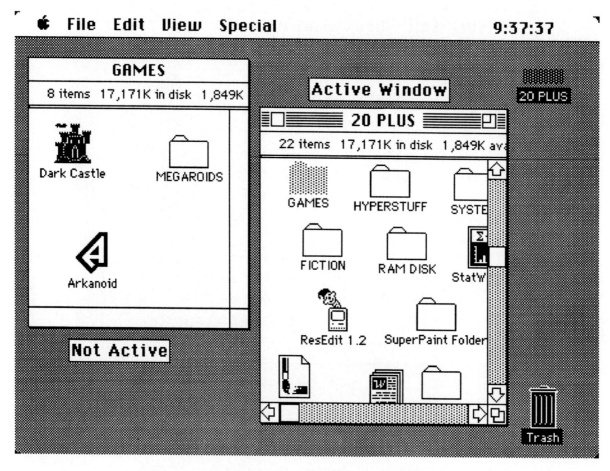

Figure 4-17: Active and Not Active Windows

4.1.14 Palettes

Palettes, like windows, are special types of screen elements since, unlike the other screen elements, palettes are not actually displays, but rather vehicles for functionality. Palettes, while similar in appearance to windows (e.g., usually delineated by a definable border, and possessing similar qualities as windows (movable on the screen with a mouse, joystick, or trackball), are distinctly different from windows. A painter uses a palette to hold pigments while working. Similarly, palettes display the available functionality to the user in the form of pictorial symbols on a flat, palette-like, image. The user simply selects one of the pictorial images to access the functionality.

Consider Color Plate 6. In the top left of the plate you will see what appears to be a collection of 18 buttons, starting with an arrow. This is actually the palette. Each of the buttons on the palette represents a different function. The user selects a function by using a pointing device, such as a mouse, to put the cursor on one of the buttons and pressing the device's selection button. The screen button would then turn a darker grey to simulate detent, and the function would be executed. Frequently used functionality should be easily accessible to the user and should be displayed on a palette if an interface is a graphical one. Like windows, palettes should be movable.

Most of the rules of thumb that apply to windows also apply to palettes. Unfortunately, little research has been done on the use of palettes. The best advice is to try several different prototypes and get user input. An in-depth task analysis (Chapter 2) should be your guide in determining which functionality should be included on a palette and which should not. Additionally, since palettes are normally only found in systems with graphical user interfaces (GUI), the functionality to be put onto a palette should be one that can be easily conveyed in a graphic. Again, paper-pencil prototypes of graphics can be shown to representative users to find the graphic that best matches the proposed function.

4.2 Constructing the Displays

At this stage, tentatively select the appropriate type of screen elements and create pencil-and-paper storyboard representations of the proposed designs. These paper-and-pencil renderings should be complete with color, labels and codes, and correct formats. In short, these hard copy models should reflect the proposed displays as closely as possible. Storyboard prototypes should be evaluated by the design team using the following criteria and their associated checklists (additional items can be added to tailor this checklist to your particular needs).

4.2.1 Content Density

Content density describes the total amount of visual information and visual noise being presented on each display. Only information that is necessary to the user, as determined by a task analysis (Chapter 2), should be displayed on the screen (Smith and Mosier, 1986, pg. 98; Tullis, 1988; Tullis, 1981). Excessive content density will result in displays that appear cluttered and are hard to read, thus inducing user errors. Endeavor to reduce as much screen clutter as possible. The percentage of the screen that is actively in use (the display loading) should not exceed 25% of the total screen (Danchak, 1976, pg. 33) and should probably be maintained between 15-20% of the total screen. In fact, NASA guidelines for the Space Station's displays, according to Tullis (1988, pg. 382), suggest that screen "density generally should not exceed 60% of the available character spaces". Figure 4-18 demonstrates different screen densities (each screen is capable of holding 10 rows of 10 Xs, thus the 50% density screen contains 50 Xs).

If excessive density is indicated on a given display, consider splitting the display into two or more separate screens. In some cases, rearranging the information without removing any of the screen elements may reduce the perceived content density and thus improve user performance. Nevertheless, if screen clutter is a problem, it is probably a good idea to review the task analysis again and reevaluate the screens to determine if **all** of the displayed information is really necessary.

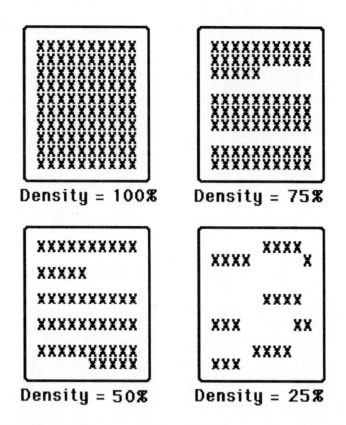

Figure 4-18: Screen Density Shown Graphically

The following techniques for reducing content density are offered by Tullis (1988, pgs. 385-393).

- ○ Use abbreviations.
- ○ Avoid unnecessary detail.
- ○ Use concise wording.
- ○ Use familiar data formats (city, state, zip code).
- ○ Arrange information into a tabular format with column headings.
- ○ Group together similar types of information (Color Plates 3, 16, and 17)
- ○ Ancillary information should be removed and make available on demand.
- ○ Use windows to display ancillary information (Color Plates 4 and 7).
- ○ Separate dissimilar type of information with graphical boundaries (Color Plates 4, 7, 16, and 17).

To evaluate the content density of screens, we strongly encourage the use of Tullis' Display Analysis program (1986a), and we also encourage you to answer the following set of questions.

If the answer to any of the following questions is **YES**, then consider redesigning the screen to display the ancillary information in windows.

1. Does the display appear congested or cluttered?

2. Is locating information difficult due to the large number of screen elements?

3. Are too many screen elements competing for the user's attention?

4. Does the screen require demarcation lines or other symbols to separate elements from each other?

5. Does the user have to focus on each element when scanning the display for important information?

6. Considering the other displays in the system, is this display less likely to be used than others because it has too much information?

7. Are more than 60% of the total available character spaces being used?

4.2.2 Content Integration

Content integration refers to how well the screen elements fit together to form an integrated presentation of information. Poor content integration will result in a screen that is difficult to use even though each of the individual screen elements are well designed. The following questions will help you and the design team to determine if the design has good or poor content integration.

A **YES** response to one of these questions indicates that the display may need reconsideration.

1. Do the elements contained in this display contain many different types of scales (e.g., linear, logarithmic) or involve disparate orders of magnitude?

2. Is it difficult to determine the relationship between the elements included in this display?

3. Does the user need to know special rules in order to interpret this display correctly?

4. Does this display require mental or paper conversion or translation of the information displayed in the elements?

5. Do dissimilar items appear to be too similar?

6. Do similar items appear to be too dissimilar?

The key to designing an integrated display is to consider that the value of the whole display should be more than the sum of its constituent parts. The integrated display should be a cognitive gestalt. If it is not, then perhaps the design team should reconsider the use of an integrated display format. A well-designed integrated display should be an integration of information, rather than requiring the user to mentally integrate the information.

4.2.3 Format Orientation

Format orientation pertains to the ability of the display format to organize and highlight meaningful information. The format should be oriented toward the intended use. Proper format orientation requires a consideration of what information is needed and how it will be used; this information can be obtained from the task analysis (Chapter 2). Often, formatting problems can be solved through the use of some type of grouping strategy.

Grouping similar elements together on a display reduces search time, improves readability, and accentuates the differences between the different groups of elements. The human eye is most sensitive to information that falls within the 5 degree visual angle apprehended by the foveal region of the retina. In other words, your eye is most sensitive to a 5 degree visual area from where your eyes fixate on the screen. A 5 degree visual angle on a CRT screen is roughly equivalent to an area that is 12 characters wide and 6 lines high. Thus, if you fixate your eyes on the center of the screen, then six characters to the right and left of your fixation define the lateral boundaries of the area of highest visual sensitivity; likewise, three lines above your fixation and three lines below define the upper and lower limits of that 5 degree area. Danchak (1976) have suggested that screens be designed so that the information is presented in "chunks" which can be accessed in a single fixation. Thus, chunks should be designed so as not to exceed 5 degrees of visual angle.

Tullis (1986b) found that for groupings with less than 5 degrees of visual angle, search time increases as the number of groups increase. Similarly, he found that for groups that exceeded 5 degrees of visual angle, search time increased as the size of the group increased. Thus, Tullis (1988, pg. 389) concluded that screens made up of groups 5 degrees of visual arc, or smaller, can be scanned much more efficiently than displays made up of larger groups. He also concluded that placing two screen elements within 5 degrees of each other will result in those areas being perceived as being grouped together.

Other than spatial orientation, screen elements can be grouped together in the following ways (Tullis, 1988, pg. 390):

- ○ presenting different screen elements in contrasting colors (Color Plate 3),
- ○ grouping using graphical boundaries (Color Plates 4, 7, 16, and 17),
- ○ presenting different screen elements in contrasting highlighting/reverse video.

The following questions will help you to evaluate your use of formatting. A **NO** response to one of these questions indicates that the display may need reconsideration.

1. Is there a meaningful relationship between how the information is displayed and its intended use?

2. Is the format conducive to presenting the important information with the necessary level of precision?

3. Is the format conducive to highlighting to attract the user's attention to the important elements?

4. Does the display automatically perform necessary calculations or conversions of the displayed information?

5. Does the information fit naturally into the display format or is it forced into the format?

6. Is there a meaningful relationship between how the information is grouped and its intended use?

7. Are the groupings conducive to separating dissimilar elements?

8. Are any of the groups larger than 5 degrees of visual arc?

4.2.4 Cognitive Fidelity

Cognitive fidelity refers to how closely the displayed information matches the way the user conceptualizes the tasks. The performance of the user will be improved if the display matches their expectations of how a given task is to be performed. Here we see the value of a good task analysis (Chapter 2); the output from the task analysis helps you to match display formats to how the user conceives of the task. A departure from user expectations may simply appear different or innovative to you, but may seem wrong to the user because the display runs counter to their expectations.

Information must be conveyed to the user at a level of abstraction that is consistent with their needs. For example, users in the control room of a process control plant are concerned with higher levels of system information, such as whether pressure is in the safe range, and may not want or need detailed information about what is going on in the memory buffers of the system. On the other hand, a user who is trying to start a piece of equipment may not be concerned with the high level details of the machine's function. **You should attempt to anticipate and match the required level of detail in the user's concept of the task set.** A well- designed display should support the appropriate decision-making process rather than impeding it.

Additionally, is the information flow consistent with the flow of the task or does it run counter to the task? The flow of the tasks in the task analysis should match the flow in the display design, otherwise the designed system will be prone to errors and inefficiency. Tullis (1988, pg. 394) offers the following guidelines for reducing errors and increasing productivity through display design.

○ Match the sequence of data element usage to the sequence of the tasks to be performed by the user (Color Plates 16 and 17).

○ Match data sequence conventions (e.g., city, state, and zip).

○ Critical data elements should supersede sequential presentation (e.g., summary displays, warning displays, etc.).

○ In cases where the task analysis reveals that frequency of use is of greater concern than sequence, put more frequently used information at the top of the screen.

○ If the task analysis reveals a hierarchical relationship exists among the data, then general data should precede specific data.

○ Should the task analysis reveal that the displayed data has chronological relationships, order the information based on the chronological relationships revealed in the task analysis.

A **YES** response to one of these questions indicates that the display may need redesign.

1. Does the user require information that is not contained in the display?

2. Does the display rely too heavily on the user's memory?

3. Does the display fail to convey all available options to the user?

4. Does the proposed format limit the ingenuity of the user?

5. Are important boundaries or limits of the relevant system functions obscure or not clearly displayed?

6. Has the display been chosen without first matching it to the user's conceptualization of the task through a task analysis?

7. Is the sequence of data element usage out of sequence with the tasks to be performed by the user?

8. Does the data sequence violate conventions (e.g., zip, state, and city)?

9. Is the more frequently used information located somewhere other than at the top of the screen?

10. Does specific data precede general data?

Once these questions have been satisfactorily answered, the next step is to create a working prototype either through HyperCard, SuperCard, ToolBook, Brickland's Demo, Protoscreens, or any of the myriad of rapid prototyping tools available. Displays should be constructed to present all necessary information to support the functions identified in the task analysis.. Initially a one-to-one correspondence can be assumed for functions and displays.

It should be noted that the construction of displays is only partially an analytical process -- it is also a partially creative one as well. Whether you lay out the display by algorithm or intuition, you must make storyboards or prototypes, evaluate them, revise them, and re-evaluate them. It is desirable to have more than one designer involved in the process, so more than one set of feasible display designs may result. When constructing displays, you **must** adhere to the following guidelines:

1. **Identify critical screen elements**. Elements that require constant monitoring should have a prominent location in the display.

2. **Consider the frequency and sequence of use**. Screen elements should be arranged on the display screen according to when and to how often each will be used.

3. **Group the screen elements into units that will be used or monitored simultaneously**. Do not expect the observer to monitor more than three or four quantitative screen elements at any one time. Dividing the user's attention between more than three screen elements only ensures degraded performance.

4. **Group the screen elements to convey a cohesive unit of performance**. Check for cohesiveness by giving the proposed display a title. (**Note** the grouping of the screen elements in Color Plate 16). Difficulty in devising a title which accurately describes the display's function may indicate the inclusion of too many unrelated screen elements.

Efforts have been made to establish systematic procedures for laying out display panels (U.S. Nuclear Regulatory Commission, 0700, 1981). Such procedures may be based on the frequency of accessing each element, the probability of transitioning from each element to every other element, the probability of a user misreading each element in each location, and/or the relative cost of misreading a given element. Unfortunately, this information may not be readily available to a designer, thereby requiring extensive prototyping and/or experimentation. Most times a full blown experiment is not required to test the usability of a display element. Observing representative users interacting with a rapid prototype may be all that is required to determine if use of a particular display type is likely to result in errors.

NOTE: the testing of screen elements is a must when using multiple screen elements in which the distance between the elements becomes a concern and in which the displays may significantly interact with each other.

4.3 Suggested Readings

The selection of screen elements is an extremely complex issue, and not one that can be adequately addressed in the space of a single chapter. What follows is a list of sources which will provide the interested reader with additional information on the design of screens.

Billingsley, P.A. (1988) Taking panel: issues in the design of windowing systems. In *Handbook of Human Computer Interaction*. Mark Helander (ed). North Holland: Elsevier, 413-436.

Smith, S.L., and Mosier, J.N. (1986) *Guidelines For Designing User Interface Software.* (Technical Report ESD-TR-86-278) National Technical Information Service.

Snyder, H.L. (1988) Image quality. In *Handbook of Human Computer Interaction*. Mark Helander (ed). North Holland: Elsevier, 437-477.

Tullis, T. (1988) Screen design. In *Handbook of Human Computer Interaction*. Mark Helander (ed). North Holland: Elsevier, 377-412.

4.4 References

Billingsley, P.A. (1988) Taking panes: Issues in the design of windowing systems. *Handbook of Human Computer Interaction*. Mark Helander (ed). North Holland: Elsevier, pg. 413-436.

Card, S.K., Pavel, M., and Farrell, J.E. (1984) Window-based computer dialogues. *Proceedings of Interact '84, First IFIP Conference on Human-Computer Interaction.* London, UK, IFIP, 355-359.

Chernoff, H. (1973) The use of faces in K-dimensional space graphically. *American Statistical Association* , 68, 361-368.

Danchak, M.M. (1976) CRT displays for power plants. *Instrumentation Technology*, 23, 29-36.

Dashevsky, S.G. (1964) Check-reading accuracy as a function of pointer alignment, patterning, and viewing angle. *Journal of Applied Psychology*, 48, 344-347.

McCormick, E. J., and Sanders, M.S. (1982) *Human Factors in Engineering and Design*. Fifth Edition. New York: McGraw-Hill Book Company.

Sinclair, H.J. (1971) Digital versus conventional clocks -- A Review. *Applied Ergonomics*, 2(3), 178-181.

Smith, S.L., and Mosier, J.N. (1986) *Guidelines For Designing User Interface Software*. (Technical Report ESD-TR-86-278) National Technical Information Service.

Tullis, T.S. (1981) An evaluation of alphanumeric, graphical, and color displays. *Human Factors*, 23, 541-550.

Tullis, T.S. (1986a) *Display Analysis Program*. Lawrence, KS: The Report Store.

Tullis, T.S. (1986b) Optimizing the usability of computer-generated displays. *Proceedings of HCI '86 Conference on People and Computers: Designing for Usability*. London: British Computer Society.

Tullis, T.S. (1988) Screen Design. In *Handbook of Human Computer Interaction*. Mark Helander (ed). North Holland: Elsevier, 377-411.

U.S. Nuclear Regulatory Commission (1981) *Human Factors Acceptance Criteria for the Safety Parameter Display System*. Draft Report, NUREG-0835.

Zeff, C. (1965) A comparison of conventional and digital time displays. *Ergonomics*, 8(3), 339-345.

CHAPTER 5
Information Coding

Careful coding of the information to be displayed can increase the display's ease of use, while decreasing the potential for user errors. This chapter presents six different types of information coding. Some of these can be used together, while others cannot. Each of these coding strategies is optimal for the display of one or more types of information. The degree to which one method is superior to another largely depends on how well a given method increases the performance of the user, shows high fidelity with the user's cognitive structures (i.e., mental model), and helps decrease information density. Properly coded information reduces human errors, training time and costs, and increases human performance.

5.0 What Is Information Coding?

The sole purpose for the design of any display is the presentation of information to a user. Increasing information results in increasing information density. Up to a point, increasing information density may result in more efficient displays. However, **large** increases in information density can lead to a predictable decrement in performance (Tullis, 1987; Tullis, 1986). The impact of information density on human performance can be easily predicted using the Tullis Prediction Model (Tullis, 1987; Tullis, 1986).

A display's ease of use can be increased, and its potential for user error decreased, if you strive to create displays that are terse and free from extraneous information. Extraneous information results in cluttered, hard to read, displays that have a potential for user error. Careful coding of information can often increase information density without creating cluttered displays.

5.1 Types of Coding

Information can be coded for display in one or more of the following ways:

1. Alphanumeric
2. Binary Coding
3. Color Coding
4. Flash Rate Coding
5. Highlighting
6. Shape Coding

The effectiveness of one coding strategy over another will be determined by how closely the coding method matches the way in which the user conceptualizes the task, the user's mental model. Use the outcome of the task analysis (Chapter 2) to match the appropriate information coding strategies to the display's design.

For example, a simple light on a control panel is a binary code. If the light is illuminated then one state exists; if the light is off then the system is in a different state. Binary codes are used in systems to indicate information that consists of only two states: on or off. Since binary codes have only two states, on or off, it is perfectly mapped, cognitively, to a two-state system (e.g., On or Off). Binary coding would be inappropriately used for displaying information that could be multimodal in nature (e.g., fluctuations in water temperature).

Inappropriate mapping will lead to an increase in human error, a decrease in human performance, and a decrease in system and data integrity. Optimal design is achieved when the chosen information codes are immediately identifiable by the targeted group of users.

5.1.1 Alphanumeric Coding

Alphanumeric coding comprises two types of codes: alpha coding and numeric coding. In alpha coding, letters are used to form the code. If you form the letters to take advantage of past learning (i.e., BUDG for Budget), alpha coding is an extremely powerful and error resistant method of conveying information. Consequently, when the coded information requires a large degree of cognitive processing, and when it lends itself to alpha coding, then alpha coding should be used (Bailey, 1989, pg. 314). Beware, though. Alpha codes formed by combinations of random letters (KJNL) that bare little or no relation to the English language are extremely prone to error (Bailey,1989, pg. 313).

If no intelligible sequence of letters can be formed, then numeric coding should be used rather than an alpha code composed of random letters, because numeric codes have been shown to be superior to random letter codes (Conrad and Hull, 1967; Conrad, R., 1959). When designing a numeric code, use the following guidelines (Kodak, 1983).

- ○ Codes comprised of all numbers should not exceed 5 or 6 digits (fewer still are preferred) (Miller, 1956).

- ○ If a code of more than 5 or 6 digits is unavoidable then the code should be broken into 3 to 4 digit segments separated by a hyphen to facilitate information processing through memory "chunking" (Miller, 1956; Klemmer,1969; Thorpe and Rowland, 1969; Bailey, 1989). For example, a telephone number is actually a numeric code consisting of 10 digits. Phone numbers are easy to remember, because they are broken into "chunks" of three and four digits separated by parentheses and a hyphen: (914) 555-9876.

○ If the code is going to contain a series of repeated digits, the repeated digits should appear at the beginning or end of the code. For example, 2567 000 rather than 2056070.

An alphanumeric code is a hybrid of the alpha code and the numeric code. An example of an alphanumeric code would be BUDG2. Hull (1975) showed that hybrid codes resulted in fewer errors than codes that were comprised of purely letters or numbers.

When designing a hybrid code, use the following guidelines.

○ When designing hybrid codes, the letters should be grouped together rather than interspersed with the digits (Miller, 1956; Klemmer, 1969; Thorpe and Rowland, 1969; and Bailey, 1989).

○ When designing a long hybrid code, group the letters at the beginning of the code and the digits at the end of the code (Miller, 1956; Klemmer,1969; Thorpe and Rowland, 1969; and Bailey, 1989). For example, BUDG345.

○ In order to prevent confusion and reduce the number of human errors, the letters B, D, I, O, Q, and Z and the numbers 0, 1, and 8 should be avoided when constructing hybrid codes (Bailey, 1989).

5.1.2 Binary Coding

Binary coding is used when the system is comprised of two states. The most common type of binary display is a light that indicates that the power to the system has been turned on. In this case, the system has two states: on or off. Binary coding can also be effective when all you want to do is to get the operator's attention and communicate that the system is not functioning normally. A good example of this is the oil light on a car's dashboard. The light illuminates when the oil level drops below a certain point. It does not tell by how much the oil level has fallen, it simply indicates that the oil should be checked because the pressure is too low.

5.1.3 Color Coding

Color coding is probably the most effective type of coding when the only information to be coded is the presence or absence of a target, as well as the target's position on the CRT. A great deal of research has been performed on the use of color as a means of conveying information.

Overall, the body of research is fairly clear on when and when not to use color as a code. Performance on **search** tasks are improved when color codes are used (Luder and Barber, 1984) (Color Plate 5). On the other hand, performance of tasks requiring **identification** of targets are actually inhibited when color coding is used. The decrement in identification performance when color codes are employed is due to the fact that the cognitive processes used in identification of targets is antagonistic to the cognitive processes involved with the decoding of color. The topic is a complex one, and beyond the scope of this discussion. The interested reader is referred to the excellent article by Luder and Barber (1984).

Like all coding strategies, using too many color codes or too many targets of the same color will result in a melange of visual noise, resulting in confusion (Color Plate 5). Even though your terminals may be able to display 16 or more different colors, no more than six different colors (including black) should be used **for information coding** per screen. If each different color is meant to convey some type of information, then even fewer colors should be used (US Nuclear Regulatory Commission, 1980). Additionally, some specific color combinations should be avoided either because of their poor readability (e.g., yellow on black, red on black, or yellow on green) or because of the negative responses which they evoke in the viewer (light green on magenta, orange on magenta, or light green on orange). Additionally, color combinations which cause aberrant visual perceptions, which can degrade performance, should be avoided. For example, use of blue letters on a red background can induce a false perception of a 3 dimensional image called *chromatic stereopsis.*

One important note: **NEVER** use the color **red** to designate normal activity (i.e. pump on, valve open, system ok, etc.). This runs counter to the MILSTD and NUREG-0700 convention of red denoting danger. It also runs counter to the cultural stereotype of red denoting danger or stop.

When designing a display using colors as a code, you should specify the colors by their wavelengths in nanometers rather than their common names (Figure 5-1 and Color Plate 1). This is important because color is a perception arising from the cognitive interpretation of incoming light, and is not an actual physical characteristic of the transmitted light. That is to say that light with a wavelength of 640 nm is detected by cones in the eye that sends a signal to the occipital lobe of the brain where the brain interprets the stimulus as being red. *Redness* does not exist as a **physical** characteristic of light, but rather is simply a retinal **interpretation** of the light's wavelength. Referring to colors by their wavelength in nanometers (Figure 5-1 and Color Plate 1) will ensure that hues are consistently displayed on all of the monitors.

Judicious use of color will result in dramatically increased user performance when searching for targets on a CRT (See Color Plates 3 and 5), particularly when color coding is used as a redundant coding strategy. Indeed, color coding is almost always used in conjunction with another coding strategy and almost never used by itself. Additionally, items having the same color are mentally grouped together by the user (Shneiderman, 1987) (See Color Plates 3 and 5). The general topic of the use of color in the design of CRTs will be revisited in greater detail in the next chapter.

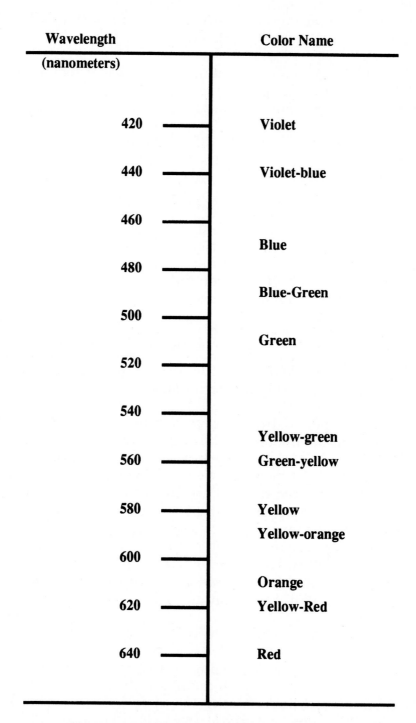

Figure 5-1: Associated Wavelengths of Colors

One final concern involves situations in which either the viewer is color blind or in which one or more of the display's color guns fail. This difficulty can be obviated through the use of redundant coding of information and through the use of white to convey all crucial information.

Some of the many variables to be considered in the design of color displays appear in Table 5-1. Table 5-2, shows an example of guidelines for designing color displays for an isotope separation control system.

5.1.4 Highlighting as a Code

There are several ways to highlight information. Table 5-3, adapted from the work of Hovey, et al. (1981), lists 11 highlighting techniques and rates each according to the reason for highlighting and the display medium used. The use of color as a highlighting technique has already been discussed. Other alternatives include underlining, enclosing in boxes, increasing brightness, and reversing the image polarity (normal image polarity is light characters on a dark background).

Like color coding, highlighted items tend to be perceived as being related (Shneiderman, 1987), and should also be used sparingly. More than two or three highlighted elements on a single display page will degrade, rather than enhance, the display's attention-getting capacity.

5.1.5 Flash Rate Coding

Flashing is a good way to attract attention, but the rate of flash needs to be carefully determined. A flash rate of 2-3 times per second (Hz) with equal on/off intervals is considered to be the best (US Nuclear Regulatory Commission, 1980), while a flash rate of 8-12 Hz may cause nausea, and flash rates of 12-20 Hz may induce seizures in individuals suffering from photo-epilepsy. Flash rates in excess of 50 Hz will not appear as flashes but as constant light to most people over the age of 30 (flicker fusion).

The background of the display should flash to attract attention, **not** the alphanumeric message. In addition, auditory signals in the 380-450 Hz range should be presented in parallel with a flashing item to attract the operator's attention.

While operators are capable of perceiving up to four distinct flash rates (Conrad and Hull, 1967; Conrad,1959), designing systems that require the user to associate more than two flash rates is **NOT** advised (McCormick and Sanders,1982; Cohen and Dinnerstein, 1958). Because it is **extremely** annoying, flashing should be reserved only for attracting the attention of the user or for indicating the urgency of a message along with an auditory signal (Van Cott and Kinkade,1972).

Table 5-1: Specifying Display Colors

Important points to remember.

1. Choose colors that indicate specific and consistent functions.

2. In choosing the type and amount of information to color code, avoid creating unplanned or obviously new patterns on the screen.

3. Patterns of color on the face of the CRT can either improve or impair user performance. Test each format for distracting visual noise before finalizing the color code assignments.

4. Color coding is beneficial if:

   a. the display is unformatted,
   b. symbol density is high,
   c. target position is unknown, but the color of the target **is** known,
   d. symbol legibility is degraded,
   e. color is logically related to the operator's task,
   f. the user's task involves search.

5. Use color to indicate the current system status (Color Plates 13 and 16).

6. Use white for very important data and information (white uses all three guns in the CRT and has high contrast against a black background.

7. Use color as a redundant coding device.

8. Select colors with high contrast for parameters and features that must "catch" the user's attention (See Color Plates 8, 9,10, 11, and 12).

9. Test the proposed selections under lighting conditions which simulate the conditions under which the display will actually be viewed.

10. Displayed colors will be distorted if colored ambient illumination is used.

11. High-ambient illumination can "wash out" displayed colors.

12. Hoods that block out light and glare are helpful if ambient illumination cannot be controlled.

13. Do not use high-pressure sodium as an ambient-light medium for viewing CRT viewing.

Table 5-1: (Continued)

14. Color should indicate function according to the user's mental model. For example, a layman's reaction to red (DANGER/STOP) would be different than a power plant operator's reaction (circuit is on). MILSTD recommends the following strategy for employing color codes:

Color	State	Result
Flashing red	Emergency	Immediate user action
Red	Alert	Corrective/override action must be taken
Yellow	Advise	Caution/recheck is necessary
Green	Proceed	Condition satisfactory
White	Normal	No "right" or "wrong" indication
Blue	Advisory	Should not be used except as a background

Intensity: Much can be done with variable intensity control on both black-and-white and color CRTs. A monochromatic format, if the flash is twice as intense as the rest of the display, will draw the operators attention as effectively as if color had been used. Fewer colors can be used if they can be adjusted for intensity.

The suggested minimum amount of control for any unit is:

1. a foreground intensity control separate from background intensity control;

2. a capability for making grid lines half as intense as the rest of the display. Reserving a specific color for the grid line will limit the graphics capabilities of the display;

3. intensity control variable enough to accommodate very low levels of ambient illumination and the higher levels normally found in office work areas (5 to 150 footcandles).

Color Identification: Before a color can be identified, it must first be detected and recognized. What one person will call orange another will call red. In addition to personal interpretation, manufacturers often use different terms

Table 5-1: (Continued)

for the same physical wavelength or may use the same term for a variety of very similar wavelengths (e.g., mauve). If only one unit is used, people can identify the colors easily enough; however, if more than one unit is used or if several manufacturers are represented, then a method for achieving uniformity is needed. By adopting the method of identifying colors by their dominant wavelengths, it is possible for several manufacturers to produce the same color (Figure 5-1 and Color Plate 1).

Manufacturers may seem to promote the use of the "standard eight" colors when demonstrating the capabilities of the unit. These "standard colors" are a carryover from earlier multicolor display units that could only generate color by having three proton guns (blue, red, green) in their fully on or off mode. The "standard eight" refers to the on/off mode of the guns and, not necessarily, to the particular hues produced on the screen. Differences in phosphors and color-generation techniques may cause red (red gun on, blue and green guns off) on one unit to appear different than on another unit displaying the same color formula. Certain tasks have come to be associated with the standard eight colors. You should be aware of the colors that are commonly used.

Due to technical advances, the guns can now be regulated to produce in excess of a million different colors, thereby making the task of color selection a major part of your job. The final selections should be based on the individual needs of the system.

CRT units seldom have 100% beam registration. Select colors discriminable with 50% misregistration of the beam. Be especially careful when using light colors such as cyan and white.

Table 5-2: Recommended Process Control Graphics Standards[1]

The following color specifications should be used when color coding process control displays.

Color	General Meaning	Use
White	N/A	Dynamic valves, dynamic alphanumeric information, boundaries/outlines
Yellow	Caution	Information in a cautionary region. Cautionary regions on graphs.
Cyan	N/A	Major headings, scales, engineering units, fluid levels, preferred flow paths on schematics
Blue	N/A	Uninstrumented (static) valve, minor headings, value numbers, component designators, borders, building walls, non-preferred flow paths, background
Broken Blue	N/A	Unavailable flow paths
Green	On	On or normal running state of equipment , normal operating region
Red	Danger	Emergency warning, failure, danger.
Magenta	Not within acceptable range of operation (radiation only)	Emergency warning Out of limits (For radiation ONLY)
Black	N/A	Background/Filler

Some points to remember:

1. Information of the greatest significance should be set apart from other display components by either increasing intensity, size, or highlighting.

2. The blink feature may be used to attract attention. However, a provision should be made for canceling the blink after it has served its purpose. Several display components blinking simultaneously would detract from the display's ability to attract attention.

Table 5-2: (Continued)

3. **Viewing distance** to **size** guidelines:

Viewing Distance (m)	Scale Base Lengths (mm)	Scale spacing 20 Divisions (mm)	Character Size (mm)
0.5	35	1.7	1.7
0.75	52	2.6	2.1
1.0	70	3.5	2.8
1.5	105	5.2	4.2
2.0	140	7.0	5.6
2.5	175	8.7	7.0
3.0	210	10.5	8.4
4.0	280	14.0	11.2
5.0	350	17.5	14.0
6.0	420	21.0	16.8
7.0	490	49.0	19.6
8.0	560	28.0	22.4
9.0	630	31.5	25.2
10.0	700	35.0	28.0

1. When displaying information concerning date and time, pick one area of the screen and reserve this area only for date and time data on all graphic presentations requiring this information. *Be consistent.*

2. If a blue background is chosen, remember that blue headings, numbers, or alpha characters will not be seen on a blue background.

3. If blue is used on both a black and a white background, the white background will cause the blue target to appear more saturated relative to the black background.

4. Yellow on white should not be used if possible due to the very low contrast.

5. In general, backgrounds should be darker than foregrounds.

6. Yellow on green should not be used due to a "vibrating" effect to the eye.

7. In general, apparent relative target hue depends on the hue and saturation of the background.

8. Extreme color contrasts can form complimentary after images due to rod receptor fatigue and should be avoided.

Table 5-2: (Continued)

9. Use the white color for very important information so that if one of the color guns fail, no important information will be lost from the screen.

10. When specifying colors such as red, green, violet, etc., specify the precise wavelengths in nanometers (Figure 5-1 and Color Plate 1).

Table 5-3: Highlighting Techniques Selected According to Use

Highlighting Method	Reason for Highlighting				Display Type	
	Alarm	Unusual Value	High-Priority Message	Data Entry Errors	Alphanumeric CRT	Graphic CRT
Brightness	2	1	1	1	1	1
Size	3	1	1	1	1	1
Image polarity	2	2	2	2	1	1
Different font	3	2	2	2	1	2
Underlining	3	2	2	2	2	2
Color	2	1	1	1	3	1
Flashing	1	3	2	3	1	1
Boxing	3	3	1	2	2	1
Arrowing	3	2	3	2	3	2
Symbolic tag	3	2	3	3	3	2
Alphanum tag	3	3	3	3	3	3

1 = Good   **2 = Workable but suboptimum**   **3 = Not recommended**

In order to enhance the readability of a message, the message itself should not be flashed on and off. Instead, the message can be flashed between full and half intensity. Alternatively, a box around the message can be flashed, or the duty cycle (the ratio of on-time to off-time) may be increased.

5.1.6 Shape Coding

Shape coding (See Color Plate 5) is useful for conveying large amounts of information because shapes are quickly recognized and easily remembered. The number of shapes that can be used is highly dependent on the quality of the display design and the information to be conveyed. One approach is to assign meanings to a set of easily distinguishable primary shapes such as circles, squares, or triangles. Often a set of symbols will be familiar to a set of users. However, care should be taken not to overemphasize the pictorial aspects of the symbol. Adding more details for pictorial realism tends to clutter the display and may increase painting time.

People can quickly learn to associate meanings with as many as 15 pictorial symbols (Van Cott and Kinkade,1972). In general, symbols should be simple and few in number. If only a few symbols are used, each symbol's shape can become its label; however, more than 15 symbols may require alphanumeric labels, thus defeating the use of the shapes. As part of your task analysis (Chapter 2), you should determine if a currently accepted symbol set exists as part of the user's job, and adopt that set of symbols if possible.

5.2 Develop Rules of Coding

When applying any given coding strategy, it is important that you establish rules of usage. These rules need not attain the sweeping status of a set of standards, nonetheless these rules will govern how and when each type of code shall be used. The implementation of rules of usage are so important that Bailey (1989) advocates creating the rules **before** deciding on a type of code. A consistent set of rules that are followed in a lawful manner will increase the ease of use of the code by the users and reduce the incidence of human error, thereby reducing corporate costs. However, rules of encoding that are inconsistently applied can be worse than no rules at all, because they lure the user into the trap of erroneous interpretation, thereby increasing human error and their associated costs.

Finally, Bailey (1989, pg. 311) points out that codes should be designed to optimize the performance of the **least skilled** users, since it is unlikely that codes designed for the least skilled users will degrade the performance of the more skilled users. Bailey (1989) suggests designing two sets of codes when there is thought to be a degradation of the performance of the more skilled set of users (e.g., allowing users to type "e" in lieu of the entire word "edit").

5.3 Notes

1. While these guidelines were originally designed for process control, they can be easily modified to fit your needs if you haven't developed your own standards/guidelines.

5.4 References

Bailey, R.W., (1989) *Human Performance Engineering: Using Human Factors/Ergonomics to Achieve Computer System Usability.* (2nd Ed) Englewood Cliffs, NJ: Prentice-Hall.

Cohen, J., and Dinnerstein, A.J. (1958) *Flash rate as a visual coding dimension for information.* WADC TR, (Wright-Patterson Air-Force Base, Ohio: Wright Air Development Center, pgs 57-64.

Conrad, R., and Hull, A.J. (1967) Copying alpha and numeric codes by hand, *Journal of Applied Psychology*, **51**, 444-448.

Conrad, R. (1959) Errors of immediate memory. *British Journal of Psychology*, 349-359.

Hovey, S. T., S. J. Dodd, and Price, J.G. (1981) *Automated Mission Planning-Penetration Analysis Systems: Human Factors Engineering Guide,* RADC-TR-81-71, Vol. S, (Rome, New York: Rome Air Development Center).

Hull, A. J. (1975) Nine codes: a comparative evaluation of human performance with some numeric alpha, and alphanumeric coding systems. *Ergonomics*, 18, 567-576.

Klemmer, E. T. (1969) The grouping of digits for manual entry. *Human Factors*, 11 (4), 397-400.

Kodak (1983) *Ergonomic Designs For People At Work.* New York: Van Nostrand Reinhold.

Luder, C. B., and Barber, P.J. (1984) Redundant color coding on airborne CRT displays. *Human Factors*, 26, 19-32.

McCormick, E.J., and Sanders, M.S. (1982) *Human Factors in Engineering and Design.* New York: McGraw Hill.

Miller, G.A. (1956) The magic number seven, plus or minus two: Some limits on our capacity for processing information. *Psychological Review*, 63, 81-97.

Shneiderman, B.J. (1987) *Designing the User Interface: Strategies For Effective Human-Computer Interaction.* Reading, MA: Addison-Wesley.

Thorpe, C.E., and Rowland, G.E. (1969) The effect of natural grouping of numerals on short-term memory. *Human Factors,* 7, 38-44.

Tullis, T. S., (1987) Design of effective screen displays. *Proceedings of the 31st Annual User-System Interface Conference.* 1-26.

Tullis, T. S., (1986) A system for evaluating screen formats. *Proceedings of the Human Factors Society's 30th Annual Meeting.* 1216-1220.

US Nuclear Regulatory Commission (1980) *NRC Action Plan Developed as a Result of the TMI-2 Accident,* NUREG-0660.

Van Cott, H.P., and Kinkade, R. G. (1972) *Human Engineering Guide to Equipment Design.* (Revised Edition) U.S. Government Printing Office, Washington, DC.

CHAPTER 6
Using Color in Displays

Color can be used in the design of displays to facilitate human visual detection, discrimination, and recognition in complex visual tasks. Understanding the complex set of interacting variables associated with the use of color is essential when optimizing human performance, especially in software design. Color can also be used to create naturalistic simulations, to enhance signal processing output , to group together similar types of information on a screen, and to separate important information from visual noise.

This chapter presents the various aspects of color presentation and the problems typically encountered, in displays ranging from CAT Scan medical images to Computer-Assisted Design and Manufacturing (CAD/CAM), and offers specific design recommendations based on the currently available information.

6.0 What Is Color?

Color is a human **perception** brought about by the brain's interpretation of the neural signals of certain retinal neurons that respond to light of a specific spectral frequency. For example, when a 500 nanometer beam of light strikes a retinal cone cell that is sensitive to light in the 500 nanometer range, the observer experiences the perception of the color green. However, the original light does not contain a physical quality of "greenness"; greenness is a psychological quality. The perception of color is simply the brain's interpretation of the signal sent to it by retinal cells that are sensitive to light in that spectral frequency.

6.1 Why Use Color When Monochrome Is Cheaper?

Color displays, whatever their mode of generation, generally cost more to purchase, maintain, and use than their monochromatic counterparts. Thus the provision of color in a display should be associated with some measurable or at least definable benefit. In some applications, the benefit may be largely aesthetic or subjective, while in others it may be directly related to user and system performance. In performance-related applications, two criteria must be met: (1) the addition of color must provide some measurable improvement in user performance and, (2) there must be no decrease in user performance in any critical task. Color can be used effectively to increase user performance by:

1. alerting the user to some change of system status,
2. improving discrimination among items on a display (Color Plate 5),
3. grouping and categorical separation of screen elements (Color Plate 3),
4. improvement of aesthetic and perceptual organization.

For example, color has been used effectively to improve the performance of antisubmarine warfare (ASW) operators (Chapanis, 1949). Antisubmarine warfare involves the detection of nearly silent targets (submarines) imbedded in a high noise environment (ocean). The problem is that of how to effectively display the fragile and transient signals of submarines relative to their noisy backgrounds (ocean). Coloring aspects of the signal and noise significantly increases the probability of target detection when compared to monochrome displays (Color Plate 5). However, the choice of color, saturation, shading, format, contrast, and resolution in the depiction of the target and the background are critical to the assurance that the operator is able to make confident, unambiguous, and consistent judgments about the presence or absence of a target signal. One could deploy some very sensitive, advanced technology to tease out the signal of interest. But, if the display format is not designed to be compatible with the operator's sensory discrimination ability, cognitive expectations, and the task being executed, then the ASW operator's performance will be degraded, resulting in the degradation of overall system performance and the consequent missing of targets.

6.2 What Determines the Effectiveness of Color?

The effective impact of color on human performance depends, to a great extent, on a complex set of interacting factors. The purpose for which the display will be used will ultimately effect the degree to which each of these factors will influence human performance. This relationship can be depicted in a three dimensional representation (Figure 6-1).

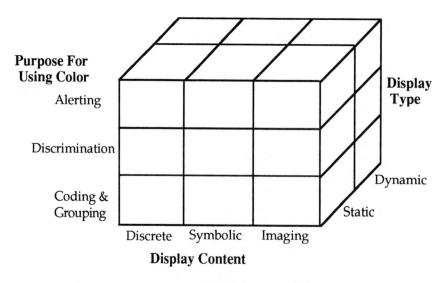

Figure 6-1: Factors Effecting the Choice to Use Color

6.2.1 Display Content

Both chromatic and achromatic displays contain a variety of content, ranging from the simple off or on "idiot light" to the most complex command-control display. For the purpose of this discussion, the following three types of display content seem useful to separate: discrete indicators and warning displays, symbolic presentation displays, and imaging displays.

6.2.1.1 Discrete Indicators

Color coding has stereotypically been used as a discrete status indicator, with green standing for safety, yellow for caution or warning, and red for danger. These color codes have been applied to colored lights, sign fields, and vehicular instruments. Some of the more complex displays, which use color coding to represent **symbolic** relationships, have tended to reserve the use of red, yellow, and green for their traditional meanings **[A practice that we recommend]**.

6.2.1.2 Symbolic Displays

In symbolic displays (Color Plate 5), color coding is used for the purpose of grouping symbols with similar meanings and separating unlike ones. In some cases, the grouping is purely symbolic. For example, some word-processing and spreadsheet programs employ color coding to indicate different categories of information (Color Plate 3). In other cases, such as military fire-control displays, different colors are used to indicate friendly versus enemy craft.

6.2.1.3 Imaging Displays

Imaging displays range from the full-color 35 mm motion picture to the simple, pseudocolor-coded satellite-view of a planet. While some imaging displays attempt to duplicate our visual perception of a familiar world, others simulate worlds which cannot be seen with the naked eye. A good example is Magnetic Resonance Imaging (MRI). MRI scans create color enhanced pictures of the interior structures of the brain without the need for intrusive surgery. Color Plates 6 and 7 show a medical display rendered using a digital image processing station to integrate input from MRI and PET (Positron Emission Tomography) scans of the brain and heart. In both cases, the coloration enhancements help doctors identify structures which may be abnormal.

Imaging displays may either be dynamic or static in their mode of presentation. All such artificially created color codes, called *pseudocolor*, have one common objective: The substitution of color for the dimension of interest in order to accent differences along that dimension and to facilitate natural groupings and spatial relationships (compare cover with Color Plate 6). For example, Color Plate 4 shows a 3D rendering of a pillow block bearing that was created with Design CAD 3D. In this case, different colors are used for each of the different components of the bearing, making them easy to discern from each other. The colors with greater saturation create the illusion of shading, which in turn creates the illusion of a three dimensional image. The quality of simulated, 3 dimensional images depends on the number of simultaneously displayed colors available, and on the number of individual picture elements (pixels) in the image. The pillow block bearing rendering, in Color Plate 4, was generated using only an NEC Multisync monitor with 800 X 600 pixel resolution and 256 colors. Some displays are available which can have 1,536 lines (more than two million pixels) and over one billion colors.

Computer-generated images are currently very costly in terms of computer time. While diffuse reflection on a computer rendered object is relatively easy and inexpensive to simulate, specular reflection (e.g., reflections on a computer rendered mirror-polished chrome ball) requires more colors and more computer time. In addition, the simulation of specular reflection, whose luminance ranges in the real world may be 1,000 or 10,000 to 1, may require greater luminance ranges than are generally found in CRTs.

However, in some cases, the maximum photographic level of realism is not required or even desirable. Wire frame images or simple diffuse shading may be sufficient to depict the surfaces desired. Moreover, high levels of realism can actually yield diminishing returns. Added realism increases the potential for image ambiguity (the viewer may see the wrong thing). A photographic image of a polished metal object, for instance, would include mirror-image reflections of its surroundings due to specular reflection. In such a circumstance, these superfluous reflections could distort the viewer's understanding of the geometry of the object.

An example of these unresolved problems is found in real-time flight simulation, in which there is an increasing demand for more realism. If the simulator is to be effective, the pilot's training on it must transfer to real-world behavior. Unanswered questions abound in this area, including the degree of realism required for effective transfer of training (Jones, Hennessy, and Deutsch, 1985). Much of the terrain for a flight simulator can be modeled with only diffuse reflection, because much of the real world has a matte appearance. However, some features, such as water, pavement, and other artifacts, exhibit considerable specular reflection as well. Correct interpretation of these features may require specular information that is not generally provided in simulators. In addition, although color shading is an effective way of achieving realism and giving an impression of three dimensions, there are no guidelines to govern how many colors are needed or how many colors can be perceived by the observer. The current procedure is generally to provide physical fidelity; that is, to simulate as much as possible the physics of light reflected from the real scene. However, this can be a very costly solution.

The question of "how many colors will suffice" is unanswered. The use of too few colors causes boundary artifacts to appear between colors (called *contouring*) when the objective might be a smooth imperceptible transition between colors. You can generally achieve this objective by using 4,096 colors (4 bits per gun) or even fewer. At the other extreme, the subjective quality, called *perceived realism*, seems to require more colors. Some in the computer animation industry believe that full color requires 24 bits or 16.8 million colors. Some even claim to see improvements between 24 and 32 bit images. Still, others argue that 16 million colors are excessive and point out that the most demanding case would require no more than one color per pixel; at the writing of this book, 16 million colors cannot be displayed simultaneously on any current display because there are not enough pixels. The argument can also be made that the viewer cannot perceive that many colors; Limb, Rubinstein, and Fukunage (1977) report a maximum of about 50,000 distinguishable colors.

Other techniques are being tried to increase realism without adding additional colors. Heckbert (1982) used look-up tables for colors that were determined by their statistical distribution rather than by equal intervals in the color space. He created images with only eight bits per pixel that compared favorably with images of 15 and even 24 bits per pixel. Pixel averaging techniques, which further decreased contouring effects and created more effective colors without increasing memory requirements, improved images even more.

Raster displays suffer from the additional problem that all elements must be composed entirely of horizontal line segments. The resulting stair-stepped or scalloping aberration associated with oblique lines can be mitigated by a greater raster density or by techniques involving recalculation of certain pixels (anti-aliasing algorithms). Both techniques result in higher costs. While this is not a consideration specific to multicolored displays (it occurs in monochrome as well), you should address the question of whether there are color dependencies in these techniques. The differential sensitivity of the eye to spatial, temporal, and orientational variations in different colors suggests that color dependencies might exist.

One recent paper was cited as addressing this point. Different pictures with different degrees of fidelity were shown to subjects who were asked to rate them for realistic appearance. The minimum number of pixels required for faithfulness of the perception in a sphere was derived from the results (Atherton and Caporeal, 1985). This technique in human evaluation of image quality may prove useful to you when answering other questions about the simulation of reality.

The relationship between color and perception of motion is another issue in the simulation of reality. One important function of color in the perception of the world is to indicate, in a normally cluttered environment, which parts of the field of view belong together and will move together. Size, motion, and color interact together in object segregation, and the color effects on perceived organization can be substantial, as is indicated by the Ishihara color vision tests and by numerous search investigations. There have been few experiments dealing with the effect of color in organizing moving arrays, and, paradoxically, color does not seem to be a prime determinant of perceived motion. For example, apparent motion can occur between different colors, rather than the same color, when the configuration allows for either perception (Ramachandran and Gregory, 1978). An analysis of the functions that color does serve in segregating still and moving objects from their surrounds and backgrounds is necessary.

Pseudocolor is used to achieve discrimination between shades of intensity in an image. For example, some satellite images of earth's resources depict vegetation and water patterns in a color coding scheme that, although logical, is not related to natural colors in the same scene. Pseudocolor is also used to depict stress and temperature gradients in mechanical components designed by computer (CAD) (Color Plate 4).

6.2.2 Purposes For Using Color

In general, color can be used to increase performance by alerting the user to changes in the system status, assisting in the discrimination between displayed elements, grouping together of similar screen elements, and increasing the aesthetics of the display.

Look at Color Plate 6. Notice how black and the differing shades of gray are used to create an illusion of modularity. The spectral bar to the left of the images has a scroll bar just to its right that allows the user to adjust the color of the displays to meet their aesthetic needs. Also notice that the arrow, in the upper left corner of the plate, has a darker gray background than the rest of the plate. The buttons on the palette change color to dark gray when a mouse is clicked on them. This is to simulate the detent of mechanical buttons, bringing the interface closer to the user's day-to-day reality. Similarly, the use of darker shades of gray to give buttons the illusion of three dimensionality is an excellent example of using color and shading to provide visual cues as to a display element's function.

6.2.2.1 Alerting the User

A change in color, or an alternation between colors, can be used to get the attention of the user and warn them that the state of the system is out of acceptable range or tolerance. Conventionally, the green-yellow-red coding is used, although this standard is often violated (for example, in nuclear power control rooms, both red and green lights are used to indicate acceptable conditions).

NOTE: The use of green for go or safe, yellow or amber for caution, and red for danger is so commonplace that it has become a stereotype. When color codings are used that are at odds with cultural stereotypes (e.g., red for go and green for stop), human performance can be **severely** degraded from a negative transfer effect. In cases where coding is at odds with cultural stereotypes, the stereotypic response can be elicited, particularly when the user is performing a highly complicated task which requires divided attention. Since the user's attention is divided, the more highly learned response (the culturally stereotyped one) is much more likely to be invoked. In the above example of a nuclear power plant, the results could be disastrous and cost millions of lives. When in doubt, code to be consistent with cultural stereotypes. An instance in which constraints **require** the system to be designed counter to cultural stereotypes will be extremely rare.

Frequently, in addition to the use of color for alerting the user, color is also used to indicate the degree to which the system is out of tolerance. An example is a thermometer that changes color as the temperature exceeds the range of tolerance. On more sophisticated displays, large symbols may be superimposed in a contrasting color to indicate a specific condition to which the operator must be sensitive and respond immediately. For example, a "breakaway X" on a military aircraft vertical situation display is a large symbol denoting that immediate action is required on the part of the pilot.

In order for the alerting function to be successful, several principles must be followed. First, the more sparing the use of the warning color, the more effective (Color Plate 5) it is as a warning (Krebs and Wolf, 1979). This principle can be expanded to the use of a warning color on adjacent displays. For example, the use of red to map an area on one display may interfere with its alerting function on an adjacent display (Frome, 1984). You **must** consider the **whole** system when choosing color codes.

Second, the number of different colors used must be few and as discriminable from one another as possible. Krebs and Wolf (1979) suggest that no more than five colors should be used, an optimum number would be three or four. The restrictions on the number of colors employed for alerting functions stem from the attempt to eliminate color confusion errors under as many conditions as possible. Specifications of colors for coding such as signal lights at sea, aviation colors, and colors for traffic control are generally available.

6.2.2.2 Discriminating Between Elements

Color, to the extent that it provides contrast, has been shown to improve the discrimination among items on a display. To assess the degree of discrimination, you will need some means of measuring or specifying the amount of contrast between colors. Luminance contrast (Color Plates 8 to 10) is defined as the difference in hue and saturation of images relative to their background (Thorell and Smith, 1990, pg 124). Color plates 8 to 10 show the differential effects of luminance contrasts on displays.

Computing **<u>luminance</u>** contrast is straightforward since it is simply the ratio of the darkest to the lightest components in a given area. You can use the following formula to compute **<u>luminance</u>** contrast:

$$C_m = (L_{max} - L_{min})/(L_{max} + L_{min})$$

where:

C_{max} = Contrast modulation
L_{max} = Maximum level of luminance of an image or background
L_{min} = Minimum level of luminance of an image or background

You can determine color contrast with the color difference formula:

$$DE = [(L^*)^2 + (u^*)^2 + (v^*)^2]^{1/2}$$

where:

L = Luminance
u and v are color coordinates in a color space known as UCS (Color Plate 1).

The color space in Color Plate 1 should be your reference when specifying the use of color in displays. Since color is simply a product of perceptions, you **MUST** give CIE coordinates when describing colors. Color Plate 1 shows that colors become less saturated moving toward the interior of the color space and more saturated moving toward the outer edges. Specifying the exact coordinates of a color in the color space very accurately predicts how the color will appear in both hue and saturation. Color Plate 2 shows lines of constant hue; the elipses indicate hues that are equally saturated.

Contrast can be used by you in two ways: (1) luminance contrast is a much more effective determinant of visibility than is hue contrast, and (2) hue contrast can aid discrimination, but only if the hues are widely separated in color space and there is little luminance contrast present (i.e., less than 10 percent) (Lippert, Farley, Post, and Snyder, 1983). Furthermore, there is evidence that red-green contrast is more effective than yellow-blue contrast in improving visibility (Frome, Buck, and Boynton, 1981; Kaiser and Boynton, 1985; and Boynton, 1986, 1979).

6.2.2.3 Grouping and Categorical Separation

One of the largest effects of color on human performance is the reduction of search time by color coding. This effect depends on color to unify items that are categorically similar to the exclusion of other items on the display. For example, Color Plate 3 shows a spreadsheet in which color is used to group together numeric values with a similar meaning. In this case, the magenta numbers indicate values representing a change in allocation. As you can see from this plate, numbers of similar color (yellow for example) appear to be grouped together. Thus, the cognitive separation between different categories can be increased thereby decreasing search time, when the user is searching for a specific class of targets (Color Plates 3 and 5). The extent to which these benefits accrue is dependent on the number of displayed items, the chromatic separation of the codes (e.g., blue-red is more easily distinguished than red-orange), the legibility of the coded symbols, and the logical relationship of the color coding to the targets.

Visual search has been extensively studied, and a number of principles for the effective use of color coding has evolved. First, if color is to be effective in helping a viewer find a symbol on a display, the symbol's color must be known to the viewer. Without such knowledge, performance is poorer on a multicolored display than on a monochrome display (Krebs and Wolf, 1979).

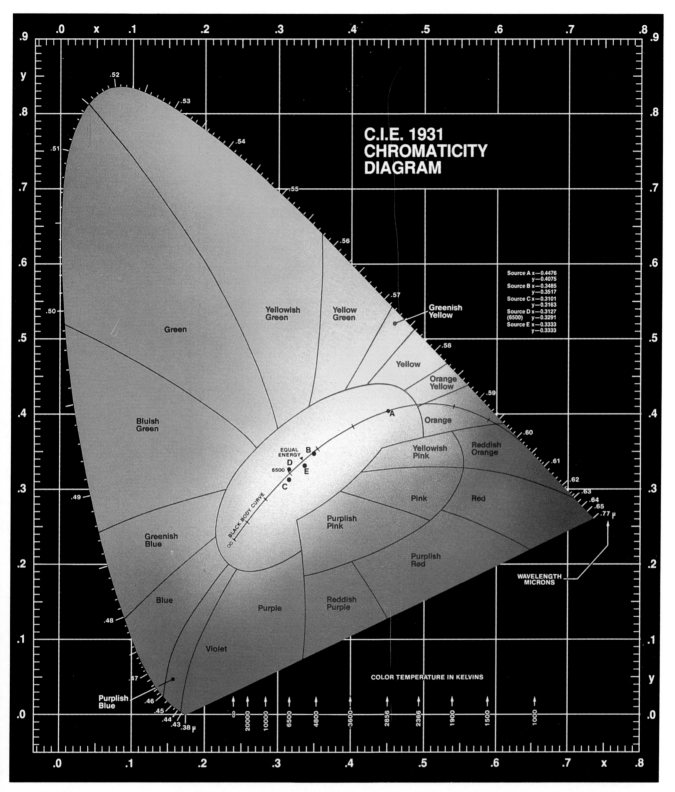

Color Plate 1. CIE 1931 Color Diagram As you can see from this plate, there are many different hues that could be considered red. You should use this color space when specifying display colors. Wavelengths of light of a given hue are displayed along the periphy of the diagram. For example, we can specify a dark red as having a wavelength of 0.77μ. Note the difference in appearance between the hue of wavelength 0.77μ and the hue of wavelength 0.60μ. Both would be identified as red, yet they appear very different when viewed together. However, by using the exact nanometer wavelength associated with a given color, you can avoid this confusion and be assured of chromatic uniformity across the displays (e.g. all reds will look exactly alike if you specify that the color red will be 630 nm). To determine what color will result when you mix two different colored lights from an emissive display, draw a straight line from the wavelength measure of one of the lights to the wavelength measure of the other. The resulting wavelength is a point on the line located between the two points of the component lights, at a distance *inversely* proportional to the amount of the component colors in the mixture. (Courtesy of Photo Research).

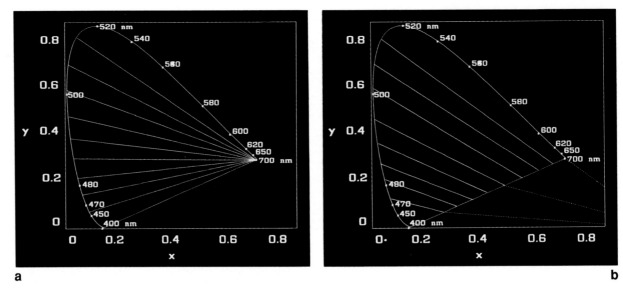

Color Plate 2. Confusion Lines for Protanopes and Deuteranopes (Color Insensitive Viewers) In Plate 2a, the colors that lay along one of the lines radiating from the lower right of the color space appear very similar to protanopic observers (difficulty discriminating reds). In Plate 2b, by contrast, all of the colors that appear on each of these lines appear very similar to deuteranopic observers (difficulty discriminating greens). (Thorell & Smith, 1990).

CORPORATE EXPENSE REPORT

	---APRIL 1986---			---QTR TO DATE---		
	ACTUAL	TARGET	%	ACTUAL	TARGET	%
SQ FOOTAGE		650	NA			
BL42/19/24		1264	NA			
EXAMPT		6	NA			
NON EXEMPT		1	NA			
TOTAL CORP H/C	6	7	86			
TOTAL H/C	6	7	86			
SALARIES	25794	23495	114	68825	78565	69
PAYROLL TX	2270	2692	84	9561	8574	65
EMP BENEFITS	952	1010	94	3889	4730	75
SUBTOTAL	29016	27197	106	82056	92089	68
OFFICE SUPPLIES	200	624	32	1129		97
PRINT SERV	80	80	100	996		NT
MACH/EQUIP				2218		NT
SOFTWARE PUR		3705		533		NT
DEPRECIATION	4256	4256	99	12144		NT
OCCUPANCY	1264	1264	100	3792	3792	100
TRAVEL EXP	863	1147	77	3226	2800	120
RECRUTING	1160	1160	102	2241		NT
MOVING EXPENSES			NT	47	7000	1
OP EXP		60	NT	164		
OTHER				70		92
TOTAL	36879	39493		108714	111681	

Color Plate 3. Color Coding of Information You can use color to represent (code) abstract meanings or functions. In the case of the display shown here, a change in the color of the data from yellow to magenta indicates to the user that the cost allocation has changed (i.e., the addition of more than one person). Using a change in color to indicate a change in the data is a very powerful cue to the user (provided they are not color insensitive, see Color Plate 2) that something about the data has changed (see Color Plate 5). However, using color to symbolize complex information (angle of aircraft approach) may be problematic depending on the task. (Thorell & Smith, 1990).

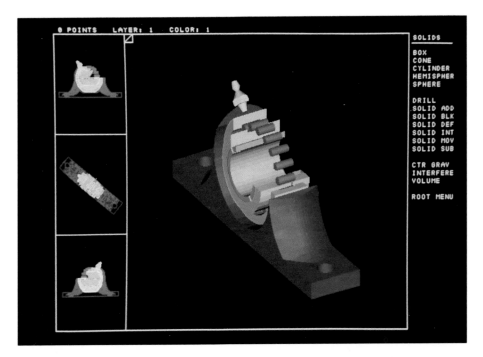

Color Plate 4. Use of Pseudocolor and Shading This three-dimensional rendering of a pillow block bearing, using Design CAD 3D, shows the effective use of pseudocoloring. Different parts are illustrated using artificial coloring (i.e., pseudocolor). In this case, the casing is shown in blue, grease inserts in yellow, inner and outer traces in yellow rings, roller bearings in red, and the bearing sleeve in light blue. Notice how distinct the different parts appear, and think about how they would look if they were all the same color (i.e. monochrome display). The illusion of three dimensions is achieved simply through the use of different shades of blue and the application of image contouring. Note how tiled windows are used to effectively show different views of the rendering simultaneously. Also note the single layer menu of functions to the right of the image. (Courtesy of Design CAD).

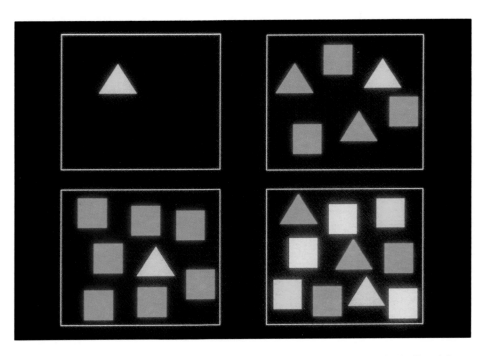

Color Plate 5. Visual Search as a Function of Color, Shape, and Number As can be seen from this plate, search time is significantly faster for the shapes of a specific color (yellow triangles in the left panel) than when there are many objects of a similar shape (top right) or similar color (lower right). (Thorell & Smith, 1990).

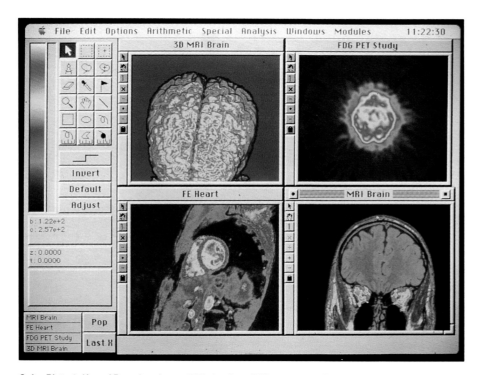

Color Plate 6. Use of Pseudocolor and Windowing Different types of medical information are effectively integrated in this display through the use of tiled windows, which can be overlapped. Different types of information appear in each window. The display of multiple windows allows the user to compare and integrate the information displayed in each of the different images. On the left border of each of the windows are a series of squares with different pictorial images. These squares are "hot" zones (buttons) of direct manipulation functionality. The resulting functionality evoked by the buttons is limited to the contents of the window upon whose borders the buttons reside. Note how shades of grey are used to create the visual illusion of buttons, buttons on the palette, the separation of windows, and the detent of the arrow button that shows its selection. Also note how pseudocolor is used to indicate areas of interest in each image. (Courtesy of William Connor of HIPG).

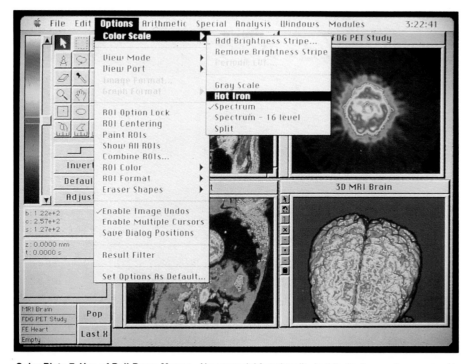

Color Plate 7. Use of Pull-Down Menus Nonessential functionality in this display can be accessed by clicking a mouse or other pointing device on a hot spot (in this case a word) on the menu bar and pulling down. Functionality that is available to the user appears in black, while unavailable functions appear in light grey. Selected functions appear in reverse video. The arrow-heads in the right margin of the menu indicate the presence of an additional, lower level, menu layer. The checkmarks to the left of a choice indicates a selected choice. (Courtesy of William Connor of HIPG).

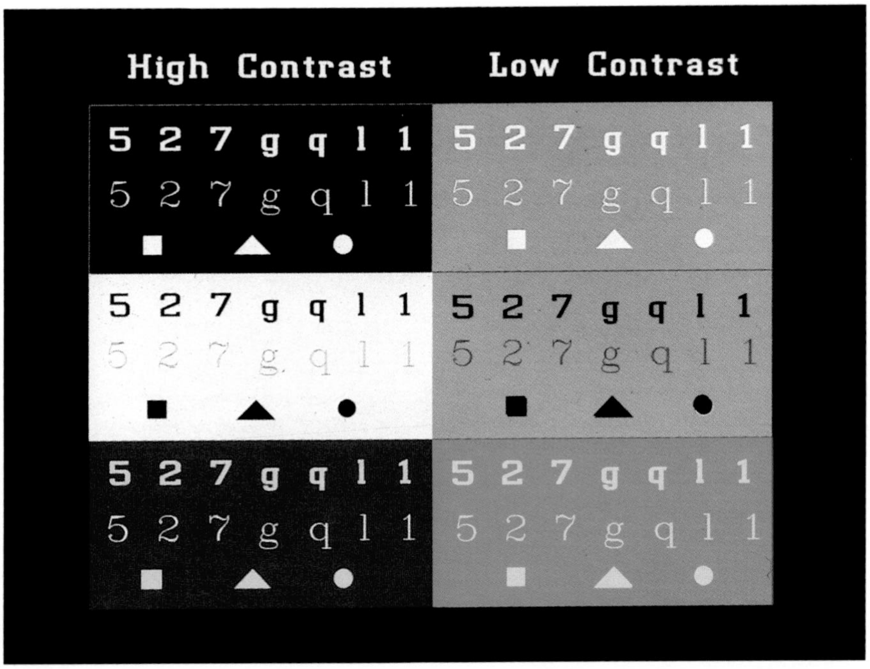

Color Plate 8. Lightness Contrast The **only** differences between the blocks of images is their lightness and color contrasts. Maximum lightness contrast is shown in the black and white block (top left). Images in the white blocks show that poor legibility (of thin fonts) can occur even if contrast levels are high (the same size font is shown in the black block). The blue block shows both high color and high lightness contrast. The grey blocks show low lightness contrast, while the green block shows both low color contrast and low lightness contrast. (Thorell & Smith, 1990).

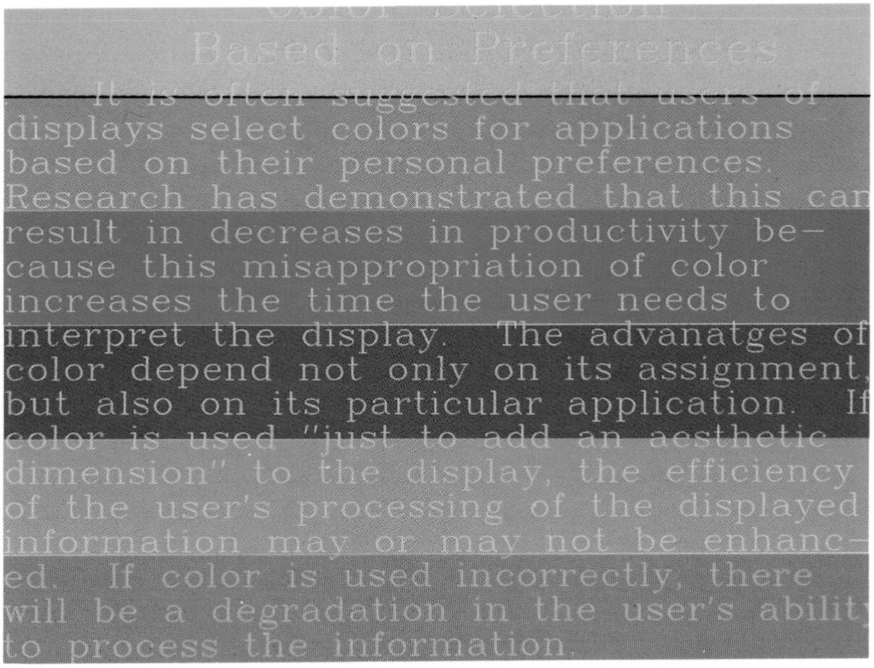

Color Plate 9. Simultaneous Contrast The grey characters in this plate look like a desaturated value of the compliment of their background color (e.g., grey text on blue appears yellowish, red appears greenish, and yellow appears slightly blue). The shift of grey to another color will depend on the size of the image relative to the background. Simultaneous contrast is greatest when the area of the background is significantly larger than the area of the target and if the luminance of the target is less than the background. (Thorell & Smith, 1990).

This text is the same color

Color Plate 10. Effect of Background Color on Neutral Images   The colors of the displayed text are identical for each of the background colors. Note the change in appearance of the letters as the color of the background is changed. Note how the contrast *appears* to change. This is called color assimilation and occurs when a foreground color *looks* like a lighter shade of its background color. Edge-dominant images, like thin lines, are particularly susceptible to this problem. Designers need to take note since this effect significantly reduces image resolution and color discrimination. (Thorell & Smith, 1990).

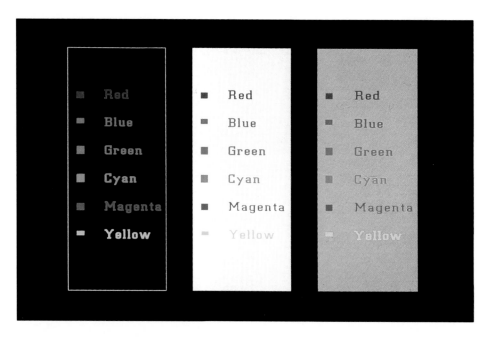

Color Plate 11. Visibility of Colors on Black, White, and Grey Backgrounds   The blocks in this plate demonstrate foreground-background color combinations that are maximally discriminable. The text show the color with high visibility, legibility, and discriminability. (Thorell & Smith, 1990).

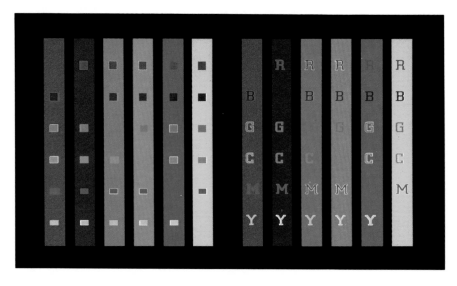

Color Plate 12. Visibility and Legibility of Various Color Combinations   Each row shows different images (a square or a letter) in a constant color on backgrounds of varying colors. Visibility and legibility are best when hue and lightness contrast are maximized. (Thorell & Smith, 1990).

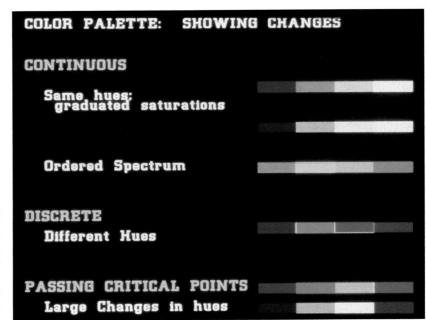

Color Plate 13. Use of Color Continua to Show a Range of Change Continual change can be effectively shown through the gradual saturation of hue or ordered spectrum. Discrete changes, on the other hand, can be shown by using discrete hues, while critical changes can be effectively shown with large hue changes. (Thorell & Smith, 1990).

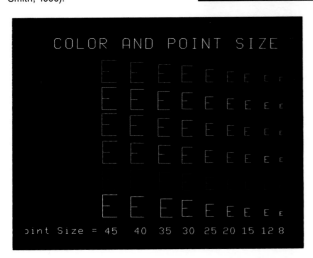
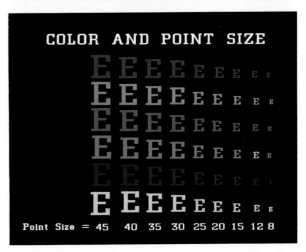

Color Plate 14. Color and Point Size of Characters You should use these two charts when making determinations as to the point size that should be used with different colors [Note: one type point = 35mm = 0.0135 inches]. (Thorell & Smith, 1990).

```
2:  white yellow
3:  white yellow cyan
4:  white yellow cyan red
5:  white yellow cyan red green
6:  white yellow cyan red green magenta

2:  green  yellow
3:  green  yellow  cyan
4:  green  yellow  cyan  magenta
5:  green  yellow  cyan  magenta  red
6:  green  yellow  cyan  magenta  red  blue
```

Color Plate 15. Color and Font You should keep in mind that color will interact with the type of font used. This figure demonstrates that thinner font styles are different when displayed in color. (Thorell & Smith, 1990).

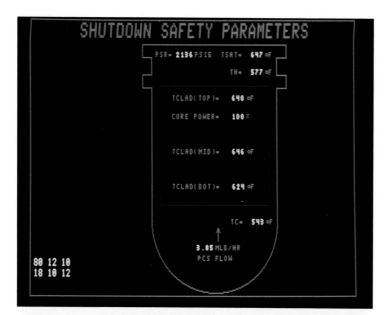

Color Plate 16. Dynamic Display The border of the display is designed to look like a nuclear reactor's containment vessel, making it similar to a mimic display; in the border is meant to symbolize the equipment to which the data relates. All of the data is displayed in the context of the pressure vessel and the fuel cladding temperature (top, middle, and bottom). In addition, power level is displayed along with the pressure and primary coolant flow. Note that only two colors, cyan and white, are effectively used to convey the important information.

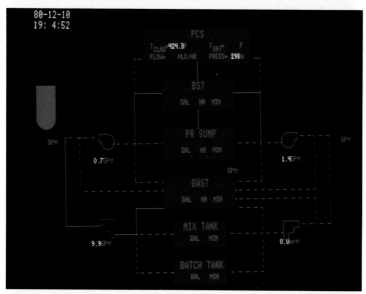

Color Plate 17. Mimic Display Color Plate 17 is a mimic that shows the relationships between different pumps, tanks, flow paths, and holding tanks. Green is used to indicate that the pump is available and currently running, while red indicates that the pump is not available. Also note that the flow rates are presented below each pump to reinforce the pump status information. For example, the green pump, which is currently running, shows that 9.9 gallons per minute are being pumped, while the red pump shows that less than 1.4 gallons are flowing per minute (natural conduction), thus reinforcing the information that the pump is not operating.

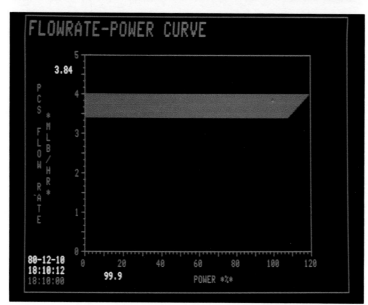

Color Plate 18. Bar Display This bar display shows a flow rate vs. power graph with a green operating hand. If the cursor is within the green band, then the user knows that they are operating in the safe range. Note how small the cursor is with respect ot the rest of the graphic. This cursor is a critical piece of information that the user needs to determine if the system is operating in the safe range. In this case, the cursor should be made to stand out much more than in the current displayed.

Second, the advantage provided by color increases as the density or the clutter on the display increases (Green and Anderson, 1956). In a simple uncluttered display, color contributes nothing to performance, while its greatest advantage is in the display of highest density. Under appropriate conditions,the use of color can reduce search time by 90 percent in a display of 60 items (Carter, 1982).

Third, the average search time increases linearly with the number of items that share the target's color, assuming again that the target's color is known to the viewer. For instance, average search time increases by about 0.13 seconds for each three-digit number of the target's color in the display area. The slope is steeper for more difficult targets (Williams, 1967). **The linear effect of the number of items of the target's color is the most powerful determinant of search time in a colored display** (Carter, 1982).

Fourth, items not of the target's color have virtually no effect on search time if their color is sufficiently dissimilar from the target's color, for example, a red and a green (Carter, 1982). Thus, a display designer can avoid decrements in search performance due to nontarget colors by selecting a color code that maintains adequate separation in color space among colors. Separation or similarity of colors can be represented by quantitative color difference formulae (Carter and Carter, 1981; Neri, Luria, and Kobus, 1986).

Additionally, items of a color similar to the target's color (i.e., a red and a red-orange) will impair search time. This effect is additive to that of some target-colored items: formulae predicting search time can have separate additive terms combining the contributions of target-colored and other-colored items on the display. The coefficients of other-colored items will be zero for colors far removed from the target color in a uniform color space (Williams, 1967). The larger the color difference between the most similar colors in a set, the shorter the reaction time (Color Plate 5), and the fewer errors made on the color matching task (Neri, Jacobsen, and Luria, 1985).

While the use of color coding may greatly increase performance in search tasks, one of the most effective applications of color coding is to organize or to unify different parts of the visual field (See Case Study 6-1). Color coding is used to organize areas on color weather maps, color medical imagery, computer-enhanced pictures, and many other applications.

6.2.3 Display Dynamics

When combined with the content of a display, the display's colors, fixed or changing, may serve to enhance or compromise the user's performance. Static displays are fixed throughout the viewing period (e.g., color landscape slides, road maps, and pseudo-colored satellite images). Dynamic displays show changes in position or value over time (e.g., the color-coded display in Color Plate 17).

CASE STUDY 6-1
Color Usage

The Earth Observational Remote Sensing System generates an overwhelming amount of data. The Landsat system, in its first generation, produced frames of imagery that contained approximately 7.5 million pixels in each of four spectral bands. These frames have been produced continuously since 1972. A down-link data rate of about 30 megabits per second is needed to deliver the data to earth. In the second generation system, the spatial resolution has more than doubled and the spectral bands have increased from four to seven, requiring a data rate of 85 megabits per second. Future systems will have many more spectral bands resulting in substantial increases in the complexity of data. A significant problem has been how people can successfully make use of such a volume of data. The issue is much more complex than interfacing with the imagery, because the data set consists of seven interrelated images in different spectral bands. Additionally, the use of such data might involve, for example, merging newly collected Landsat data with existing geographic information expressed in visual imagery.

Other unanswered questions concern the choice and the number of colors to be used in displays of this type. There is a limit to the number of colors that can be used for organizing data and still remain comprehensible. Evidence suggests that this number is small. In the Landsat observation, the limit may be approached or exceeded in the future generation systems (e.g., one current prototype has 128 spectral bands). Another problem is the limited number of hues, intensities, and saturations that can be discriminated by the user.

Color, by its very nature, may contain an answer to this interfacing problem. Colors exist in a three-dimensional volume of hue, brightness, and saturation, allowing relationships among data to be expressed in a variety of color schemes that could not be done in a single dimension of monochrome. The achromatic axis is special, as are the red-green and yellow-blue axes. Thus, dimensions of hue, brightness, and saturation can be used as three different coding strategies.

Despite the appeal of such an approach, unanswered questions remain. For example, are there advantages to be gained by paralleling the data dimensions with intrinsic color dimensions? Insofar as a metric can be established in the original data, you could try to preserve the metric by mapping it onto the metric axes of the color space. As a simple first pass, a principal component analysis could be performed on the original data, mapping the first component onto luminance, the second onto the blue-yellow axis, and the third onto the red-green axis (Buchsbaum, 1987).

Similarly, the planes corresponding to the equilibrium hues could be used as landmarks in color displays (e.g., if a variable is coded onto the red-to-yellow axis, passing through orange in the middle, the perceptual consequences may be quite different than if it is coded onto the orange-to-yellow-to-green axis, passing through yellow in the middle). In the first case, the end-points are poorly defined.

6.3 Human Performance With Multicolored Displays

The way a user perceives and responds to color in a display is directly influenced by a large number of variables. These variables include the physical parameters and constraints of the workstation, the physiological and psychophysical aspects of human color vision (Coren, Porac, and Ward, 1984), and social factors. Grouping these variables under physical, psychophysical, and psychological topics provides a logical framework for categorization. For some variables, this is relatively easy. For example, temporal stability, gamma correction, convergence, and phosphor decay are all physical aspects of the workstation. However, many variables subsume two or more of these categories. Even with physical variables, the primary concern is a psychophysical one (i.e., how the eye responds to the physical variation in the light emitted from the CRT). All of the factors that influence human perception and performance using multicolored displays are listed alphabetically in Table 6-1.

6.3.1 Interactions Among Variables

Although the color **perceived** by an individual depends on each of the variables in Table 6-1, interactions among them may also serve to produce unanticipated color changes. **NOTE:** Much of the knowledge on color appearance was obtained under controlled experimental conditions such as a small field, a dark surround, and precisely measured physical stimuli. Thus, interactive effects can pose particular problems that you won't find in journal articles or textbooks. These complications may be illustrated by an example. The spectral composition of a source of light is obviously a prime determiner of its color appearance; however, the correlation between the spectral composition and color appearance may be destroyed if the light is too small, too dim, too far out in the peripheral field of view, or viewed under too bright or too highly colored surround conditions (See the effect of this on font appearance in Color Plates 14 and 15). If the object is too small, its color may be incorrectly perceived, even if it is of normally sufficient intensity and is foveally viewed.

Consider Color Plates 14 and 15 and note how the color and readability of the letters change as the font gets smaller and thinner. Also note the effect that different colored backgrounds have on colored foregrounds (Color Plates 10-12). While a special color set may be required to ensure a match between foregrounds and backgrounds that increase visibility, a good rule of thumb is: Use high color and luminance contrast ratios (> 7:1). Luminance contrasts in excess of 7:1

sharpens edges. If your goal is to smooth edges, however, then use contrast ratios of < 3:1. For displays which will be looked at for long periods or in environments with reduced illumination, contrast ratios should be between 3:1 and 6:1.

However, even the specification of the critical size is subject to interactive effects of other variables. The classic limit, less than 10 to 20 minutes of arc, refers to a circular area of that diameter; this configuration results from research conducted on the phenomenon that employed optical systems to provide the monochromatic stimuli. In multicolored displays, the geometry of the visual stimulus may be different, such as an outline drawing or an alpha-numeric symbol. The critical dimensions (construction element, total area, plane angle, solid angle, stroke width) for this type of symbol are unknown. The spatial distribution and integration area are undoubtedly important and, for colored displays, the pixel count is a factor.

Table 6-1: Factors Influencing Performance in Color Displays

Absolute luminance	Luminance contrast
Adaptation level	Modulation: spatial, temporal
Age	Number of colors
Amount of displayed information	Number of task relevant dimensions
Attention	Phosphor decay
Brightness	Proximity effects
Chromaticity	Redundancy of color code resolution
Color coding	Sequence of colors
Color contrast	Simultaneous contrast
Color induction	Size of target
Color vision anomalies	Spectral bandwidth
Convergence	Spectral composition
Diffuse reflection	Spectral reflection
Foreground/background effects	Surround or background
Gamma correction	Temporal stability: additive-spatial
Glare	Temporal, subtractive
Layout, font, grouping	Type of task: discrimination, recognition
Location in visual field	User characteristics

6.4 Design Principles For Using Color Displays

Research to-date has led to a number of design principles for the use of color in displays. This section presents principles for implementation and provides exemplary applications.

6.4.1 Principles of Color Appearance

The requirement that the colors perceived by the viewer are the ones intended by the display designer is basic to the use of color for any purpose. To meet this first requirement, the desired physical stimulus (the appropriate spectral radiant power distribution) must be produced on the display and the observer must respond to this distribution as anticipated.

The following is a list of principles that **must** be taken into consideration when designing a display:

1. The colors perceived by the user may be different from those experienced by the designer due to unanticipated responses by the user's visual system.

2. The most varied and highly saturated colors are perceived best when foveally viewed and presented against a somewhat darkened surround.

3. Too great an external illumination will cause the colors on the display to appear dark and unsaturated. Too highly chromatic an external illumination may cause deviations in color appearance due to chromatic induction (Benzschawel, 1985; Walraven, 1984).

4. If a color is to be recognized correctly, you must be sure it is large enough to avoid aberrations in the color. (See the changes in color as a function of type size in Color Plate 14).

5. If symbols on a display are to be viewed with peripheral vision, color must be used with caution. The further the image is from the fovea, the more likely the colors will be judged the same; they will be seen as white or very unsaturated in the periphery of the retina (Burnham, Hanes, and Bartleson, 1963; Kinney, 1979; Moreland and Cruz, 1958).

6. Loss of color vision in the user's peripheral retina can be compensated for by increasing the target size (Gordon and Abramov, 1977). The increases in size that are required, however, makes this an impractical solution for some purposes.

7. Highly saturated colors of equal luminance will often fail to appear equally bright. For example, monochromatic reds or blues may appear several times brighter than colors of less saturation. Techniques are available to make different colors on a display appear equally bright to the human observer (Kinney, 1983; Ware and Cowan, 1984).

8. A large variation in the luminance of a colored light will often result in a change to its color appearance (the Bezold-Brucke Effect). Some colors are more affected than others and the direction of the change differs in

different portions of the spectrum. The general rule is that the spectral colors tend to shift in appearance toward blue and yellow as their intensity is increased. Thus, yellow-reds and yellow-greens appear bluer. Moreover, these hue shifts can occur when the perceived brightness of a colored light is manipulated rather than its physical intensity (Walraven, 1984).

9. Another change in perceived hue occurs when white light is added to colored light. This is a common method of obtaining a less saturated color, but it also results in hue shifts for some colors. Unsaturating a blue, for example, may cause it to appear violet. The differences, while frequently small, could be important in applications in which it is essential that the hue remain constant despite variations in saturation (Walraven, 1984).

> **NOTE:** Considerable evidence has been amassed that the blue system of color vision has poorer spatial and temporal resolution than do the red and green systems (Frome et al., 1981). This has led some experts to discount the use of blue entirely for symbology on multicolored displays. In view of the many interactions, a more reasonable approach is to consider the application. If the information must be presented in a small or brief form, it is best to use luminance or shape differences to encode it. Larger and longer symbols can be color-coded, with red-green differences being more effective than blue-yellow (Benschawel, 1985).

6.4.2 Evaluating the Effect of Color on Task Performance

For the most part, the impact introducing color on the performance of a given task should be evaluated using objective methods. Thus, accuracy of a user's performance should be compared for targets of different colors, or for colored targets versus monochrome. Color may be the only dimension in which the targets differ from non-targets, or color may be combined with other attributes such as brightness, size, and shape. The number of colors employed, the specific color set, and their contrast with the background illumination are all variables that can interact and should be evaluated.

The time required for successful visual search has figured prominently in research and usability tests evaluating the effectiveness of color in displays. Typical usability tests require subjects to search for a specific target on a display. Here are the two most common techniques.

1. The time required to locate the target is recorded when the test user says "stop", identifies some distinguishing feature, or indicates success by pointing at or touching the target (Christ, 1975).

2. The tendency to look at irrelevant objects, assessed objectively by the number of eye fixations on targets of the wrong attribute (color, size, shape, etc.) relative to those made on objects that share the defining criterion characteristic is recorded (Williams, 1967).

While these are the two most common methods, other evaluation techniques are possible. Carter and Carter (1981) had subjects search for a self-luminous three-digit target among other similar three-digit targets on a dark background. The variables included the number of other objects on the screen that shared the target's color, the total number of objects on the display, and the color difference between the target's color and that of the other objects. Each of the variables had a profound effect on both search time and relative fixation times.

Much of the information on the types of tasks for which color is effective in improving performance is derived from studies using these methods. For example, of the 42 studies comparing color codes and achromatic codes reviewed by Christ (1975), all used either accuracy of identification or search time as dependent measures of performance.

Subjective methods have also been used to assess the effectiveness of color in displays. Typical users are asked to rate subjective pleasantness or personal preference for specific colors or for color versus monochrome. These methods almost universally result in support for the use of color.   Subjective assessments have suggested that the use of color seemed to make tasks easier and more natural. This is true whether or not there is any measurable change in performance with color (Christ, 1975; Kellogg et al., 1984).

Color may have an impact on the total task by reducing operator workload and yet not show a measurable effect if assessed with respect to those tasks involving only the color display. For example, Krebs and Wolf (1979) found performance improvements when a combined performance score for both tasks was computed (Figure 6-2). The advantages of color increased with increasing task difficulty. Luder and Barber (1984) also used a multi-tasked environment with similar results, thus emphasizing the need to assess total performance of a human-machine system in a complex task, in order to reveal the advantages or disadvantages of color.

6.4.3 Color Problems

Designs that look as though they should work on paper don't always work when implemented on a CRT display. Before changing the design, consult Table 6-2, which lists the most common problems associated with color CRT displays.

One of the biggest complaints made by CRT users is visual discomfort. This effect is often compounded by the use of color. Tables 6-3 and 6-4 offers some suggestions for color combinations that increase user comfort ratings. Displays that will be viewed for long periods of time should use medium contrast, a dark background, and desaturated colors. Color Plate 12 shows the differences in visibility and legibility of different color combinations, while Color Plate 15 shows the interaction between color and font.

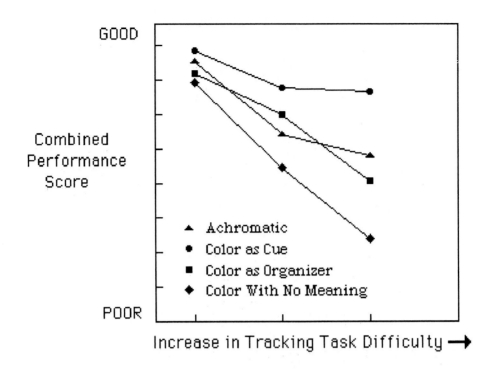

Figure 6-2: Effect of Color Coding on Tracking Performance.

6.5 Choosing the Right Colors

The seemingly simple question of which colors should be used on a multicolor display is fraught with complications and unanswered questions. It is essential to know, beforehand, the purpose for which the display is to be used (Chapter 2). For example, a simple alerting function requires fewer and different colors from those needed to simulate reality. In selecting color for coding purposes, questions concerning specific colors, number of colors, cultural stereotypes, and possibilities of color continua for continuous quantities must all be addressed.

6.5.1 Specific Colors to be Used for Coding

The limits to the number of categorically different colors that can be employed are based on information available for surface colors, rather than emissive ones. However, there is an upper limit of surface colors that can be employed, without error, in ideal conditions. That number of colors, whether emissive or surface, is exactly 11 (Berlin and Kay, 1969; Chapanis, 1965; Evans, 1948; Halsey and Chapanis, 1954). There is a potential set of 11 real reflecting colors that, under appropriate viewing conditions, will never be confused by people with normal color vision. The 11 colors can be grouped as bright, unique colors (white, red, green, yellow, and blue), bright blends (orange, purple, and pink), and dark colors (gray, black, and brown). Two of the names from the word counts (gold and silver) are excluded because they are "object substance" names (Evans, 1948).

Table 6-2: Common Color Problems and Their Solutions

Problem	Probable Cause(s)	Solution
Color Identification	Insufficient contrast Images are too small Color vision deficiency	Use high lightness and hue contrast Ensure images are at >20 minutes of arc Use colors that can be discriminated by all users
Color Discrimination	Insufficient hue differences Insufficient saturation differences Color vision deficiency	Ensure a min. of 40ΔE units between hues Ensure at least 1 saturation JND Use colors that can be discriminated by all users
In Periphery:	Use of colors only visible in the foveal region.	Use colors visible in the periphery
Color Discrimination of Blue Images	Image too small	Ensure images are > 20 minutes of arc
Blurry Edges	High spatial frequency (small or thin images too close together) Low contrast Light image on dark background Neutral images and color surround	Increase image contrast Use combinations other than red-green or blue-yellow. Increase lightness and hue differences Use dark image on light background Use desaturated colors
Afterimages	Continuously viewing saturated colors	Use desaturated colors
Color Fringes	Misconvergence	Align convergence
Depth Effects	Extreme hues and high saturation	Use similar hues and desaturation values
Equal size images appear unequal	Extreme differences in hues, saturation, and lightness	Use similar hue, saturations, and lightness values

(Adapted From Thorell and Smith, 1990)

Table 6-3: Comfort Ratings for Color Displays

Text Color	Red	Blue	Green	Cyan	Magenta	Yellow	White	Black
					Background Color			
Red	-	N	N	S	N	S	N	N
Blue	N	-	S	S	N	S	N	N
Green	N	S	-	S	S	N	N	N
Cyan	N	S	N	-	S	N	N	S
Magenta	N	N	S	S	-	S	N	N
Yellow	N	O	N	N	S	-	N	S
White	S	O	S	N	N	N	-	O
Black	N	N	N	S	N	S	S	O

O = Optimum   S = Suboptimum   N = Not Recommended

(Adapted From Thorell and Smith, 1990)

Table 6-4: Color Values for Extreme Viewing Conditions

	Room Lighting		Visual Angle		Viewing Distance	
	Bright	Dim	Central	Periphery	Short	Long
IMAGE COLOR VALUES						
Saturation						
Saturation	X		X	X	X	X
Desaturation		X	X	X		
Brightness						
Dim	X		X		X	
Bright	X	X	X	X	X	X
BACKGROUND VALUES						
Dark	X	X	X	X	X	X
Light	X		X		X	
IMAGE SIZE						
Very small	X		X		X	
Large	X	X	X	X	X	X
FONT WEIGHT						
Stick	X	X	X		X	
Bold	X	X	X	X	X	X

(Adapted from Thorell and Smith, 1990)

Oddly, orange is missing from the word count list, and purple was uncommon. Perhaps this is because these colors can be completely described as combinations of red-yellow and red-blue, respectively (Fuld, Wooten, and Whalen, 1981; Sternheim and Boynton, 1966). This list thus comprises the achromatic colors, the psychologically unique colors, and three blends. The reason for the lack of a commonly accepted name for the blue-green combination is not known.

While 11 colors appear to be the limit for surfaces, there are several reasons why fewer than 11 colors are not confused on video screens. One important reason is the requirement for reliable and consistent color video production and calibration. A second reason is that color-coded characters in many video displays are almost always brighter than their background, thus eliminating brown, gray, and black. It would theoretically be possible to employ all 11 discriminable colors in the video display, particularly if it were designed to appear as a surface. To achieve this effect, the video display could be produced on a thin surface and viewed under appropriate surround conditions so that the colors change under ambient illumination to appear as if they are reflecting surfaces.

Carter and Carter (1982) presented a unique approach to choosing specific colors to be used for coding. They used the conventional idea of color as a three-dimensional space and suggested that, if the space were perceptually uniform, then colors (represented by points in space) could be chosen to be as far from each other as possible in this space. They had previously shown (Carter and Carter, 1981) that, as the distance between color points increase, discriminability of color codes is improved. In this conception of the problem of choosing colors, the capabilities of the display to be used are taken into account as boundaries on the achievable colors in color space. Carter and Carter offered a computerized algorithm to choose a high-contrast set of colors tailored to the capabilities of the device to be employed. The merit of this system is obvious.

6.5.2 Choosing Colors for Extreme Viewing Conditions

When viewing displays under extreme conditions such as excessive brightness, extreme visual angle, or long viewing distance, careful consideration should be given to the types of colors and fonts employed. Table 6-4 provides you with suggestions for designing displays that will be viewed under extreme circumstances.

6.5.3 Choosing Colors Based on Viewing Angle

A very important consideration in any type of display design is the angle at which the display will be viewed. Viewing angle is particularly crucial in the design of chromatic displays, since colors which fall in the visual periphery will be less discriminable and less perceptible than those which fall in the foveal region. Table 6-5 presents you with some suggestions as to the colors that should be used, given a certain viewing angle.

Table 6-5: Color Suggestions For Different Viewing Angles

Peripheral Viewing:	Cyan	Blue	Green	Yellow	Red	Magenta
0-40 Degrees		X	X	X	X	
40-50 Degrees		X		X		
50-60 Degrees		X				
>60 Degrees						

(Adapted from Thorell and Smith, 1990)

As you can see from Table 6-5, the eye becomes progressively less sensitive to colored targets as the visual angle increases. This is because chromatically sensitive cells (the cones) in the retina are concentrated in the fovea and decrease dramatically in the periphery. Consequently, colored objects in the user's peripheral vision will be hard to discriminate and even harder to detect. However, Table 6-5 shows that some sensitivity to blue light remains in the 50 to 60 degree range. This is due to the fact that the retina is optimally sensitive to blue light. Interestingly enough, the cells in the peripheral vision are insensitive.

NOTE: In low levels of illumination, the cones stop responding and the rods take over. The rods are most sensitive to light with a wavelength of 500 nm (blue-green). In order to maximize target detection in extremely low levels of illumination, then the target's wavelength should be 500 nm.

On the other hand, if it is important for the user's eyes to remain dark adapted, that is night commando patrol, the display should be predominantly shades of red since the rods are relatively insensitive to light of > 600 nm.

The following rules of thumb for designing peripherally viewed targets are based on Thorell and Smith (1990; pg. 221):

- ○ Target should be large
- ○ Use area-fill
- ○ Use highly saturated targets or backgrounds
- ○ If color must be used in the periphery beyond 40 degrees, **do not** use red or green.
- ○ If the target is beyond 50 degrees **do not** use yellow
- ○ Do not use color beyond 60 degrees. Use white only.

Table 6-6: Color Ordering For Physical Impressions

Physical Impression:	Magnitude (Lowest to Highest)					
	White	Blue	Green	Yellow	Red	White
Stress Simulation		X	X	X	X	
Height or Depth		X	X	X	X	X
Temperature						
Nonconducting Materials	X	X		X	X	
Conducting Materials		X		X	X	X

(Adapted from Thorell and Smith, 1990)

6.5.4 Color Continua

If color coding is to be used to depict spatial variation of a continuous quantity such as stress or temperature across a surface or position in-depth, there are a number of possibilities for the color continuum (Color Plate 13 and Table 6-6). One could use the spectral continuum from violet, through blue, green, yellow, orange, to red; the range of perceived brightness such as white, yellow, blue, black; or a range based on color temperature, red (cooler) to blue (hotter) or on a perceived temperature, as red (hot) to blue (cold) (Table 6-6).

An intuitive arrangement, using the spectral continuum, for coding three-dimensional representations may be presented with red on top, orange as the next layer, and so on. Another intuitive scheme is the use of saturation variations of a single hue to depict changes in intensity, the most intense shown as the most saturated (Color Plate 13).

In practice, pseudocolors are frequently used to depict temperature gradients or rates of change (Color Plate 13). The temperature relationship may be appropriate because of long-standing associations between color and temperature (red with warmth and blue with cold). In fact, this association between color and temperature is one of the few psychological effects of color to be replicated over the years (Payne, 1964). The red-to-blue spectrum may be equally appropriate for associating most-to-least gradients in depictions of pressure and stress or, generally, any gradient of activity or potency. In studying the meaningful connotations of colors, Osgood (1971) found systematic effects of color on the judged activity or potency of the objects with which they were associated. Regardless of the object being judged, those depicted in colors toward the red end of the spectrum were judged to be "passive". Some of these associations between color and attributes of objects may be cross-cultural (Oyama, Tanaka, and Chiba, 1962).

However, there have been very few empirical evaluations of such schemes, and in at least one, the outcome was unexpected. For example, Frome (1984) used six sets of hue per value combinations to spatially separate but relate information in CAD displays. When designers were asked to evaluate the color schemes, there was favorable agreement that red should be the top layer, green the bottom, and aqua the interior layer. Before the study, many people wrongly guessed that they should use intensity or brightness as the code for layer. The underlying basis for their choices is not known; one hypothesis is that the lowest level is most closely associated with the base material of the printed circuit board, which virtually in all cases is green. More research on this topic is required in order to develop a reasonable rationale for the choice of a code for color continua.

6.6 Rules of Thumb For Designing Color Displays

The information presented, thus far, can be condensed into a collection of rules of thumb, which can be used when designing new systems.

6.6.1 General Rules

1. Color is highly beneficial if used for redundant coding of information or if:

    a. the display is unformatted,
    b. symbol density is high,
    c. target position is unknown/target color is known,
    d. symbol legibility is degraded,
    e. color is logically related to the operator's task.

2. Use color to indicate current status.

3. Choose colors that indicate specific and consistent functions.

4. Too many colors can detract from the legibility of a display.

5. No more than six different colors (including black) should be used on one screen/page. If each color is to carry a specific meaning, even fewer colors should be used.

6. Some specific color combinations (e.g., red on black, yellow on white, yellow on green) and any brightly colored background should be avoided (See Color Plates 11 and 12).

7. Specify colors by their wavelengths in nanometers (Color Plate 1) to ensure that hues are consistently displayed on all monitors.

8. Use white for very important data and information presentations (white uses all three guns in the CRT and has high contrast on black background).

9.   Select colors with high contrast for parameters and features that must "catch" the user's attention.

10. Red should **NEVER** be used to designate normal activity (i.e., pump on, valve open). This runs counter to the MILSTD and NUREG-0700 convention of red denoting danger.

11. Color should indicate function according to the operator's mental set/model. For example, a lawyer's reaction to red (DANGER/STOP) would be different than a power plant operator's reaction (circuit on).

12. If a blue background is chosen, remember that blue headings, numbers, or alpha characters will not be seen on a blue background.

13. If blue is used on both a black and white background, the white background will cause the blue target to appear more saturated relative to the black background.

14. In general, backgrounds should not be brighter than foregrounds (e.g., yellow on white) because of the very low contrast.

15. Yellow on green should not be used due to a perceived "vibrating" of the target.

16. In general, apparent relative target hue depends on the hue and saturation of the background.

17. Displays which have extreme color contrasts between foreground objects and the background color can form complementary afterimages due to rod receptor fatigue and should be avoided. For example, after staring at a yellow target for more than 10 seconds on a black background, when the eye is suddenly averted, a green afterimage will be perceived.

18. Place a small pattern of red, green, and blue in a corner of the display to confirm that each color gun is working.

19. Always use white for all important dynamic information. The failure of one color gun would then still leave other colors visible.

20. In choosing the type and amount of information to color code, avoid creating unplanned or obvious new patterns on the screen.

21. Patterns of color on the CRT face can either impede or enhance operator performance. Test each format for distracting visual noise before finalizing the color-code assignments.

22. If color pattern is intended to display a function, select colors that indicate system state. Use muted colors for filling in symbols and unit markers on scales.

23. Simulate lighting conditions under which the display will be operated.

24 Colors will be distorted if colored ambient illumination is used.

25. High ambient illumination can wash out colors.

26. Screen hoods that block out light and glare are helpful when ambient illumination cannot be controlled.

27. Do not use high-pressure sodium as an ambient-light medium for CRT viewing.

Table 6-7: Color Guidelines

Color	State	Result
Flashing red	Emergency	Immediate user action
Red	Alert	Corrective action must be taken
Magenta	Emergency Warning	Out of limits or specifications (radiation-related information only)
Yellow	Advise	Caution, recheck is necessary
Green	Proceed	Condition satisfactory
White	Normal	Dynamic information & Boundaries
Blue	Advisory	Used only as a background/filler hue
Black	N/A	Background/filler hue
Cyan	N/A	Major headings, scales, engineering units, fluid levels, or preferred flow paths on schematics

Table 6-8: Character Size

Viewing Distance (m)	Scale Base Lengths (mm)	Scale spacing 20 divisions (mm)	Character Size (mm)
0.50	35	1.7	1.7
0.75	52	2.6	2.1
1.0	70	3.5	2.8
1.5	105	5.2	4.2
2.0	140	7.0	5.6
2.5	175	8.7	7.0
3.0	210	10.5	8.4
4.0	280	14.0	11.2
5.0	350	17.5	14.0
6.0	420	21.0	16.8
7.0	490	49.0	19.6
8.0	560	28.0	22.4
9.0	630	31.5	25.2
10.0	700	35.0	28.0

6.6.2 Intensity

1. If the flash of a monochrome target is twice as intense as the rest of the display, the user's attention will be drawn as effectively as if color had been added. Thus, fewer colors can be used if they can be adjusted for intensity.

2. The suggested minimum amount of intensity control for any unit is:

   a. a foreground intensity control separate from the background intensity control;

   b. a capability for making grid lines half as intense as the rest of the display; reserving a specific color for grid line will limit the graphics capability of the display;

   c. intensity control variable enough to accommodate very low ambient illumination and the higher levels normally found in office work areas (5 to 150 fc).

6.6.3 Target Grouping and Viewing Distance: (See Table 6-8)

1. Information of greatest significance should be set apart from other display components by either increasing intensity, size, or highlighting.

2. When displaying information concerning date and time, pick one area of the screen and reserve this area only for the date and time data on all graphic presentations requiring this information. **Be consistent**.

3. Group screen elements into units that will be used or monitored simultaneously. Do not expect the user to monitor more than three or four quantitative elements at one time.

4. Group screen elements to convey a cohesive unit of information. Check for cohesiveness by giving the proposed display a title. Difficulty in devising a display title may indicate the inclusion of too many unrelated elements.

Often efforts have been made to establish systematic procedures for laying out display panels (e.g., guidelines for laying out the control rooms of nuclear power plants). Such procedures may be based on the frequency of accessing each element to every other element, the probability of misreading each element in each location, and/or the relative cost consequence of misreading an element. Unfortunately, these numbers may not be readily available to you and may require extensive simulation and/or experimentation. This level of effort, while perhaps unwarranted for single display systems, may well be worthwhile for multiple displays in which the distance between elements becomes significant.

6.7 Additional Reading

Banks, W. W., Hunter, S. L., and Noviski, O. J. (1985) *Human Factors Engineering: Display Development Guidelines*, LLNL UCID - 20560.

Banks, W. W., and Pihlman, M. (1989) MIPS and BIPS are megaflops: Limits of undimensional assessments. *Proceedings of the 33rd Human Factors Annual Conference.*

Coran, S., Porac, C., and Ward, L.M. (1984) *Sensation and Perception.* (2nd Ed.) New York: Academic Press.

Dertouzos, M. L., (1990) Redefining Tomorrow's User Interface. *Proceedings of the CHI'90 Conference on Human Factors in Computing Systems .*

Dertouzos, M. L., (1989) *Made in America: Regaining the Productive Edge,* Cambridge, MA: MIT Press.

Gilb, T., (1988) *Principles of software Engineering Management* . Reading, MA: Addison-Wesley Publishing Co.

6.8 References

Atherton, P.R., and Caporeal, L.R. (1985) A subjective judgement study of polygon based curved surface imagery. *Proceedings of CHI '85 Human Factors in Computing Systems,* pg. 27-34.

Berlin, B., and Kay, P. (1969) *Basic Color Terms, Their Universality and Evolution.* Berkeley, CA: University of California Press.

Benzschawel, T. (1985) *Human Color Vision and Visual Displays.* Technical Report 11327. Yorktown Heights, NY: Thomas J. Watson Research Center.

Boynton, R. M. (1979) *Human Color Vision.* New York: Holt, Rinehart and Winston.

Boynton, R. M. (1986) A system of photometry and colormetry based on cone excitations. *Color Research and Application,* 1:244-252.

Buchsbaum, G. (1987) Color signal coding: Color vision and color television. *Color Research and Application,* 12:266-269.

Burnham, R.W., Hanes, R. M., and Bartleson, C.J. (1963) *Color: A Guide to Basic Facts and Principles.* New York: John Wiley.

Carter, E.C., and Carter, R.C. (1981) Color and conspicuousness. *Journal of the Optical Society of America,* 71:723-729.

Carter, R. C. (1982) Visual Search with color. *Journal of Experimental Psychology: Human Perception and Performance,* 8:127-136.

Carter, R.C., and Carter, E.C. (1982) High contrast sets of colors. *Applied Optics,* 21:2936-2939.

Chapanis, A. (1949) How to see. *In Human Factors in Undersea Warfare.* Panel on Psychology and Physiology and the Committee on Undersea Warfare. Washington, D.C.: National Research Council.

Chapanis, A. (1965) Color names for color space. *American Scientist,* 53:327-346.

Christ, R. E. (1975) Review and analysis of color coding research for visual displays. *Human Factors* , 17:542-570.

Coran, S., Porac, C., Ward, L.M. (1984) *Sensation and Perception.* (2nd Ed.) New York: Academic Press.

Eastman Kodak Company (1944) *Influence on Color Contrast on Visual Acuity.* Technical Report 4541. New York: National Research Committee Section 16.3 - Camouflage OSRD.

Evans, R. M. (1948) *An Introduction to Color.* New York: John Wiley.

Frome, F. S. (1984) Improving Color CAD systems for users: Some suggestions from Human Factors studies. *IEEE Design and Test Computers*,1:18-29.

Frome, F. S., Buck,S.L., and Boynton, R.M. (1981) Visibility of borders: Separate and combined effects of color differences, luminance contrast and luminance level. *Journal of the Optical Society of America*, 71:145-150.

Fuld, K., Wooten, B.R., and Whalen, J.J. (1981) The elemental hues of short-wave and extraspectral lights. *Perception and Psychophysics,* 29:317-322.

Gordon, J., and Abramov, I. (1977) Color vision in the peripheral retina II: Hue and saturation. *Journal of the Optical Society of America,* 67:202-207.

Green, B.F., and Anderson, L.K. (1956) Color coding in a visual search task. *Journal of Experimental Psychology*, 51:19-24.

Halsey, R., and Chapanis, A. (1954) Chromatically-confusion contours in a complex viewing situation. *Journal of the Optical Society of America,* 44:442-454.

Heckbert, P. (1982) Color image quantization for frame buffer display. *SIGGRAPH '82 Proceedings.*

Jones, E.R., Hennessy, R.T., and Deutsch, S. (Eds.) (1985) *Human Factors Aspects of Simulation.* Committee on Human Factors, National Research Council. Washington, DC: National Academy Press.

Kaiser, P.K., and Boynton, R.M. (1985) Role of the blue mechanism in wavelength discrimination. *Vision Research,* 25:523-529.

Kaiser, P.K., Herzberg, B., and R.M. Boynton (1971) Chromatic border distinctness and its relation to saturation. *Vision Research,* 11:953-968.

Kellogg, R.S., Kennedy, R.S., and Woodruff, R.R. (1984) *Comparison of Color Versus Black and White Visual Displays as Indicated by Bombing and Landing Performance in the 2B35 TA-4J Flight Simulator.* Technical Report TR-84-22. Brooks Air Force Base.

Kinney, J.A.S. (1979) The use of color in wide-angle displays. *Proceedings of the Society for Information Display* , 20:33-40.

Kinney, J.A.S. (1983) The brightness of colored self-luminous displays. *Color Research and Application,* 8:82-89.

Krebs, M.J., and Wolf, J.D. (1979) Design principles for the use of color in displays. *Proceedings of the Society for Information Display,* 20:10-15.

Limb, J. O., Rubinstein, C.B., and Fukunage, K. (1977) Digital coding of color video signals - a review. *IEEE Transactions on Communications,* COM-25, 11:1349-1385.

Lippert, T. M., Farley, W.W., Post, D.L., and Snyder, H.L. (1983) Color contrast effects on visual performance. *Society for Information Display Digest,* 83: 170-171.

Luder, C.B., and Barber, P.J. (1984) Redundant color coding on airborne CRT displays. *Human Factors* , 26:19-32.

Moreland, J.D., and Cruz, A.C. (1958) Color perception with the peripheral retina. *Optica Acta,* 6:117-151.

Neri, D.F., Jacobsen, A.R., and Luria, S.M. (1985) *An Evaluation of Color Sets for CRT Displays.* Technical Report 1068. Groton, CT: Naval Submarine Medical Research Laboratory.

Neri, D.F., Luria, S.M., and Kobus, D.A. (1986) The detection of various color combinations under different chromatic ambient illuminations. *Aviation, Space, and Environmental Medicine* ,57(6):555-560.

Osgood, C.E. (1971) *The Measurement of Meaning.* Urbana, IL: University of Illinois Press.

Oyama, T., Tanaka, Y., and Chiba, Y. (1962) Affective dimensions of colors: A cross-cultural study. *Japanese Psychological Research* 4:78-91.

Payne, M. C. (1964) Color as an independent variable in perceptual research. *Psychological Bulletin,* 61:199-208.

Ramachandran, V.S., and Gregory, R.L. (1978) Does color provide an input to human motion perception? *Nature* , 275:55-56.

Sternheim, C.E., and Boynton, R.M. (1966) Uniqueness of perceived hues investigated with a continuous judgmental technique. *Journal of Experimental Psychology,* 72:770-776.

Thorell, L.G., and Smith, W.J. (1990) *Using Computer Color Effectively: An Illustrated Reference.* Englewood Cliffs: Prentice-Hall.

Walraven, J. (1984) The colours are not on the display: A survey of nonvertical perceptions that may turn up on a colour display. *Displays,* 6:35-42.

Ware, C., and Cowan, W.B. (1984) *Specification of Heterochromatic Brightness Matches: A Conversion Factor for Calculating Luminance of Stimuli Which are Equal in Brightness.* Ottawa Ontario, Canada: National Research Council of Canada.

Williams, L.G. (1967) *A Study of Visual Search Eye Movement Recordings.* Technical Report 12009-IR. Minneapolis, MN: Honeywell Systems and Research Center.

CHAPTER 7
From Screens to Dialog

Single screens do not, normally, a computer system make. In order to convey information to the user, the screens must be organized into some kind of logical framework. The interaction that occurs between the user and computer is a type of communication, not unlike the communication between one person and another. The structure of the dialog, or the way in which the screens are linked and interact to give a user the information that they need to perform some task, must be designed to be just as easy and efficient for the user to understand and operate as the screens you've just designed. It is almost axiomatic that the more screens placed in a system, the more complex the associated dialog will become for the user. Systems with complicated or convoluted dialogs are notorious for "losing" users or for spawning errors. The ease of use of a system can be greatly increased, and the number of "lost" users decreased, by providing users with "safety-nets", such as a summonable history trace or "escape-hatch" options.

7.0 Making the Connection

By this point in the design process, you should have a collection of screens composed of one or more screen elements. If the system you are designing contains multiple screens, some functionality must be used to connect the screens together. Probably the most important concern here is the level of computer experience each user has obtained (information contained on the User Profile Worksheet). The greater mismatch between the experience level of the user and the type of connection chosen, the greater the probability for human error; this is particularly true if the users are novices. For example, if the users are novices, it is probably a mistake to link the screens using a command language. Making inexperienced or infrequent users remember and recall a lexicon of commands places unnecessary demands on their cognitive processes, resulting in increased errors. A more concrete action-oriented linkage such as a graphical user interface or a direct manipulation interface would be more appropriate. Again, an in-depth task analysis (Chapter 2) will help you determine which type of screen linkage is most appropriate for your user group.

NOTE: As the number of screen linkages increase, the system's complexity increases resulting in an increased probability that the user will become disoriented or "lost" while moving between screens (navigation error).

7.1 Linking With Command Language

In systems that use command languages to activate functionality or navigate users between screens, the computer's operating system interprets the commands the user inputs and translates them into a machine-readable form. These commands are often English-like, though sometimes they aren't. In actuality, the words used to describe the desired operation are irrelevant to the computer, which can only process the typed commands once they have been translated into machine-readable form. You might wonder then why so many command driven interfaces are hard to use. The answer is a complex one, but at least part of the problem stems from the nature of human memory and part from computer culture.

It is a well-known fact in the field of psychology that it is easier for humans to recognize words and concepts than it is for humans to recall them. This is not too surprising when you consider that recognition simply requires picking a target from a list, where the target itself is acting as a memory cue. Recall, on the other hand, asks the person to pull a piece of information out of long-term memory. The task is roughly analogous to trying to find a book in the Library of Congress with and without a card catalogue for assistance. The bottom line is that command languages require users to recall commands from memory in order to access the system's functionality.

The second part of the problem stems from the computing culture. Computer science has always been somewhat of an elitist field, almost to the point of having an alchemistic feel. The whole "hacker" phenomenon is tribute to this. Computer science, like other fields, has developed its own set of jargon, or incantations to keep with the alchemist metaphor. For twenty years or so, computers were the sole domain of the computer scientist. Consequently, the command languages, such as UNIX, were spawned from the jargon of the CS field (Consider the UNIX commands in Table 7-1). It is only when the uninitiated began using computers in the midseventies that problems with command languages started to emerge. These neophytes had degrees in business, biology, and even art! Many of them had never even seen a computer, let alone used one. So it is only natural that the commands used in command language interfaces, such as UNIX (one of the more notoriously difficult languages), seemed strange, arbitrary, and even threatening. Similarly, like the lost art of alchemy, the lore of the jargonic origins of the commands became lost, and the commands themselves were just accepted out of convention. They may at one time been easy for those familiar with the jargon to remember because they knew of the link. The new breed of users, though, just found them to be arcane and found themselves having to engage in feats of mental gymnastics to remember the commands.

However, command languages, once learned, are a concise and rapid means of specifying the functions which the user wants the computer to perform, particularly if the software permits the chaining of commands. For example,

Table 7-1: Common UNIX Commands

Command	What It Does
cat *file*	Displays contents of named file
cd *dir*	Displays contents of named directory
cp *files dir*	Copies named files into named directory
date	Displays the current date and time
echo *args*	Displays the arguments to the command
ed *file*	Edit the named *file*
ls *dir*	Lists the files in the named directory
mkdir dir	Creates a directory named *dir*
mv *file* $_1$ *file* $_2$	Move *file* $_1$ to *file* $_2$ (or rename *file* $_1$ to *file* $_2$ if no additional directory reference is given)
mv *files dir*	Moves named *files* into directory *dir*
pwd	Displays the current directory path
rm *files*	Removes the named *files*
rmdir *dir*	Removes an empty directory *dir*
sort *file*	Alphabetizes the contents of *file*
who	Displays a list of logged on users

using the UNIX operating system, to get a list of the users of the system, alphabetized and written to a file, type the following at that system prompt ($):

$ *who | sort > users*

The command **who** presents the user with a list of all of the users currently logged on the system. The sort command takes the input and alphabetizes it. The ">" is a redirect symbol which tells the computer to take the output of the sort command and place it into a file called "users". By using three simple commands, the user has told the computer to do a great deal. Nevertheless, the command language syntax, who | sort > users, is cryptic, and it is easy to see how novice users could be intimidated. Shneiderman (1987) presents the following example:

GREP --V ^$ FILEA > FILEB

This example is also drawn from UNIX. In this case, it is not obvious that this string of commands is used to delete blank lines from a file. What, after all, does GREP do? The function of DATE is straightforward and so is WHO, but GREP? The point is, the more unusual the command name, the harder it will be to recall the command when needed, thus leading to an error.

7.1.1 Sources of Human Error Using Command Language

There are five major sources of error in command language interfaces:

1. Users forgetting the commands and their syntax,
2. Invisibility of changes to the system,
3. Typing errors
4. Semantic closeness of commands,
5. Poor abbreviation schemes.

7.1.1.1 Forgetting the Commands and Their Syntax

Forgetting the names of the commands is probably the most frequently made error by novice and intermediate user errors of a command language dialog. Introductory psychology teaches us that humans have a great deal of difficulty recalling target items from memory. Humans are much better able to recognize an item rather than recall it. Infrequent use of a system makes this effect much greater, since the ability to recall items increases with practice. To make matters even worse, command languages like UNIX have a syntax that is cryptic and hard to form associations with existing mental models. In other words, the more cryptic and bizarre the syntax, the harder it will be for users to recall the commands. Inability to recall the commands leads to increased user errors.

All is not lost. A mnemonic is a technique that improves the memory. You may have learned the phrase, **E**very **G**ood **B**oy **D**oes **F**ine, in elementary school as a way of remembering the notes on the E major scale. This is a mnemonic, just as ROY G BIV is a mnemonic for the colors of the visible spectrum. These mnemonics work even after twenty or more years. Why do mnemonics work? That is a topic of some debate. For our purposes, let's assume that the mnemonic superimposes a familiar structure on unfamiliar material. By imposing a familiar structure on the unfamiliar material, we are fitting the material into the person's mental model.

Similarly, in order to make command names easy to remember, they should be mnemonic. The best way to make them mnemonic is to make them familiar. The mistake made with the GREP command is that it is alien and has no analog in the day-to-day world. CUT and PASTE on the other hand are the names of actions that we have been performing ever since first grade. They are familiar and unthreatening. CUT and PASTE takes advantage of the user's mental model of cutting and pasting that was formed in the dark ages of first grade art class. By tying the functionality to the mental model, and tying the command name to the functionality, you are making a highly structured command set that has as its basis a firm grounding in the user's mental model. Thus CUT and PASTE will be remembered long after the function of GREP has faded from memory. (Note: one of the authors had to remind himself of the function of the GREP command for the purpose of writing this book. Though the last time he'd used the command was only two years past, he'd forgotten it because GREP has no analog in the real world and no foundation in his mental model to "cement" the meaning into his memory).

7.1.1.2 Invisibility of Changes

Command interfaces are notorious for their lack of feedback. The example cited in Chapter 1 was so vivid, yet so typical, that it is presented again here as a reminder of what **NOT** to do.

> "In the UNIX command language, the command "Cat," followed by a filename, generally displays the file. The command "Chmod," when followed by a filename, makes that file inaccessible (that is, undisplayable) to all users. However, there is no feedback (no immediate, visible effect) when the Chmod is issued. The system simply returns the usual system prompt. Later, however, if the user asks to display the file through the "Cat" command, the file is *not* displayed, and an error message is issued . . . In this example, a single command, the "Cat" command, has two different results in two different instances: in one it displays a file; in the other, it does not display the file and issues an error message instead. . . this inconsistency is a *paradox* that users must resolve in their mental model of the system. To resolve it, they must *hypothesize* what went on in the "black box" when the Chmod command, since they received no immediate, visual feedback from that action." (Mayhew, 1992)

When designing a command-driven interface, avoid this type of situation by giving users adequate feedback to the effects of the issued commands. In the case of the Chmod command, much of the confusion could be avoided if a set of commands, such as Show Access or Show Invisibles, were included so that users could check on the status of the files. Better yet, instead of giving users an error message that confuses them, give them a message that provides them with information. For example:

> **The selected file has been rendered inaccessible.**
>
> **Contact the system administrator to gain access.**

Too many systems give users cryptic error messages. One of the authors got the following error message when using an application for the Macintosh:

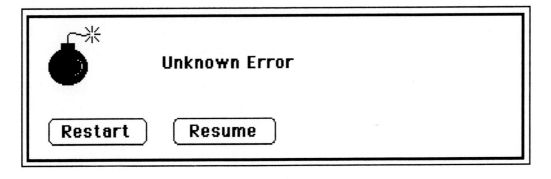

While the Macintosh family of computers are one of the easiest, if not the easiest, family of computer systems to use, one wonders why users are given such unhelpful error messages. After all, great pains have been taken to make sure that the system is user friendly, sometimes to the extent of being condescending (e.g., it is our **opinion** that the happy face icon when a disk is inserted and the counting down fingers of System 7.0 crosses the line between user friendliness and being condescending to mature users). In light of the fact that so much effort has been spent making sure that the Macintosh is nonthreatening and that developers adhere to their user interface guidelines, it is hard to understand why Apple has chosen to include some of the most cryptic and nonuseful error messages that we have ever seen. All too often, we have gotten the "bomb" dialog box (a bomb dialog box indicates a fatal error), with the following message:

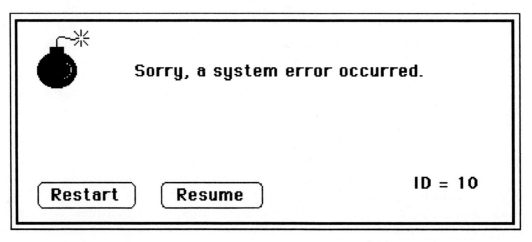

In this situation, the user has one choice: hit restart to reboot the system. Resume is nonfunctional, yet it is not greyed-out to indicate its unavailability, as put forth in the Macintosh interface standards. In addition, the ID number of the error has absolutely no meaning to the user, so why include it? Macintosh does not give the user a list of error ids in the troubleshooting section of the documentation so the id serves no purpose except to take up real estate. One might suggest that the number is used for reference when users call customer support. However, Apple has traditionally not had a customer support line (though that may have changed by the time this book is published). Since the system obviously knows the nature of the problem, otherwise it could not place the identifier characters "ID = 10" into the dialog box, why couldn't useful instructions be placed into the dialog box instead? If, as in this case, the only action that the user can take is to restart the system, then why not tell the user this? Finally, this error message occurs **every** time the author tries to start the program, so he has no idea as to why the program cannot run. If it is not running because of insufficient memory, then the system should tell the user this so they can go to the Control Panel and increase the amount of available memory. One of the authors even got this completely meaningless dialog box.

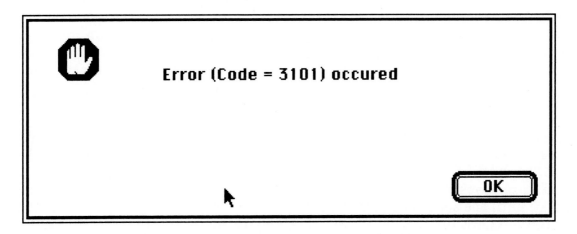

The problem of insufficient information being given to the user is not unique to the Apple Macintosh. In fact, it is troubling that such an easy to use system has such user hostile error messages. All too often, diagnostic and help messages are the last things to be done in a system design (**note**: we are **not** saying this is what happened in the case of the Macintosh system). As a result, slippages in production schedules often result in insufficient attention being given to the construction of these very useful messages. This is unfair to the user, since the reaction of the user all too often is to sit, looking at the screen, blaming themselves for the problem, and wondering what "they" did wrong.

When using command language interfaces, give the user specific and unambiguous feedback as to the action that has been taken as a result of their issuance of a command. In the event of an erroneous input, provide error feedback that is unambiguous and that suggests a specific corrective action rather than giving the user hostile and ambiguous feedback that leaves them feeling confused as to what action to take next and penalized by the system.

7.1.1.3 Typing Errors

Probably the most frequent cause of error in using command language interfaces is typographical errors. Since this is probably the easiest type of error to correct, one wonders why more systems aren't designed to be more forgiving of typos.

Most programming languages have the string operation functions that give them the ability to *parse* input strings. If the system has the capability of being case insensitive (i.e., taking the input string whether it is in upper case or lower case), then the system probably has the capability of analyzing the input string. Thus, if a user intends to type the command **SAVE** but instead types **SAVR**, because E and R are next to each other on the keyboard, the interface should be intelligent enough to interpret that the user intended to type **SAVE**. We realize that it is impractical to suggest that the system be intelligent enough to resolve ALL typographical errors, but it should be robust enough to resolve the most common errors, which are a result of hitting a key in close proximity to the intended key. Table 7-2 lists the most likely keystroke confusions that users are likely to make when entering information. The user's keyed input should be parsed and compared to the available lexicon of commands. When a mismatch is found, the system should refer to a "confusion" table such as Table 7-2 and attempt to "correct" the input by replacing the incorrect letters automatically.

7.1.1.4 Semantically Similar Commands

Another source of difficulty arises when two or more commands perform related, but subtly different tasks. For example, some systems use KILL and DELETE, or DELETE and PURGE, or DELETE and ERASE. In most systems, DELETE removes the file from viewed access, but doesn't write over that area on the disk until the space is needed. Many systems with a DELETE function also have a RESTORE function that calls back deleted material, provided it hasn't been overwritten. Thus, the DELETE command is said to be **reversible**. On the other hand, PURGE, ERASE, and KILL have traditionally been irreversible versions of the DELETE command (i.e., they irretrievably remove the file from the disk). KILL, PURGE, DELETE, and ERASE are semantically-related words that perform subtly different functions. Novices or users in conditions of stress can confuse these commands, resulting in devastating losses.

NOTE: We **strongly** urge designers **NOT** to build irreversible commands into their systems. The costs of mistakes are just too high. If you must include irreversible commands, a checkpoint should be included that informs the user that they are about to invoke an irreversible step and requests that the user verify their intention. For example, the MS-DOS command:

C> Erase C:*.*
Are you sure (Y/N)?

would erase the entire file in the root directory of the hard disk (C:) if invoked. To prevent accidental erasure, the operating system asks for verification: **Are you sure (Y/N)?**

7.1.1.5 Poor Abbreviation Schemes

Confusion is often caused by poor abbreviation schemes. Some command strings are too long to type out (e.g., Make Directory). Thus, abbreviation strategies are developed to shorten the command string in order to reduce workload (e.g., MKDIR for Make Directory). Unfortunately, situations occur in which abbreviation schemes may be inconsistent or appear to have no identifiable pattern. This should come as no great surprise, because large software projects are often divided into different development groups that take responsibility for building one component of the system. If each group has a different abbreviation scheme for the developed commands, then problems will be created for the user. The following abbreviation schemes can often be used with good results (Shneiderman 1987):

Table 7-2: Keystroke Confusions For a QWERTY Keyboard

Correct Keystroke	Confused Keystroke	Correct Keystroke	Confused Keystroke	Correct Keystroke	Confused Keystroke
A	S	N	M	2	1
B	V	N	B	2	3
B	N	O	P	3	2
C	X	O	I	3	4
C	V	P	O	4	3
D	S	Q	W	4	5
D	F	R	E	5	4
E	W	R	T	5	6
E	R	S	A	6	5
F	D	S	D	6	7
F	G	T	R	7	6
G	F	T	Y	7	8
G	H	U	I	8	7
H	G	U	Y	8	9
H	J	V	B	9	8
I	U	V	C	9	0
I	O	W	Q	0	9
J	H	W	E		
J	K	X	Z		
K	J	X	C		
K	L	Y	U		
L	K	Y	T		
M	N	1	2		

(Adapted From Bailey, 1989, pg. 308)

1. **Truncate to the first 1 to 3 letters** (e.g., DIRECTORY becomes DIR).

2. **Remove all vowels** (e.g., COPY becomes CP, and MOVE becomes MV).

3. **Use the first and last letters** (e.g., SORT becomes ST).

4. **Use the first and last letter of the words that comprise the command phrase** (e.g., MAKE DIRECTORY becomes MKDR).

5. **Use the first letter of each word that comprises the command phrase.** (e.g., REMOVE DIRECTORY becomes RD.

6. **Use standard abbreviations.** (e.g., QUANTITY becomes QTY) (Shneiderman, 1987).

In general, if no conflicts arise, and if the commands are clear, truncate to the first three letters of the command (DIRECTORY becomes DIR). In cases where the command is constructed from a word or phrase, the first three letters of each word should be used (CHANGE DIRECTORY becomes CHADIR). If simple truncation is inappropriate to your needs, then vowel dropping is the next viable alternative.

Development managers should agree on **ONE** simple abbreviation rule and ensure that the strategy is followed by each member of each design group (Ehrenreich and Porcu,1982). This will prevent the design of inconsistent commands. The rule that is used must be effectively communicated to the user via documentation or training.

Command language metaphors should be avoided if the system functions are going to be used infrequently because commands can be easily forgotten if not used regularly or if the syntax is complex. However, if you must use a command interface rather than a graphical user interface, remember that the more logical the command names, the easier they are to remember and recall at the desired moment.

7.2 Linking With a Menu

Due to the high number of errors associated with command languages, the next logical step in the evolution of interfaces was to design a system that only relied on user's ability to recognize a command, rather than recall one. Menu metaphors take the burden of remembering commands off the user, since the available options are displayed, thus reducing errors associated with users' inability to remember commands. This is particularly important in high stress situations, because stress inhibits recall. The user need only pick the desired option from the list of available options. Anyone who has used a computer in the last five years has no doubt encountered the Menu Metaphor. A hypothetical word processor menu appears in Figure 7-1.

```
┌─────────────────────────────────────────┐
│                                           │
│            WORDMEISTER III                │
│                                           │
│         1.  Edit Document                 │
│         2.  Create Document               │
│         3.  Save Document                 │
│         4.  Merge Document                │
│         5.  Print Document                │
│                                           │
│         Please Input Your Choice          │
│         (1-5) >  ____                      │
│                                           │
└─────────────────────────────────────────┘
```

Figure 7-1: Basic Menu

While the menu format may seem to be the answer to your prayers, this means of linking screens is actually much more complex than it might seem. There are actually three <u>basic</u> types of menus that can be created (Figure 7-2). Shneiderman (1987) identifies a fourth class of menu, the linear menu (i.e., a menu composed of a number of interdependent menus). We would argue, however, that linear menus are simply a special type of single menu.

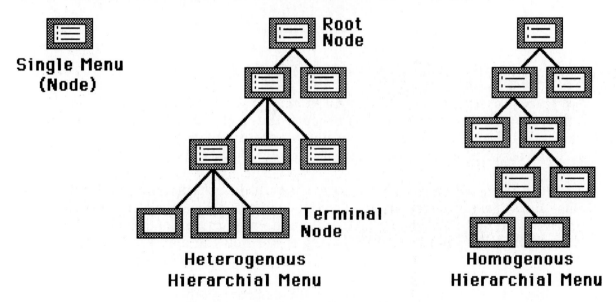

Figure 7-2: Types of Menu Structures

Single menus present the user with a number of functions (three in Figure 7-2) that can be selected. The user selects one of the functions and the computer performs the requested activity. Hierarchical menu constructs are simply a collection of single menus arranged in a superordinant-subordinate fashion (Figure 7-3). Normally, the options on a menu are numbered, but a function is sometimes selectable by the first letter of its name (e.g., in Lotus 1, 2, 3 ™), or through the use of a checkbox or radio button (Figure 7-3).

7.2.1 Single-Level Menus

Single-level menus are composed of a single screen, displaying a collection of discrete functions. In Color Plate 4, a single menu is located on the right side of the screen. This single menu provides the CAD user with the available types of solids. Similarly, Figure 7-3 shows a single-level menu from the printer setup dialog box from a hypothetical wordprocessor. Selecting an option in a single level menu causes an action to be initiated, rather than presenting the user with another menu. As you can see from Color Plate 4 and Figure 7-3, single-level menus are the easiest menus to use, because the only choices available are on the screen in front of the user. To greater simplify the user's decision processes, thereby increasing their productivity, we suggest providing users with information regarding which options are available and which are not. Notice in Figure 7-3 that some of the items are shown in a lighter gray. The items presented in light gray are the ones which are not currently available. An even more extreme design would be to not even show items that are unavailable.

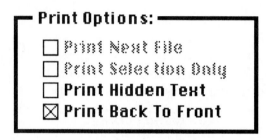

Figure 7-3: Single Level Menu With Checkboxes

Navigation errors, errors that occur during navigation between screens, cannot occur with single level menus because the user is not traversing between different menu layers. When multiple menus are linked together in a hierarchical structure, each menu panel is referred to as a node.

A special form of single-level menu is the pull-down type menu typically found in systems with a graphic user interface (GUI), such as Macintosh or MicroSoft Windows. In Figure 7-7 and Color Plate 7, you see that the menu remains hidden until the user clicks on an invisible "hot spot," overlaying a word on the menu bar, and "pulls down" the menu, revealing the available options. Options are selected by dragging the mouse, or other pointing device, downward until the desired option is selected, indicated by reverse video. Options that are not available, or unselectable, in a given mode are depicted in gray rather than black, and are said to be "grayed out," and do not highlight when the cursor of the pointing device passes over their hot spots. By graying out unavailable options, you are decreasing the number of options that the user must decide between, thereby decreasing the number of decisions to be made, which in turn decreases decision time and decreases error likelihood, which in turn leads to a more effective and productive system.

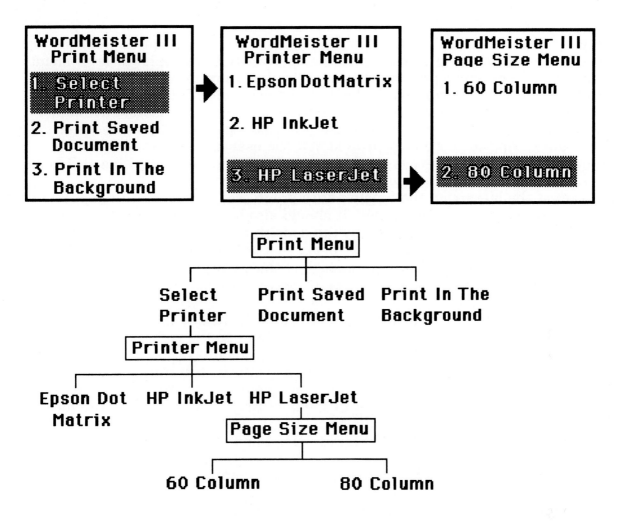

Figure 7-4: Example of Menu Subordination

7.2.2 Hierarchical Menus

Hierarchical menu system are often implemented in systems with a large number of functions. In order to decrease the user's mental workload, similar functions are grouped together to form categories, usually as a follow up to a Task Analysis of the system. Each distinct category of functions are grouped together to form a series of ingle menus, where each single menu represents a category of function. These categories are then arranged into a hierarchical structure which, usually, is arranged from general to specific functions, as the user traverses the structure from the most general node (called the *root node*) to the most specific node (called the *terminal node*) (See Figures 7-1 through 7-4). The root node is always a single menu since its options initiate a function or a change in mode.

Consider Figure 7-1 which shows the root node of an imaginary word processor. The types of functions are classified into Edit, Creation, Saving,

Merging, and Printing. As shown in Figure 7-4, selecting an option from the root node, such as Print, results in the user being presented with a lower level menu comprised of 3 different printing options: selecting a printer, printing a file, or initiating background printing. If the user chooses option 1, they are taken to the next lower menu in the hierarchy. Since there are multiple printers available, printing a document is not as easy as simply selecting option 2 from the first menu and having the document printed out; the user must select one of three printers. Once the user selects the LaserJet, they are presented with a still lower level menu asking them to input a page size. As you can see from the tree diagram of the hierarchy, the functionality progresses from general to specific as you traverse lower in the hierarchy. It should also be clear that the danger of a user becoming "lost" in the hierarchy (navigation error) increases as the number of layers increases. The number of layers of menus is called the *depth* of the menu, while the number of options on each of the menus is called the *breadth* of the menu.

While most pull-down menus are single menus, the one displayed in Color Plate 7 is actually a hierarchical menu. The arrows on the right of the items in the options menu indicate the presence of an additional layer of menus; this type of construction is unlike hierarchical menu structures in traditional, nongraphical interface systems, in which one menu screen must be cleared before reaching the next lower level in the hierarchy. Traditional hierarchical menus are more susceptible to navigation errors than pull-downs, because higher level menus are erased as the next lower level menus are displayed. Pull-down menus, such as the one displayed in Color Plate 7, eliminate this problem by displaying all levels of the hierarchy to the user, simultaneously.

As a hierarchy of menus increases in-depth (i.e., the number of levels), the probability that the user will commit one or more navigation errors also increases. Each navigation error increases the user's search time since the user has to backup through the layers to the point at which they became lost. This is a tremendously time consuming process. However, the solution is not as easy as reducing depth by including more options on each menu layer since this increases the breadth of the layer. While decreasing depth through increasing breadth may dramatically decrease the probability of occurrence of navigation errors, eventually, a point of diminishing returns will be reached. Increasing the number of displayed options will increase the information density of the screen. Too many menu options will increase the user's search time and decision times to the point that the increased decision time overrides the savings and degrades user performance. This dilemma can be particularly problematic in situations where a fast response time is essential (e.g., control rooms of nuclear power plants, aircraft cockpits, early warning systems, etc.).

Hierarchical menus can either be homogeneous or heterogeneous and either complete or incomplete. Homogeneous menus have hierarchies that contain the same number of options on all of the menus (See Figure 7-2, each menu contains 2 items), whereas heterogeneous hierarchies have menus with a different number of options. Similarly, complete hierarchies have the same number of menus along each branch of the hierarchy, from root node to terminal node, while incomplete hierarchies have differing number of menus per each branch. Not surprisingly, menu hierarchies that are complete and homogeneous are the easiest to optimize.

7.2.3 Optimizing Homogeneous Menu Hierarchies

Whenever a menu's hierarchy is reorganized, such that search time is minimized, the menu's structure is said to be *optimized*. If the menu choices on each level are not grouped together, then the menu structure is said to be *ungrouped*. Depth can often be reduced through increasing breadth, with little or no increase in search time, if similar functions are lumped together into groups, such a menu is said to be *grouped*. Assuming that the user doesn't make any errors in his or her search, and that the user stops his or her search once the goal is achieved (i.e., a self-terminating search), then the average time the user will spend searching through a homogeneous menu can be computed using the following simple equation developed by Lee and MacGregor (1985) and Paap and Roske-Hofstrand (1986):

$$E[T] = h[c(m+1)/2 + s + r]$$

where:

$E[T]$ = the average <u>expected</u> time for a user to access the terminal node of a homogeneous, hierarchical menu,

h = the number of levels in the hierarchy,

c = the average time for a user to decide whether an option should or shouldn't be selected,

m = the number of options on a single level of the hierarchy,

s = the average time needed to press a key, touch an option on a touch screen, or select an option using a mouse,

r = the time required by the computer for processing the key press, the screen touch, or mouse click, and replacing the current menu screen with the next menu screen in the hierarchy.

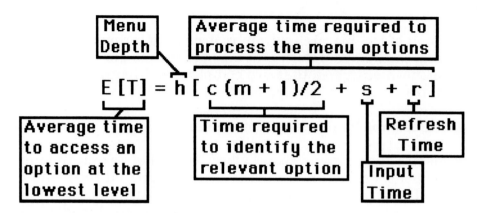

Let's look at an actual example. Consider the homogeneous menu that appears in Figure 7-4. This menu has five levels, h = 5, and two options per panel, m = 2. If we assume that a typical users takes 3 seconds to decide between each of the two options, then c = 3. Assuming that it takes the user .05 seconds to strike a key and it takes the screen .01 second to refresh, then s = .05 and r = .01.

$$E[T] = h[c(m+1)/2 + s + r]$$

$$E[T] = 5[3 \text{ seconds } (2+1)/2 + .05 \text{ seconds } + .01 \text{ seconds}]$$

$$E[T] = 5[(9 \text{ seconds}) /2 + .06 \text{ seconds }]$$

$$E[T] = 5[4.5 \text{ seconds } + .06 \text{ seconds}]$$

$$E[T] = 5[4.56 \text{ seconds}]$$

Expected Time to access the lowest level option = **22.8 seconds**

Now consider what happens to expected access time when you reduce the depth of this menu to 1 by taking all 32 terminal options or nodes and place them on a single level menu with 32 options. A menu hierarchy such as this has a 0 possibility of navigation errors since the user does not navigate through the body of a hierarchy. What is the cost then, in terms of access time, of reducing depth by increasing the breadth? In this case, m = 32 and h = 1 (because it is a single level menu). If we assume that c, s, and r have the same values, then c = 3, s = .05, and r = .01.

$$E[T] = h[c(m+1)/2 + s + r]$$

$$E[T] = 1[3 \text{ seconds } (32+1)/2 + .05 \text{ seconds } + .01 \text{seconds}]$$

$$E[T] = [(99 \text{ seconds}) /2 + .06 \text{ seconds }]$$

$$E[T] = [49.5 \text{ seconds } + .06 \text{ seconds}]$$

Expected Time To Access The Lowest Level Option = 49.56 seconds

As can be seen from this illustration, increasing the breadth of the menu increases the access time by 54%, yet the number of terminal options in both cases is 32. Thus, as the breadth of the hierarchy increased to 32, the depth decreased to 1, the average access time increased by 54%.

What then is the solution? How is the menu structure optimized for ungrouped homogeneous hierarchical menus? Lee and MacGregor offer the following equation for computing the optimal number of **m** options per each menu layer:

$$m(\ln m - 1) = 1 + 2(s + r)/c$$

The optimal value for **m**, given values for **s** and **r,** can be found through the application of Newton's Method from Calculus. A detailed example of this is beyond the scope of this work. The interested reader can find a section on Newton's method of root approximation in any introductory calculus text. Fisher, et al. (1990) tells us that **m** increases without bound (i.e., to infinity). Since **c** is the amount of time spent deciding if an option should or should not be rejected, then **c** is a function of the value of **m**. Thus, as **m** approaches infinity, so does **c** relative to **s** and **r**. Fisher et al (1990) note that the lower limit of **m**, then is 3.56. With this information in mind, **m** can be optimized for values of **s** and **r** using Newton's method.

Lee and MacGregor (1985) suggest that the optimal number of menu choices, **m**, rarely exceeds eight. But, if options with similar functions were grouped together, would search time decrease? Yes, because the user doesn't have to search through the whole collection of functions if the first few don't match their needs (Paap and Roske-Hofstrand,1986). For example, the spreadsheet shown in Figure 7-5 has a header menu which groups functions together by how wide of an area is effected by a selected function: on a file, on the spreadsheet, or on the data. MacDonald, Stone, and Liebelt (1983) showed that categorical grouping of menu options, such as this, was superior to alphabetical and random grouping in reducing search times.

Thus, if a broad menu structure is chosen as a means of decreasing the probability of navigation errors, then you should group the options together, if possible, to decrease search time and thereby increase user performance. This strategy will be even more effective if the grouped items are identified with a label that indicates the name of the grouping category. However, while grouping can obviate the increased response time observed in broad menus, this effect does not extend infinitely.

Paap and Roske-Hofstrand (1986) offer the following equation for finding the optimal number of menu option, **m**, when the menu hierarchy is homogeneous and when the items can be divided into equally sized groups:

$$E[T] = h\{c[(g+1)/2] + c[(m/g + 1)/2] + s + r\}$$

where:

h, c, m, s, r =   The same value as before.

g =   Number of equally sized groups that **m** items are grouped into

Assuming 32 items and a single menu level, as we did before, and assuming 4 groups of eight items each, then the equations can be solved like this:

$$\text{E[T]} = 1\{3 \text{ seconds } [(4+1)/2] + 3 \text{ seconds } [(32/4 + 1)/2] + .05 \text{ seconds} + .01 \text{ seconds}\}$$

$$\text{E[T]} = \{3 \text{ seconds } [2.5] + 3 \text{ seconds } [(9)/2] + .06 \text{ seconds}\}$$

$$\text{E[T]} = \{7.5 \text{ seconds} + 13.5 \text{ seconds} + .06 \text{ seconds}\}$$

$$\text{E[T]} = 21.06 \text{ seconds}$$

Compare E[T] = 21.06 for the grouped single menu of 32 items with E[T] = 49.56 for an ungrouped single menu of 32 items, and you find that grouping the items has given you a savings of **28.5%**! In fact, if you compare E[T] = 21.06 for the grouped single menu, with the original E[T] = 22.8 for the hierarchical menu structure, then you find out that not only has the grouping strategy offset the effects of reducing depth, but has given us a performance **increase** of 8%!

MICRO ACCOUNTANT					
File		**Spreadsheet**		**Data**	
Save Print		Add Column		Graph	
New Import		Delete Column		Transform	
Open		Change Width			
A	**B**	**C**	**D**	**E**	**F**
REVENUES	1991	1990	1989	1988	1987
La Mirage	586,987	432,540	356,194	816,994	853,96
Cafe Ole'	243,321	275,188	187,445	200,089	211,34
Uncle Ed's	89,065	189,987	245,654	387,312	298,33
Total:	919,387	897,715	789,293	1,404,395	1,363,6

Figure 7-5: Spreadsheet With Categorized Menu Options

The benefit of grouping is clear. However, there still remains the question of whether grouped menus can be optimized still further to give you even better performance. The answer to that question is yes. Paap and Roske-Hofstrand (1986) found that the optimal number of menu items can increase dramatically over the number of items in ungrouped menus. Paap and Roske-Hofstrand offer the following equation as a means of determining the optimal number of menu items, **m,** that can be included in a grouped menu. As before, Newton's method should be used to approximate with the following optimization equation:

$$m(\ln m - 1) = 1 + (s + r)/c$$

7.2.4 Optimizing Heterogeneous Menu Hierarchies

Unfortunately, unless the menu's hierarchical structure is very carefully planned, its structure will almost **never** be homogeneous. More often, the menu structure will be heterogeneous with some branches having more nodes than others. The hierarchies of heterogeneous menus are extremely complex and each one differs depending on the number of nodes and levels. For example, over a million different heterogeneous structures are possible for a menu structure with 64 terminal nodes (Fisher, Yungkurth, and Moss, 1990). Due to the sheer complexity caused by the number of possible variations, the optimization of heterogeneous structures requires the use of a computer program. Luckily, Fisher, Yungkurth, and Moss (1990) have developed a special program, TIME, for performing this analysis. You are referred to their excellent article for further elaboration on optimizing heterogeneous hierarchies.

7.2.5 Menu Navigation Strategies

Early menus had a purely tree-shaped structure. This type of structure was particularly prone to navigation errors, since the selection of an incorrect option would ensure a navigation error since the user would have no way of reaching their destination without backtracking through the entire menu hierarchy. However, the reduction in the cost of both RAM and disk storage have led to the evolution of larger and larger applications. Larger applications usually mean larger menu structures with larger numbers of options. For example, the PRODIGY service had, at the time of this book's writing, an excess of 800 applications, each of which has a menu as its primary interface. That's a lot of menus!

As an attempt at trying to deal with this explosion of available options, software designers began building menus that incorporated two new forms of navigation: cross navigation and backward navigation. These types of navigation can be seen in Figure 7-6.

The first of these strategies is cross navigation. Cross navigation simply provides the user with an option to navigate to an adjacent node rather than traversing further down the hierarchy. By providing this type of capability, the user can cross the branches of the hierarchy if they discover themselves traversing down the wrong branch. It should be noted, however, that the construction of menus with cross navigation require careful attention and should not be attempted without having first performed a detailed task analysis. If care is not taken in the design, cross navigation can actually serve to **increase** navigation errors because of the complex organization of this type of menu.

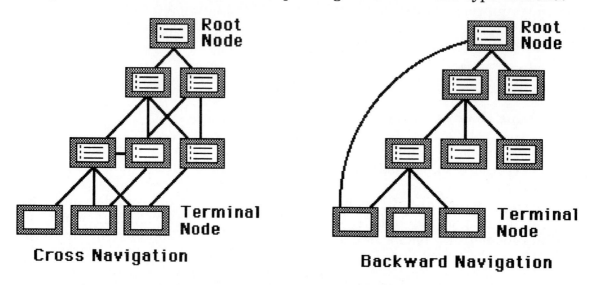

Figure 7-6: Navigation Strategies

Backward navigation offers the user a good compromise. Backward navigation provides the user with an option that will navigate them back to an earlier menu rather than further down the hierarchy. The best use of this design is the inclusion of an option on **EVERY** menu, so the user can navigate back to the root node of the menu at any time. This is what we term a *safety-net*. Like a safety-net, the backward navigation option is there to "catch" the user should he or she become lost within the hierarchy. The user can be safely returned to the top of the menu by simply selecting this option. This feeling of safety is important, particularly if the users are computer novices. It also encourages users to explore which may in fact be the most powerful and most effect method of training users to operate the system, particularly since users often refuse to read documentation and would prefer to learn through exploration (Carroll, 1984; Carroll and Mack, 1984; Weimer, 1990a, 1990b, 1990c).

7.2.6 Hybrid Designs

Hybrid designs are becoming more and more common, particularly in graphical user interfaces (GUI) (See Section 7.3). Hybrid designs combine single-level menus with form fills and other types of dialogs (e.g., some have buttons that open overlapping windows when the button is activated with a mouse). Figure 7-7 shows a hypothetical hybrid interface. The specific design requirements for the component parts (i.e., single-level menus, input fields, and so forth), hold for the hybrid as well. However, hybrids have emergent features that result from the combination of the different kinds of dialog elements. Recall from Gestalt Psychology that wholes do not equal the sum of their parts, because the whole has emergent properties that are not present in the constituent parts. The combination of the different elements cause unique properties to "emerge", hence the term emergent properties.

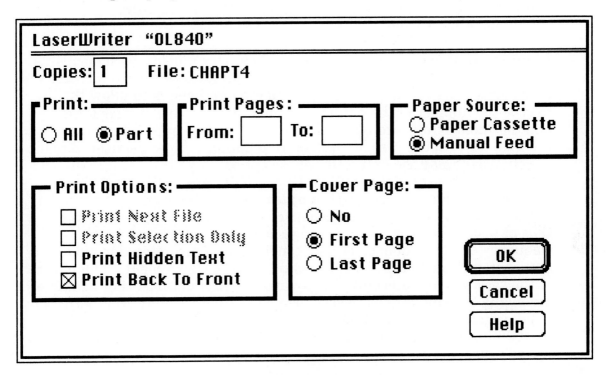

Figure 7-7: Hybrid Dialog

The real trick with hybrid interfaces is capitalizing on the emergent features rather than getting burned by them. The only way to test the emergent properties is through a working prototype. Mocking up a design in HyperCard, SuperCard, MacroMind Director, Protoscreens, or Brickland's Demo II will allow you to see the emergent properties and then to change the design in real-time, if necessary. By manipulating a rapid prototype, design characteristics can be optimized and user performance increased.

7.2.7 Menu Design Guidelines

In order to ensure the best possible menu designs, follow these guidelines.

1. **Menus should be self-explanatory**. Choose descriptive labels for the menu options, preferably action verbs, that unambiguously describe the function that the selected option will perform. In the case of higher level "parent" options, choose category labels that describe the functions of the child menu.

2. **Gray-out, or render invisible, inaccessible options**. To decrease the possibility of human error and decrease decision time, gray-out or hide inaccessible or inappropriate options (See Figure 7-7). Graying out refers to displaying the unavailable option in a light gray font and making it unable to be selected as an option, as opposed to simply deleting it from the menu.

3. **Limit the number of required keystrokes**. One problem with menus, as pointed out in section 7.2.8, is their inefficiency. One way to increase the efficiency of menus, in the case of numbered options, is to allow the user to type the number of the option and then press return, rather than making them scroll through each option with the keyboard arrows or the TAB key. In the case of alphabetized options, allow the user to make a selection by typing the first letter of the option.

4. **Choose an ordering scheme that optimizes performance.** The ordering of the menu options has a huge impact on performance. Based on the type of task to be performed, arrange menu options according to frequency of use, sequence of use, convention, interoption dependencies, alphabet, or functionality. There is no "best" arrangement. The nature of the task should determine the arrangement of options. For example, arranging 5 menu options based upon their function may be a perfectly valid design choice, but a task analysis of may reveal that 2 of the items are used 98% of the time. In that case, those two items should be the first two menu items.

5. **Use the task analysis results to drive the menu design.** As pointed out in the section on menu optimization, there are sometimes thousands of different ways to design a menu. The best advice is to design the menu so that it increases the performance of the tasks identified in the task analysis.

6. **Whenever possible, make menus broader to minimize depth**. While broader menus will mean increased decision time, the increases in decision time may more than offset the time lost due to the navigation errors that will be made if the designed menu is too deep. Table 7-3 offers some rules of thumb for decreasing breadth. As shown in the section on menu optimization, menu optimization is complex, and the reader should realize that these rules of thumb are a simplification.

7. **If a menu occupies the full screen, arrange items vertically.** Some research suggests that vertical arrangements of items are searched more rapidly by users than horizontal arrangements (See Figure 7-8).

8. **Consider pie menus as an alternative to 1 or 2 level pull-down menus when the list of items at each level is short** . The circular arrangement of pie menus (See Figure 7-9) results in faster reaction times than vertical menus, since the user does not have to pass over unneeded items.

Table 7-3: Rules of Thumb For Designing Broader Menus

Task/Usage Variables	Maximum Suggested Breadth
Menu options are *complex* and/or Menu options *cannot* be grouped	Up to 10 options per screen
Menu options are **not** *complex* and/or Menu options *can* be grouped but Usage is *infrequent* and/or Users are *novices*	11 to 20 options per screen
Menu options are **not** *complex* and/or Menu options *can* be grouped and Usage is *frequent* and/or Users are *experts*	> 21 options per screen

(Adapted from Mayhew, 1992, pg. 147)

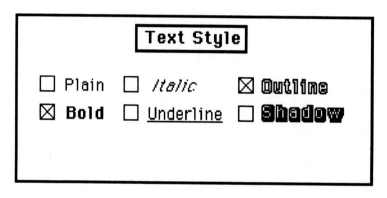

Figure 7-8: Vertical Option Arrangement

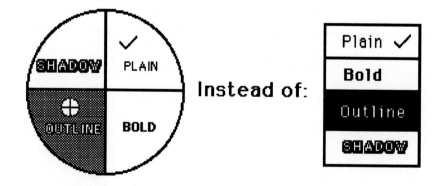

Figure 7-9: Vertical Option Arrangement

9. **Category labels should be self-explanatory and mutually exclusive.** The items on the higher nodes of hierarchical menus are simply category names that describe the menus that comprise the lower nodes. The arrangement of hierarchical menus should be such that the items in a lower level menu should have some functionality in common. In this way, the label of the higher level menu option that leads the user to this lower level menu, uniquely describes the functionality contained in the lower level menu.

10. **Item labels should be grammatically consistent.** If some of the item labels on the first menu begin with action verbs, then they all should begin with action verbs. Do not mix verbs and nouns as labels. Action verbs generally make good labels.

11. **Reoccurring items should always be in the same screen location.** For example, we have suggested the inclusion of cross navigation functionality (PREVIOUS MENU or MAIN MENU) as an option on every menu node of a complex hierarchy. Anytime functionality appears on every screen, it should occur at the same location, that way the user always knows where to look for it. The best way to do this, in most systems, is to make the reoccurring item the last item on the menu.

12. **If item labels cannot be made unambiguous, use item descriptors**. An item descriptor is a single line of text that appears, usually, at the bottom of the screen and provides the user with additional information about the selected item. Although item descriptors may decrease user errors and increase user satisfaction, the presence of additional text to be processed by the user may increase the time needed to make a choice.

13. **If possible, always provide a menu default**. This is particularly true if menu items are arranged by frequency of use. If the cursor defaults to the top of the screen, and if the items are arranged by frequency of use, then the user need only press return to select the item. In the case of menus that use checkboxes or radio buttons for making selections, show the default selection as a checked box or a highlighted button (See Figure 7-7).

14. **If possible, use checkboxes to alert the user to the fact that multiple, simultaneous choices are possible.** Consider Figure 7-7. Each item in the Print Options menu is preceded by a checkbox. This looks visually distinct from a numerical menu or a pop-down menu. Traditionally, in the Macintosh system, checkbox menus have been used to indicate that multiple items are selectable, while radio buttons have been used to indicate discrete functions. Checkboxes can be used to indicate discrete functions by graying out the remaining items once an item has been selected, and restoring them if the selected item is de-selected.

15. **Provide the user with visual feedback concerning menu selection.** Consider the X's in the checkboxes in Figure 7-7 and the checkmarks in Figure 7-9 and Color Plate 7. These marks indicate to the user which items are currently selected or which ones are the current system defaults.

16. **In systems that have limited real estate, consider using pop-down or user-invoked menus.** Pop-down menus and user-invoked menus allow functionality to be temporarily hidden and provides the user with additional work space. Consider Color Plate 6. It would be extremely useful to be able to hide the palettes at the left of the display, in order to be able to expand the size of one or more of the tiled windows.

17. **Provide the user with a visual cue to indicate lower level hierarchies when using hierarchical pop-down menus.** Consider Color Plate 7. The arrows to the right of the item labels indicate the presence of a lower level menu. By selecting one of these items and dragging the arrow cursor to the right, the user causes the next menu level to appear. This strategy is an extremely good one because it allows the designer to provide the user with additional functionality, while allowing the user to keep all functionality within plain sight.

18. **Provide expert users the capability to side-step the menu process.** Menus are tedious and time-consuming for expert users. There are a number of ways to avoid this. First, the designer can provide a menu option that toggles the system into a command language mode; many on-line services provide this solution. Function keys and macros can also be provided that allow the expert to access functionality without forcing them to traverse the entire tree structure of the menu.

This has been a brief overview of the most salient guidelines for the design of menus. There are probably as many different possible guidelines as there are different systems. The usefulness of any of the presented guidelines will be determined by the structure of the task which will be revealed to you through an in-depth task analysis.

7.2.8 Drawbacks to Menus

The characteristics of the task (Is the task time dependent? Is it performed infrequently?) and of the user population (Are they computer novices? Are they computer literate?) will determine the degree to which each of these drawbacks will affect performance. The answers to these questions can be determined through an in-depth task analysis and the construction of a User Profile using the User Profile Worksheet.

7.2.8.1. Lost Users

As the depth of the menu hierarchy increases so does the probability that users will become lost within the depths of the menu (navigation errors) and will waste a great deal of time trying to retrace their steps to get out of the menu, if they ever do. We have actually seen some menu hierarchies that have been so deep and so poorly constructed that traversing their structure was akin to traversing through a maze. The problem of lost users is very easily remedied. Decrease the depth of the menu hierarchy by increasing breadth and provide a safety-net option on each menu that will return the user to the root node of the menu structure.

7.2.8.2. Menus Are Inefficient For Experts

Menus are extremely inefficient by their very nature. Forcing the user to go through screen after screen to access a single function that could have been activated by typing the command name of the function is extremely inefficient, and not advised if the User Profile reveals that the user population is extremely skilled in using command language interfaces. In the case of novices or infrequent users, menus can be extremely efficient, since it is faster for them to go through each screen than it is for them to search their memory for the command name. Recall that recognition memory is much more accurate and faster than recall memory since recognition memory is cued. In a computer science metaphor, the process is similar to trying to find an item in a data base with or without the appropriate index.

7.2.8.3 Menus Take Valuable Real Estate

For menus of any complexity, the entire screen is required to display the menu. This problem can be partially offset through the use of pop-down menus. Whether the real estate problem is actually a problem will depend upon the structure of the task.

7.2.8.4. Menus Are Inflexible

True, menus are inflexible when compared to command language interfaces which can be concatenated, given multiple parameters, and so forth. Some flexibility can be built into menus by giving the users the capability of customizing the items that appear in the menus. Very often, menu customization is not a viable option because of the programming logistics required. Again, the true determinant of the degree of impact of the inflexibility is the structure of the task and the nature of the user population.

7.2.8.5 Impractical for large numbers of choices

Menus are impractical when the system includes a large number of functions. How many functions are too many? That's hard to say with any accuracy. Again, an in-depth task analysis and user profile should be your guide.

While we cannot give you a number as to how many is too many, we can offer an anecdote. One of the authors used to work on a project that had ~ 300 screens. It was menu-driven, and it was his job to make the system easier to use. Not an enviable task. Nevertheless, 300 terminal screens is definitely too many to be accessed by a menu. The first thing we did was, you guessed it, a task analysis. Through the task analysis we determined which screens were necessary for completing the job, which ones were similar in function, and which ones were redundant or unnecessary. Using the task analysis as our guide, we eliminated unnecessary functions and screens, collapsed screens together that had similar enough functionality to be combined, and we redesigned other screens. In the end, we were left with a system that had approximately 100 screens and a menu structure that was only three layers deep!

7.3 Linking With a Graphical User Interface

A graphical interface (GUI) is one in which users perform functions by manipulating small graphics , called icons (Figure 7-10 and Color Plate 7). Because the manipulation of on-screen graphical objects to achieve some goal or activity is the salient feature of graphical user interfaces, these interfaces are also sometimes known as *Direct Manipulation Interfaces*.

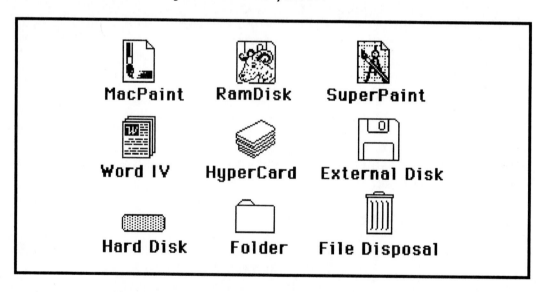

Figure 7-10: Typical GUI Icons

In a GUI, the icons take the place of commands. Each program creates its own unique icon to prevent confusion. For example, Word IV is the word processor that this book was written with, and it generates files whose icons look like sheets of paper with writing on. Similarly, SuperPaint and MacPaint are paint programs and create files with icons that resemble an artist's canvas. Finally, you might notice that the icons for the different disks resemble the disks themselves. The use of icons clearly reduces some types of errors simply due to the fact that word processor file icons are very distinct from paint program files.

The GUI interface has a decided advantage over the command interface, insofar as the graphical symbols remain visible, eliminating the need for the user to recall commands. Functions in a GUI interface are performed through using a pointing device to initiate an action through the manipulation of icons, pulling down pull-down windows, and through direct manipulation of on-screen objects. For example, the picture of a folder symbolizes a directory. In order to place a file into the directory, rather than typing a series of commands instructing the computer to move the file from one directory location to another, the user simply selects the icon with a pointing device (i.e., mouse, trackball, joystick, touch screen, etc.) and drags the picture across the screen until it is superimposed over the folder icon. The copying process then occurs.

Another salient feature is the use of pull-down menus and windows in lieu of traditional menus (Figure 7-11). Pull-down menus are menus contained in windows which can be opened by using a pointing input device, such as a mouse, to select on an invisible "hot spot" that overlays the words on the menu bar and pull down. Menu items, in this case **by Name,** are selected using the pointing device, or in some cases through a keyboard macro (e.g., the universal keyboard macro for QUIT in the Macintosh universe is ⌘-Q).

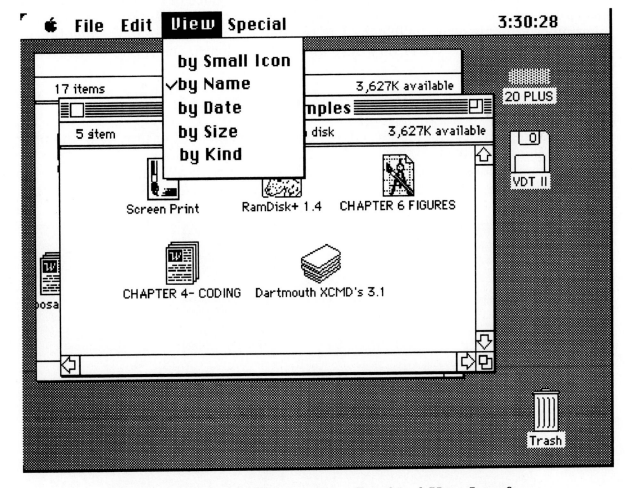

Figure 7-11: Apple Macintosh's Graphical User Interface

As shown in Figure 7-11, windows hold a collection of objects. Those objects can be the icons associated with files, or they can be menu commands. Windows can also be a very effective aid to programming; the source code could be displayed in one window, the programs output in another window, and a dynamic debugger in still a third window. The two major advantages of windows are the removal of the burden of having to remember commands, and the simultaneous presentation of information from multiple tasks.

7.3.1 Benefits of Graphical User Interfaces

Graphical user interfaces, due to their physical manipulation metaphor, have a number of unique advantages over other interface dialogs.

7.3.1.1 GUIs Are Intuitive and Easy to Learn

Graphical user interfaces offer the advantage of being very intuitive, because the physical analogy capitalizes on the user's existing mental models of interacting with the real world. In the real world, when you want to put a piece of paper into a manila folder, you pick up the paper and place it inside of the folder. In like fashion, GUI interfaces use icons of folders in place of directories. To move a file into a folder, you simply use a pointing device to select the file and superimpose the file over the folder. The relation of the interface to the mental model of the user make GUIs very easy and quick to learn, serving to reduce training time and cost.

7.3.1.2 GUIs Provide the User With Immediate Feedback

Due to the physical metaphor, GUIs also have the benefit of providing the user with immediate feedback regarding the outcome of their actions. When a user performs some action, the GUI system provides them with a visual reaction in the form of a change in the visual signature of the physical objects. See Figure 7-12.

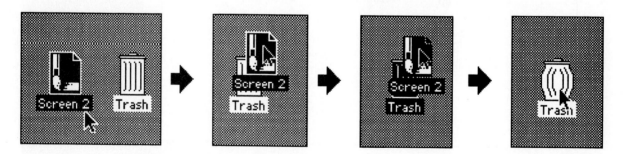

Figure 7-12: GUI Immediate Feedback

7.3.2 GUI Drawbacks

For all their advantages, GUIs, like menus, offer some disadvantages.

7.3.2.1 GUIs May Frustrate Expert Users

Like menus, the inefficiency of interacting with a GUI dialog can frustrate expert users who are interested in getting the task performed as quickly and efficiently as possible. Anecdotally, one of the authors has repeatedly observed expert computer users complaining about Macintoshes and Windows, making the claim that it was easier to get things done when all you had to do was to issue a few commands. This is in stark contrast to the claim that GUIs are easy to use, and tends to underscore our claim that a profile of the user population is a must when designing an interface.

7.3.3.2 Actions Are Not Always Obvious

GUIs are as intuitive as one might think. Anyone who has initially tried to use an Apple Macintosh or Windows without a manual will realize this. Consider the buttons on the GUI in Color Plate 7. Are the functions of each button immediately obvious? Since GUIs do not offer the user prompts, the user is left to rely upon the icons to "infer" the action to be taken. If the graphics on the icon are vague, then the action to be performed can be obscured.

7.3.3.3 Actions May Not Be Easily Designed Into a Graphic

Since GUIs are so reliant upon the intelligibility of the graphics of its icons, it is of the utmost importance that designers pay close attention to the graphics used. Nevertheless, there will be times when designers will be unable to develop a graphic that conveys the underlying action. For example, what graphic would you use for the command UNDO?

In spite of their problems, the GUI dialog style, like menus and commands, have their place. Only through task analysis can you determine which dialog type best suits your needs.

7.4 Linking With Hypertext

Related to the graphical user interface metaphor is the Hypertext metaphor. Originally coined by Ted Nelson in the mid-sixties to mean nonsequential writing, Hypertext now refers to a means of linking and retrieving data, text, screens, or displays in a nonsequential format.

In a hypertext system, the screens or displays are connected using linkages. Buttons, which can be visible or invisible, are placed on the screen or in the text and are activated when a pointing device selects them. The button, when selected, engages the linkage[1] and navigates the user to the linked screen or opens a window.

Consider the example which appears in Figures 7-13 through 7-15. Figure 7-13 shows a typical hypertext system in which certain words in the text have buttons overlaid on them. These buttons, when selected, will either navigate the user to a separate screen or initiate some function. Figure 7-14 shows what happens when the button overlaying the word thalamus is selected. The button overlaying thalamus in Figure 7-13 is linked to a window which opens and displays a digitized photomicrograph of the thalamus. In multimedia systems, buttons can open windows that display live action, digitized film/video clips, or play digitized voice.

The bent arrow, which appears at the lower right corner of the window displaying the photomicrograph (Figure 7-14), when selected, activates a reverse linkage which closes the window, in this case, but which could just as easily navigate the user back to the screen which he or she was viewing immediately preceding. You will recall that backward navigation was one of the safety-net features discussed in the section on menus. In the event that a user of a hypertext system is navigated to the wrong screen, he or she can use the bent arrow to backward navigate. Other backward navigation, safety-net, features appear at the bottom of the screens displayed in Figures 7-13 through 7-15. The house icon, the arrow icons, and the "Where am I" button each provide the user with a different degree of rescue should he or she become lost.

First, the arrows are buttons which navigate the user to the next/previous page/screen of a multiple page segment. This allows the user to page through the node the same as they would page through a book. Selecting the right button would advance the user through the pages, while the left button would cycle them through the pages in reverse sequence. In either event, the arrows are simply buttons with linkages to other screens. In this case, the right buttons are forward linkages, and the left buttons are reverse linkages.

The house icon is analogous to the root node option in a menu metaphor. The house is used to indicate a safe haven, in this case the HyperCard home stack. Selecting this button assures the user that he or she will **ALWAYS** be navigated to the home stack, thus creating a safety-net for the novice.

Finally, there is the "Where am I?" button. This is a very important button. Selecting this button in Figure 7-14 causes the window, shown in Figure 7-15, to appear. This window shows a map of the immediate hypertext space. Hypertext, as you'll remember, refers to nonsequential text, data, or screens. The arrow and the emboldened linkage and node indicate that the user is at the thalamus node. The checkmarks indicate which nodes the user has already visited.

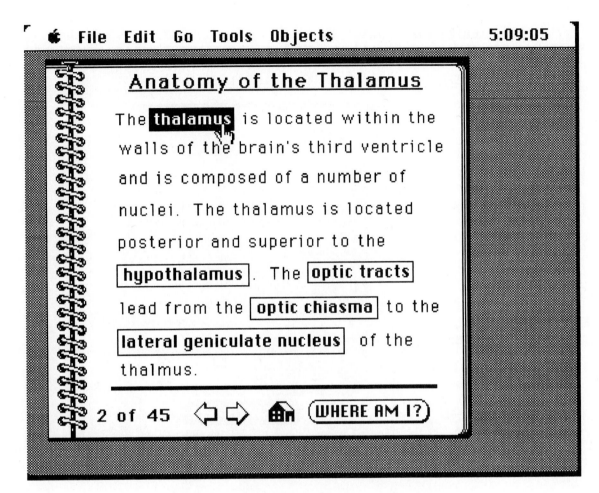

Figure 7-13: Typical Hypertext System

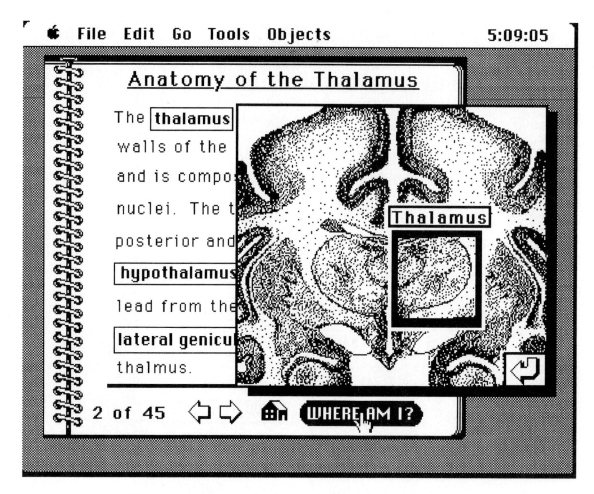

Figure 7-14: Hypertext With Photomicrograph

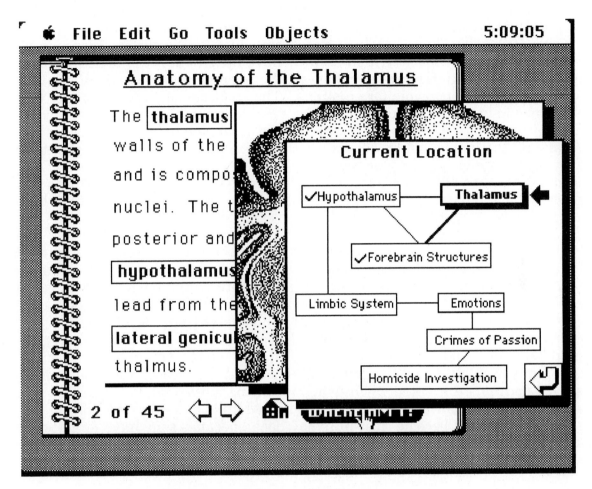

Figure 7-15: Hypertext Structure Map

Look closely at the map in Figure 7-15. The thalamus node is linked to the Forebrain Structures node and the Hypothalamus node. The Hypothalamus node is linked to the Limbic System node which is linked to the Emotions node which is linked to the Crimes of Passion node which is linked to the Homicide Investigations node. This structure may seem odd at first. After all, crimes of passion and homicide investigation seem to have little to do with structures of the forebrain and median forebrain. However, the hypothalamus is part of the limbic system, which is responsible for emotions. The emotions of rage and anger have been shown to be directly tied to the limbic system and to play a large part in crimes of passion. The system designer placed a linkage between crimes of passion and the limbic system because of the associative link the two topics have with anger. Similarly, many homicides fall under the category of crimes of passion. This type of linkage structure forms the basis of the hypertext approach. Hypertext by its very nature is **nonsequential**. The nonsequential nature of hypertext is both its greatest strength and its greatest weakness.

The nonsequential nature of hypertext allows the user extremely rapid access to related content which they may not have been able to access through using a book. How many neuroscience books contain chapters on homicide investigation?

The nonsequential nature of hypertext is also its greatest weakness. Hypertext systems are extremely difficult to develop (what associative linkages should be made?) and are extremely susceptible to navigation errors. In fact, a recent study by Nielsen and Lyngbœk (1989) showed that 56% of the readers they observed became disoriented when using one of the most popular hypertext systems. Readers typically access the associated links of associated links of associated links and become "lost in hyperspace", because they have forgotten the associative linkage net they have followed to get where they are, so backward navigation is difficult or impossible.

Nielsen (1990) has pointed out that many of these navigation problems can be obviated by providing the user with an history of where they are and where they've been (Figure 6-12), the provision of a fish-eye overview diagram in larger systems (Furnas, 1986), backward linking, time-stamping of nodes, or footprints or checkmarks. The problem with using such techniques as footprinting, checkmarking, and time-stamping is that eventually so many nodes will become marked that an additional problem will be created for the user.

Unfortunately, hypertext systems are so new that no real rules or standards have been developed as to how best to implement them. Nonetheless, the non-sequential linkage of information is appropriate in some instances. Only an in-depth task analysis can determine if this structure is appropriate for your system. While hypertext systems are extremely prone to navigation error, a careful task analysis coupled with prudent usage of footprinting, backward navigation, and safety-nets can help eliminate the occurrence of many of the navigation problems. Additionally, in restricted task domains, a task analysis can help reveal the **natural** mental associations which the user makes between the different types of information and will thus suggest the most appropriate linkages between nodes, which will further reduce the occurrence of navigational errors.

7.5 Usability Testing of Displays

7.5.1 Metrics and Measures

The screens should be usability tested when they are still at the storyboard stage. However, this is the final point, that is linking the screens together, at which you should consider usability testing. If you do not perform a usability test at this point, you run the risk of giving the users an untested product. You wouldn't dream of releasing an untested drug or an untested jet engine, because someone could die. If you are putting untested displays into the control room of a nuclear power plant, **thousands** could die. Performing objective tests of display formats or configurations, is **crucial** at this point. If for no other reason, making changes to the display will be extremely difficult beyond this point since the displays will be in production. The design manager **MUST** build sufficient time into his or her schedule to allow the creation and usability testing of a prototype. Prototyping and usability testing of the initial design phase will save the corporation money in the long run through reducing the need for later enhancements to patch problems with the software that would have been caught if the system had been prototyped and adequately tested. It is our opinion that 90% of the calls received by help desks and technical support centers stem directly from problems which could have been caught had the software been appropriately prototyped and tested. Prototyping and usability testing of screens and functionality will **SAVE MONEY** for the company through reducing the calls to technical support staff and reducing the amount of retrofitting/enhancing of the next version of the software. The actual savings can be computed by figuring the cost per error (Chapter 1).

There are several different usability metrics. Some of these are as follows.

Minimum Metric Set

1. Time required to complete the task and subtasks,
2. Time to train (time required to understand program operation),
3. Number and types of human errors made,
4. Perceived ease of use (ratio of positive to negative responses on Likert scale questionnaires and interviews),
5. Amount of work completed over a fixed period of time,
6. Time required to detect and fix errors,
7. Time to recognize errors have been made,
8. Discriminability accuracy (in percent) of targets over time and under different work loads,
9. Videotapes of user interaction with the software to identify inaccurate or inappropriate interaction behaviors,
10. Percent utilization of display space on screen.

Optional Metric Set (Requires Special Equipment)

11. Pupil changes over time measured in percent, variance, or S.D.,
12. Facial temperature changes over time,
13. Pupil and/or face temperature changes related to specific application interaction,
14. Amount of eye motion preceding hand actions,
15. Amount (frequency and magnitude) of eye motion,
16. Tracking frequency of eyes on the display,
17. Amount (frequency and magnitude) of hand motion,
18. User interest level over time (derived from pupil size and temperature time profiles) correlated with verbal reports.

While this list is not exhaustive, it should illustrate a number of different measures of usability possible in a testing situation. It is also desirable to use automated data collection (usually software capture of session keystrokes) if possible or data collection equipment which is unobtrusive with respect to the users performance. The initial component characteristics of a desirable, unobtrusive observation system are as follows.

1. An observation workstation to act as a host computer to control and receive data from the other components,

2. Analysis programs and image processing tools to observe the workstation,

3. A low resolution color, videotape camera to watch the user's hand motion,

4. Video recording of user workstation, full screen display, and audio recording of session (omnidirectional microphone in lab),

5. An eye-gaze system which determines where a user is looking and pupil size by following the gaze point without special headgear (desirable but expensive),

6. A low resolution infrared camera to obtain digital data on the amount and variation of temperature changes over time of the user's face **(OPTIONAL)**,

7. A shell interface to the application to collect user's keystrokes, inputs, and mouse moves,

8. Observation room with one-way glass.

Recent technological advances have made it practical to put together this type of system. Lightweight eye-tracking systems and headtrackers are now commercially available at fairly low cost, due to increased market demand. The need for eye-tracking cannot be overestimated. Without eye-tracking it is impossible to determine where the user is looking on the screen.

The need for such a high-tech, flexible configuration is justified by the difficulties in finding the most useful and easily measured metrics, and deriving conclusions as to application usability. At this point, you may not know what metrics are important, how easily they are measured, or how they are correlated. The opportunity to study what goes on while the user is working with an application without touching or interfering with the user is only possible with cameras and systems such as the eye-gaze system or head-tracing device.

Figure 7-16 shows a side view of the camera configuration. The eye-gaze camera system is mounted beneath the user's workstation monitor, and the IR camera observing the face is in-line with the eye-gaze camera but set back farther. The eye-gaze camera has a narrow field of view of about 6 degrees, while the other has a wider angle of view to include the user's face. The user's keyboard and mouse are located at the front of the table and are in view of the low resolution color camera. The dedicated PC, which is part of the eye-gaze system, is not shown. Neither are the rest of the user's workstation, nor the video connection to the workstation display shown. It would be best if the observation workstation be located nearby, but not in the same room with the user.

With the system in place in the user's environment or similar environment, the actual testing session would proceed from an experimental design and data collection plan. The plan could originate from productivity requirements desired by the management of a project or organization sympathetic to this research. The designation of user test subjects could be determined by the plan and by the requirements for a statistically meaningful sample. The experimental design and plan would include the metrics for which data would be taken and the usability attributes for which information was desired. The user would be informed of specific tasks to be performed and the time limit.

The session could begin with the eye-gaze subsystem being calibrated to the eye of a new user subject. The user would start up the application. Either modified I/O drivers or an application shell would capture all subsequent user keyboard and mouse interactions. The user would try to complete the tasks outlined in the test plan. From the observation computer, the collected user inputs, video, and thermographic data would be monitored, and some real-time analysis done to verify that the data collection was working properly and that the rates of data collection were set appropriately. Eye-tracking applications written using eye-gaze software tools would display real-time data on the eye-gaze subsystem monitor. At the conclusion of the session, the user would be interviewed. Subsequent analysis, and the comparison of the results of many different user sessions with the same task assignment would reveal information about the quality of the application's user interface and the productivity of the users.

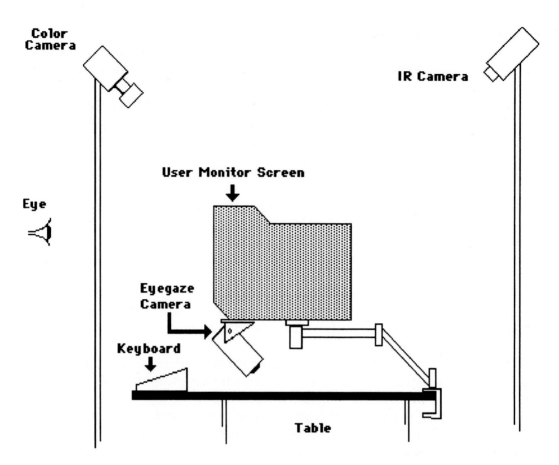

Figure 7-16: Usability Lab Configuration

Important questions which will have to be addressed include the following:

- Which metrics should be used?

- What are the best ways to obtain data for metrics?

- How accurate are the experimental measurements and calculations?

- What relationships, if any, exist between the different metrics?

- What are the correct relationships between the metrics and the usability attributes?

- Does the user move so much that headtracking will be necessary?

- Will the user need to sit in a high back chair to limit head motion?

- Can observation work in the user's environment?

- Does the eye-gaze subsystem give misleading data when the user's eyes becomes unfocussed when thinking?

- Do other physiological measurements need to be take (pulse, etc.)?

- How can we correlate the user task performance with the physiological feedback?

- How can we interpret the IR face data: What can we learn from medical thermography?

- How can we compare similar function prototypes or applications?

- How can we determine the significance of observation results?

- How can we use observation results to influence design of user interfaces?

- How relevant are observation results on the selection or development of the best user interfaces?

The time estimate to conduct a test should be estimated based on the following activities:

A. Detailed research plan and schedule
B. Select and acquire hardware/software
C. Integrate components in phases
D. Design of appropriate experimental session database
E. Design of appropriate cross-session database
F. Design and write observation data acquisition and control
G. Design and write observation analysis
H. Pilot testing sessions
H. Experimental testing
I. Test and evaluate results
J. Prepare report
K. Peer review of report
L. Publication of report

7.6 Summary

For quick reference, we have summarized this chapter's information into Tables 7-4 and 7-5. The information in the Table 7-4 matches user characteristics to dialogs, suggesting combinations that give optimal user performance. Comparison information can be obtained from the User Profile Worksheet. Table 7-5 matches the different dialog types with the characteristics of the task being performed (See task analysis data forms).

Table 7-4: Comparison of Dialogs and User Characteristics

User Characteristics	Commands	Menu	GUI	Form Fill
Knowledge and Experience	High	Low	Low	Low
Typing Skill	Moderate to High	Low	Low	Moderate to High
System Experience	High	Low	Low	Low to Moderate
Task Experience	High	Low	Low	Moderate to High
Application Experience	High	Low	Low	Low to Moderate
Use of Other Systems	Infrequent	Frequent	Frequent	Moderate to Frequent
Computer Literacy	High	Low	Low	Moderate to High

(Adapted From Mayhew, 1992)

Table 7-5: Comparison of Dialogs and Task Characteristics

Task Characteristics	Commands	Menu	GUI	Form Fill
Frequency of Use	High	Low	Low	Moderate to High
Primary Training	Formal	None or Informal	None or Informal	Informal to Formal
Turnover Rate	Low	High	High	Low to Moderate
Task Importance	High	Low	Low	Moderate
Task Structure	Low	High	Moderate	High

(Adapted From Mayhew, 1992)

7.7 Notes

1. In object-oriented languages, such as HyperTalk or SuperTalk, these linkages are instructions embedded in the object's handler. More often than not, these objects are buttons, which call a handler when a mouse clicks on the button object. A typical handler and its accompanying linkage might be:

On MouseUp
     Go Card ID 3456
End MouseUp

7.8 Suggested Readings

The linking of screens is an extremely complex issue, and not one that can be adequately addressed in the space of a single chapter. What follows is a list of sources which will provide the interested reader with additional information on linking screens to form a dialog.

Barnard, P.J., and Grudin, J. (1988) Command names. In *Handbook of Human Computer Interaction*. Mark Helander (ed). North Holland: Elsevier, 237-256.

Carlson, D.A., and Ram, S. (1990) Hyperintelligence: The next frontier. *Communications of the ACM* , 33(3), 311-322.

Carroll, J.M., Mack, R.L., and Kellogg, W.A. (1988) Interface metaphors and user design. In *Handbook of Human Computer Interaction*. Mark Helander (ed). North Holland: Elsevier, 67-86.

Paap, K., and Roske-Hofstrand, R.J. (1988) Design of menus. In *Handbook of Human Computer Interaction*. Mark Helander (ed). North Holland: Elsevier, 205-236.

Nielsen, J. (1990) The art of navigation through hypertext. *Communications of the ACM* , 33(3), 297-310.

Verplank, W.L. (1988) Graphic challenges in designing object-oriented user interfaces. In *Handbook of Human Computer Interaction*. Mark Helander (ed). North Holland: Elsevier, 365-376.

Ziegler, J.E., and Fahnrich, K.-P. (1988) Direct manipulation. In *Handbook of Human Computer Interaction*. Mark Helander (ed). North Holland: Elsevier, 123-134.

7.9 References

Carroll, J.M. (1984) Minimalist Training. *Datamation. 30,* 18, 125-136.

Carroll, J.M., and Mack, R.L. (1984) Learning to use a word processor: By doing, by thinking, and by knowing. In *Human Factors in Computing Systems,*. Thomas, J.C. and Schneider, M. (Eds.). Norwood, NJ: Ablex Publishing Corporation: , 13-51.

Ehrenreich, S. L., and Porcu, T. (1982) Abbreviations for automated systems: Teaching operators and rules. In *Directions in Human-Computer Interaction*. Badre, A., and Shneiderman, B. (Eds.). Norwood, NJ: Ablex Publishers, 111-116.

Fisher, D.L., Yungkurth, E.J., and Moss, S.M. (1990) Optimal menu hierarchy design: Syntax and semantics. *Human Factors*, 32, 665-683.

Furnas, G.W., (1986) Generalized fish-eye views. *Proceedings of the ACM CHI '86 Conference on Human Factors in Computing Systems.*

Hutchins, E.L., Hollands, J.D., and Norman, D.A. (1986) Direct manipulation interfaces. In D.A. Norman and S.W. Draper (Eds), *User Centered System Design*. Hillsdale, NJ: Lawrence Erlbaum Associates. pg. 87-124.

Lee, E., and MacGregor, J. (1985) Minimizing user search time in menu retrieval systems. *Human Factors*, 27, 157-162.

MacGregor, J., Lee, E., and Lam, N. (1986) Optimizing the structure of database menu indexes: A decision model of menu search. *Human Factors,* 28, 387-399.

McDonald, J.E., Stone, J.D., and Liebelt, L.S. (1983) Searching for items in menus: The effects of organization and type of target. In *Proceedings of the Human Factors Society's 27th Annual Meeting* , 834-837. Santa Monica, CA: Human Factors Society.

Miller, D.P. (1981) The depth/breadth trade-off in hierarchical computer menus. In *Proceedings of the Human Factors Society's 25th Annual Meeting* (pp. 296-300). Santa Monica, CA: Human Factors Society.

Nielsen, J. (1990) The art of navigation through hypertext. *Communications of the ACM* , 33(3), 297-310.

Nielsen, J., and Lyngbœk, U. (1989) Two fields of hypermedia usability. *Proceedings of the HyperCard II Conference.* York, UK.

Paap, K.R., and Roske-Hofstrand, R.J. (1986) The optimal number of menu options per panel. *Human Factors*, 28, 377-385.

Shneiderman, B. S. (1987) *Designing The User Interface: Strategies for Effective Human-Computer Interaction*. Reading, MA: Addison Wesley.

Snowberry, K., Parkinson, S.R., and Sisson, N. (1983) Computer Display Menus. *Ergonomics*, 26, 699-712.

Weimer, J. (1990a) Internal Prodigy Services Company Technical Report.

Weimer, J. (1990b) Internal Prodigy Services Company Technical Report.

Weimer, J. (1990c) Internal Prodigy Services Company Technical Report.

INDEX

D

Appendix A: Sample CRT Display Guidelines

HARDWARE

Controls and Input Devices

Keyboard Feedback

1. An indication of control activation should be provided.

   Example: When key is pressed, a snap feel, audible click or associated sound or integral light should occur to let user know that key has been actuated.

Key Actuation Force

1. The force required for key displacement should be 0.25 to 1.5 N.

2. The force required for key displacement should be 0.3 to 0.75 N for repetitive keying tasks.

3. Less force should be used when the key being actuated is used continuously.

Key Rollover

1. N-key rollover capability should be implemented for the reduction of keying errors.

Key Travel

1. Key displacement should be 0.03 to 0.19 inches for numeric keys and 0.05 to 0.25 inches for alphanumeric keys.

2. Displacement variability between keys should be minimized.

Key Color/Labeling

1. All controls should be appropriately and clearly labeled in the simplest and most direct manner possible.

2. Functional highlighting of the various key groups should be accomplished through the use of color-coding techniques and/or templates.

   Example: Actuation keys may be green, control keys black, and emergency/safety keys colored red.

3. Key symbols should be etched to resist wear and colored with high contrast lettering/templates.

4. Color of alphanumeric keys should be neutral (beige or gray) rather than black, white, or one of the spectral colors.

5. Spectral colors (red, yellow, green or blue) should be avoided for coloring alphanumeric keys and reserved for use in highlighting functional key groups.

6. Keys should be matte finished.

7. Keys should be labeled with a nonstylized font.

8. Raised, tactile cues should be provided on the "home" keys of the QWERTY keyboard and on the 5 key of the numeric keypad.

Key Dimension/Spacing

1. The linear dimension of the key tops should be from 0.385 to 0.75 inches, with 0.05 inches preferred.

2. Separation between adjacent key tops should be 0.25 inch.

3. Push-button height for decimal entry keypads should be from 1/4 to 3/8 inch.

4. Key height for alphanumeric keyboards should be from 3/8 to 1/2 inch.

Keyboard Slope

1. Keyboards should have a slope of 15 to 25 degrees from the horizontal, with 12 to 18 degrees preferred.

2. The keyboard slope should be adjustable.

    Example: Moveable keyboards should be fitted with collapsible legs that allow for easy adjusting of keyboard height.

Keyboard Thickness

1. The thickness of the keyboard should be less than 50 mm. (acceptable) with 30 mm or less preferred.

Special Function Keys

1. When dedicated controls are used to indicate/activate functions the keys should be grouped together.

2. Function controls should be easily distinguished from other types of keys on the computer console.

3. Each function control should be clearly labeled to indicate its function to the user.

4. When function keys are included with an alphanumeric keyboard, the function keys should be physically separate.

5. Keys with major or fatal effects should be located so that inadvertent operation in unlikely.

Numeric Keypad

1. Terminal keyboards should be provided with an auxiliary numeric keypad.

2. The configuration of a keyboard used to enter solely numeric information should be a 3x3x1 matrix with the zero digit centered on the bottom row.

3. The layout of keyboard numeric pads should be calculator style.

Alternate Input Devices

Light Pens

1. Movement of the light pen in any direction on the screen should result in smooth direct movement of the cursor in the same direction.

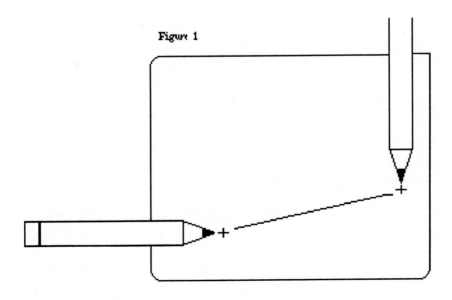

Figure 1

2.   Direct placement of the light pen at any point on the screen should cause the cursor to appear at that same exact point and remain steady in that position so long as the pen is not moved.

3.   When using the light pen for the creation of free-drawn graphics, the refresh rate (ability of the cursor to keep direct tracking with the light pen) should be high.

Joysticks

1.   Joystick controls should be used for tasks that require precise or continuous control in two or more related dimensions (any measurable extent, as length, width, etc.).

2.   In rate-control applications, which allow the cursor to go beyond the edge of the display, indicators should be provided to aid the in bringing the follower back onto the display.

Figure 2 (side view)

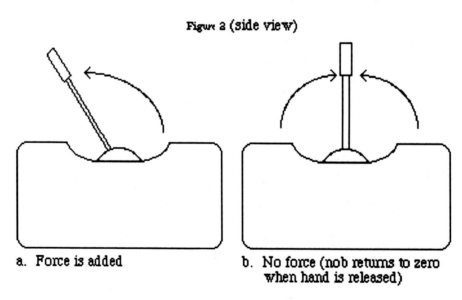

a. Force is added   b. No force (nob returns to zero
                                                              when hand is released)

Isotonic Joysticks

1.   Isotonic joysticks, which are used for rate control, should be spring-loaded so that the joystick knob returns to the vertical position or the cursor returns to center of the screen when the hand is removed.

2.   Isotonic joysticks should not be used in connection with CRTs unless they are both instrumented for zero-set (when joystick knob is in vertical position).

3.   Isotonic/displacement joystick knobs should be 1/4 to 5/8 inch in diameter and 3 to 6 inches long.

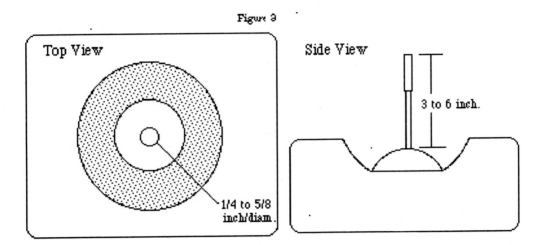

Figure 3

6.   Movement of the joystick should only take 12 to 32 ounces of pressure

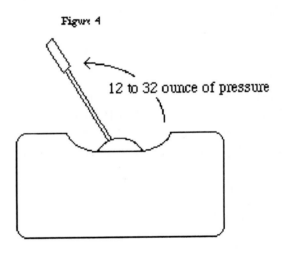

Figure 4

12 to 32 ounce of pressure

7.   Full movement of the joystick in any direction should not exceed 45 degrees.

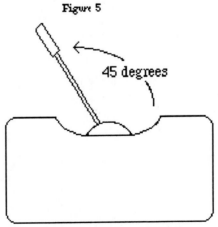

Figure 5

45 degrees

Full movement in any direction
should not go past 45 degress.

8. Isotonic/displacement joysticks should be provided with the following clearances:

    a. Distance from display to joystick   15-3/4 in.
    b. Area around joystick   4 in.
    c. Joystick to shelf front.   4-3/4 to 9-7/8 in.

9. Movement of the joystick should be smooth in all directions, and rapid positioning of the cursor should be achieved without noticeable cursor lag.

10. Movement, friction, and control ratios should meet the requirements of the rapid and precise positioning of the joystick.

11. For greater precision and control, pencil attachments may be used.

12. The movement of the joystick to cursor ratio should be sufficiently high when using the joystick for free-drawn graphics.

13. Delay between the movement of the joystick and response from the display should not exceed 0.1 seconds.

14. When position accuracy is more critical than positioning speed, isotonic displacement joysticks should be used rather than isometric ones.

15. Isotonic displacement joysticks should be used for data pickoff and drawing.

Isometric Joystick

1. The isometric joystick should be used for such functions as data pickoff.

2. Isometric joystick should not be used in situations where the user must maintain a constant force on the joystick for a sustained period of time.

3. Finger-grasped isometric joysticks should have the same dimensional characteristics as isotonic joystick.

Figure 3

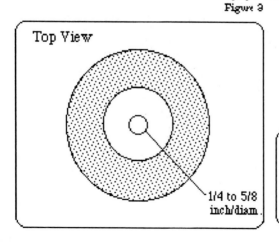

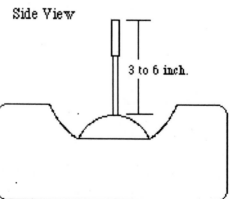

4. Hand-grasped isometric joysticks, when integral switching (e.g. switching to a file containing large amounts of whole data) is required, should have a stem length between 4.3 to 7.1 inches long and have a maximum grip diameter of 2 inches.

5. Area clearance around hand-grasped isometric joysticks should have the following minimum clearances:

   a. Around the sides: 4 inches
   b. Rear of joystick: 2 inches

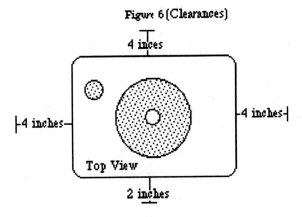

Figure 6 (Clearances)

4 inces

4 inches   4 inches

Top View

2 inches

6. Hand-grasped isometric joysticks should have a maximum resistance force of 26.7 lb for full output.

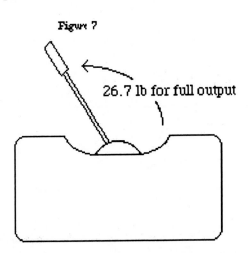

Figure 7

26.7 lb for full output

7. The isometric stick should have little resistance when force is applied, but when force is applied to the stick when it is in its full upright (zero position) position there may be resistance.

8. Movement of the joystick in any direction should be somewhat equivalent to the movement of the cursor on the computer screen.

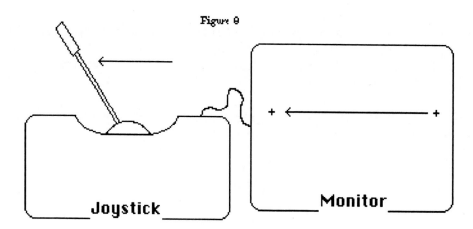

Figure 8

Joystick   Monitor

Track Ball

1. A track ball control should be used for such tasks as data pickoff.

2. When using the track ball, do not allow the follower to leave the screen in any application.

3. To prevent wrist and arm injuries when using the track ball, arm and wrist support should be used.

4. The track ball control should be capable of rotating in any direction.

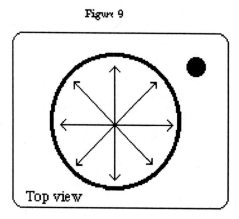

Figure 9

Top view

6. When moving the track ball in either the X or Y direction, there should be no other cursor movement in any other direction, movement of the cursor should only be in the X and Y direction.

7. Upon taking over control of the track ball, the controller should put their hand on the ball slowly to prevent any sudden movements of the cursor.

8. Movement of the track ball in respect to the movement of the cursor on the the screen should correspond.

9. Track balls should be used in graphic applications requiring position and selection.

GRID AND STYLUS DEVICES

1. Grid and stylus devices should be used for data pickoff, when entering points on a screen, creation of free-drawn graphics, and similar control applications.

2. Transparent grids which are used as display overlays should conform to the the size of the display.

3. Grids that go beyond the boundaries of the display should be centered, directional, and also show the maximum extent of its boundaries.

4. Movement of the stylus (pointed object which controls the cursor) in any direction on the grid surface should result in smooth movement of the cursor in the same direction.

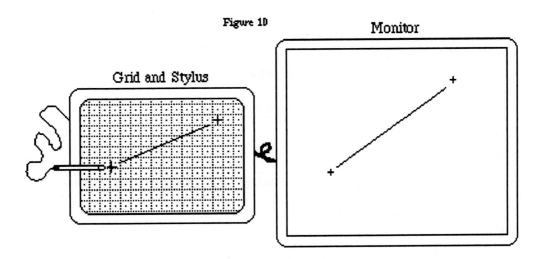

Figure 10

Monitor

Grid and Stylus

5. Specific placement of the stylus at any point on the grid surface should cause the follower to appear at the corresponding coordinates and to remain steady in position so long as the stylus is not moved.

6. Refresh rate (tracking rate of the cursor in respect to the stylus) for the follower should be sufficiently high to ensure the appearance of a continuous track whenever the stylus is used in creation of free-drawn graphics.

X-Y CONTROLLER (MOUSE)

1. The mouse controller should be used for main item selection, scrolling (moving a directory in its window so that you can see a different part of it), data retrieval, and data entry.

2.   The mouse controller should have physical dimensions of:
     a. width   1.5 to 3 inches
     b. length   3 to 5 inches
     c. thickness   1 to 2 inches

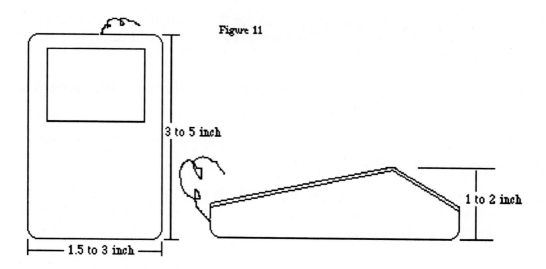

Figure 11

3.   The design of the controller and placement of the maneuvering surface should allow the user to consistently control the movement of the mouse without any visual reference to the controller.

Displays

Flicker

1.   The refresh rate of the CRT screen should be kept at 60 Hz to insure it does does not create flicker to the end user.

Contrast Ratio

1.   The contrast between the screen and information to be displayed on the screen is best provided at a ratio between 5:1 and 10:1.

2.   If a light or electrostatic filter is used or if the room lighting is extreme, this ratio would need to be adjusted. A control to adjust the contrast for the VDT should be required.

Glare

1.   Prevent glare from overhead lights by positioning the screen such that no lights are reflected on the screen.

Screen Resolution

1. The images on the screen should maintain the illusion of a continuous image. The viewer should not have to resolve scan lines or matrix spots.

SCREEN STRUCTURES AND CONTENT

Cursor

1. This is the symbol that indicates the position where the next character will appear or where the user's attention should be focused.

2. The cursor should be noticeable, but not detract or obscure any other information displayed on the screen.

3. The cursor should be easy to move from one location to another.

4. A box or block is the preferred shape for the cursor. Arrows should be used with GUI interfaces for selecting, and I bars for inputting text.

5. The cursor should blink at about 3 Hz.

Text

6. Consistent format should be maintained from one display to another.

7. Upper and lower case letters should be used appropriately.

8. Display paragraphs should be separated by at least one blank line.

9. Any text that includes instructions for a task to be performed in sequential order, should have each sequence numbered consecutively.

10. Text should be properly punctuated.

11. Short, simple, concise sentences are the most effective.

12. Use explicit vocabulary at a level easily understood by the user.

13. The meaning for any text should be verified for clarity by users prior to adapting it for general use.

Labels

1. All controls should be appropriately and clearly labeled in the simplest and most direct manner.

2. Labels should be horizontal and read left to right.

3.   There should be clear identification of what the label is identifying.

4.   Physical location or limitations including distance vibration time response should be considered.

5.   Control labeling must indicate the functional result of the control movement, that is, ON, OFF, Increase, Decrease.

6.   Words should be chosen on the basis of familiarity and understanding.

7.   Similar names for different controls and displays should be avoided.

8.   Control and display labels should convey their meaning in the most direct manner by using simple words and phrases.

9.   Abbreviations may be used when they are familiar to the user.

10.   Units of measure should be included when appropriate.

11.   Labels should be printed in all capitals; periods should not be used after abbreviations.

12.   Mechanical labeling should be graduated in size to reduce confusion and search time.

13.   Label names should be easily discriminated from surrounding labeled fields or messages.

14.   All labeling and control identification must be verified for clarity and understanding by user to eliminate any variability in interpretation. This is necessary before implementing any changes to an existing system.

Messages

1.   The computer should be capable of providing two levels of message communications: an immediate prompt on the primary screen, and a secondary, detailed, and comprehensive meaning of the message for the less experienced user.

2.   Messages should be constructed using short, meaningful, and common words.

3.   Messages should be concise, factual and be stated in the affirmative and active voice.

4.   Any message that cannot be clearly conveyed within these guidelines should be considered as text.

5. Prior to implementation of any message system, the meaning and instructions should be verified by user to eliminate variability.

6. Sentences should be kept as simple in structure as possible.

7. Number of items to be remembered in one message can be up to 5, but no more than 7.

Abbreviations

1. Abbreviations should only be used where speed of recognition is essential or usage of the full word is not a common form.

2. Standard and commonly accepted abbreviations should be used if available.

3. Abbreviations should not include punctuation.

4. When user/industry specific abbreviations are used,

   a. abbreviations should be consistent;

   b. a dictionary of abbreviations should be available, both online (if possible) and in a hard copy for every user (or in a common user library);

   c. any changes or additions to the list of accepted abbreviations should be approved only once a consensus of the all the effected managers has been reached;

   d. user/industry specific abbreviations should be distinct from standard and commonly accepted abbreviations.

5. Prior to implementation of nonstandard abbreviations, user/industry abbreviations should be evaluated by user(s) to establish conformity of its distinct meaning.

ALPHABETICAL AND/OR NUMERICAL SYMBOLS

1. Each character (any conventional mark, sign or symbol) within the display should be uniquely designed to avoid similarity of characters.

   Example: The I and the **1** are clearly distinguishable as in this sentence.

2. For a given font (an assortment of printing type of a specific size or style), it should be possible to clearly distinguish between the following characters:

                                    X and K
                                    O and Q
                                    T and Y
                                    S and 5
                                    I and L
                                    U and V
                                    I and 1

Character Size and Proportion

1. Character height should be 16 minutes of arc to 26.8 minutes of arc, with 20 minutes of arc preferred.

2. The ratio between character height and character width should be from a low of 1:1 to a maximum of 5:3. For example,if the character is 1 inch in height the width should be between 3/5 of an inch to 1 inch.

3. The ratio between character height and stroke width (the width of the line that makes up the character) should range between 5:1 to 8:1.

4. The minimum spacing between characters directly following one another should be one stroke width. An example of this is in the word STROKE. If the characters were too close together the word would appear to be connected. Any more than one stroke width would be too much space.

5. The minimum spacing between words should be one character width. Any more than one character width would appear to be too much space.

6. Spacing between lines should range from 50%-150% of the character height.

    Examples :

    50% Spacing: This is fifty percent spacing.

    100% Spacing: This is one-hundred percent spacing.

    150% Spacing: This is one-hundred and fifty percent spacing.

Character Case

1. Labels or statements should be in capital letters.

2. Text, with the exception of labels, should be printed according to in upper and lower case letters.

    Example of a label: TELEPHONE
    Example of text: This telephone requires money to be operated.

SCREEN ORGANIZATION AND LAYOUT

Screen size

1. The screen (computer display) should allow the user to read the smallest sized target or characters with 100% accuracy.

2. The farther away the viewer is away from the screen, the larger the screen dimensions should be to accommodate the distance.

Grouping

1. Information that is constantly being used together should be grouped in an orderly fashion so that it is easily obtained.

2. Information should be organized so that information used most frequently is the most easily to obtained.

3. Information should be grouped according to its function. A task analysis (Chapter 2) will suggest the displays that should be grouped together.

4. When grouping together displays, they should be grouped by the level of importance or sequence of use in performing the task. A task analysis (Chapter 2) will suggest the order of importance and the sequence of usage.

5. All displayed data necessary to support a subtask should be grouped together, if a task analysis suggests that performance will be improved.

6. Grouping similar items increases performance by decreasing search time.

Display Density

1. The ratio of screen displayed information to empty space should be no more than 50%, and preferably less than 25%.

2. Grouping of information and displays decreases clutter.

3. Avoid displaying information on screen that is unnecessary (e.g., programmer's or sysop's notes) to the user's task.

4. All data related to one task should be placed on a single screen whenever possible.

5. Information on the screen should be limited to what the user needs to perform the task.

Windows (division of the screen into sections)

1. Windows should have, thick, easily distinguishable borders.

2. Tiling windows should have 3 to 5 columns of blank spacing between them, if the screen size allows it.

3. Specific areas of the window should be reserved for information such as commands, status messages, menu bars, and input fields; these areas should be consistent on all screens.

4. Windows should be expandable to allow viewing of all the information within that window.

Screen Specifications

1. Specific areas of the screen should be reserved for information such as commands, status messages, menu bars, and input fields (user input); these areas should be consistent on all screens.

2. The display layout and the input/output formats should be agreed on by the managers of all of the design teams in order to insure consistency.

3. Items such as page number indicators and the time and the date should be placed at the same location at the top of each display page.

4. The first four lines (at least) should be reserved for information such as alarm messages, error messages or other information that is urgent and required for the completion of the task.

5. Procedures for user actions should be verified to be understood by all users.

6. Every screen should have a unique identification or a title to distinguish it from other screens and identify its function in completing the task.

7. Screen titles should be on a separate line from the text.

8. Status information should be displayed near the top-right corner of the screen.

9. Location information should be on display at all times to reduce time spent by searching for that information.

10. If color is intended to indicate *function*, then colors should indicate the state of the system.

11. Colors with high contrast to the background should be selected for symbols and features that must "catch" the user's attention.

12. In general, backgrounds should be darker than foregrounds.

13. Extreme color contrasts should be avoided.

14. Colors should be specified as a precise wavelength rather than a hue (red, green,violet, etc.).

15. Difference in brightness should not be used as a coding mechanism. However, if you have no other choice, then use a more saturated color.

16. Each color should represent only one category of displayed data.

Screen Coding

Number of Colors

1. If color discrimination is required, do not use more than eight colors.

2. A one-color format can be used if the highlight/flash is twice as intense as the rest of the display.

Maintenance of Colors

1. Do not use colored illumination with color-coded CRT's.

2. Color displays should be periodically adjusted to maintain proper registration of images.

Color Applications for Mimics

1 Choose colors that the users can identify the objects with.

2. Show the users different storyboards showing the objects in different colors and get a consensus before assigning any colors.

Misuse of Color

1. More than 8 colors may make a screen confusing or unpleasant to use.

2. Color codes should not be contrary to color meanings that already exist in the user's job.

3. Color codes should not be contrary to color stereotypes (e.g., red for go and green for stop).

Shape Coding

1. Shape coding should be used for visual separation and discrimination between different categories of data on graphic displays.

2. Sets of shapes should be limited to a maximum of 15 different symbols.

3. When shape coding is used, storyboards of the basic symbols should be shown to users prior to design and should be 100% identifiable by every user

4. Symbols should subtend a minimum of 20 minutes of arc.

5. The stroke width to height ratio should be 1:8 or 1:10 for symbols of 0.4 in or larger when viewed up to a distance of 7 ft.

6. A drawn, painted, etched, or projected structure, representing a scene or an object should be shown to the users and determined to have the same meanings to all of the users.

7. Standard symbols used to represent equipment components should be used in piping and instrumentation drawings.

8. No more than 20 different symbols should be used.

9. Symbols should be solid forms without unnecessary detail.

10. Redundant visual features should be minimized between members of a symbol set.

11. Graphic coding methods should be used to present standardized qualitative information to the user or to draw their attention to a particular portion of the display.

Coding Redundancy

1. Redundant coding (e.g., color and shape) increases performance, particularly on search tasks.

2. When speed of comprehension and detection is important, graphical/pictorial/iconic coding should be used rather than text messages.

3. Multidimensional coding of displays is recommended, given the task supports multidimensional coding, and given that the user is not under conditions of heavy workload.

Standardization

1. The assignment of shape codes should be consistent for all displays and should be based upon an established standard, or agreed on by a consensus of the managers of all of the design teams.

Mixing Symbols and Words

1. Words and symbols should not be used alternately.

2. Equipment components, process flow, or signal paths should be indicated using pictorial symbols. Numerical or coded data should reflect inputs and outputs associated with equipment.

Labeling Conventions

1. When letters are used, perhaps to supply footnotes for symbols, upper and lower case letters should be used to improve readability.

2. For search and identification tasks, or whenever there is any doubt as to whether some users will be able to understand the symbol, both symbolic and word labels should be used.

3. When using pictorial symbols of what function is being used (e.g., an icon of an open book with a "D" on it might be the symbol for the dictionary or spell check function), keep the symbols as simple as possible, and keep it consistent with any included features that are currently being utilized.

Pictorial Symbol/ICON

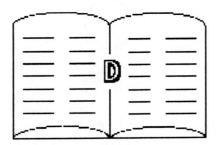

Don't use two symbols that look very similar to mean two different things.

Dictionary   Thesaurus

4.   Sufficient lumination should be provided so the user is able to identify what is on the display screen from the maximum viewing distance.

5.   The symbols should always be in the proper/natural orientation to decrease comprehension time.

6.   Icons (pictorial symbols) should not be used when display resolution is low.

7.   If there is a doubt about what the icon means, the icon should be redesigned. Icons by their very nature are meant to be self-explanatory

Magnitude

1.   When symbols are sized differently as a means of coding, all intermediate symbols should be spaced logarithmically between the first and last symbol (large » small). This saves space on your screen.

   <u>**Example:**</u>

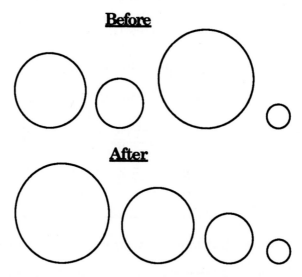

2.   When the symbol size is proportional to the data value, the area in which the symbol will be represented should be a scaled parameter, rather than a linear dimension.

3.   For area coding (the use of one symbol that increases its total area or size as a means of coding), a maximum of all six sizes should be used. It is recommended that only three be used.

Example:

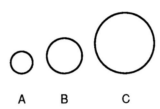

       A   B   C

4.   Length coding is quite similar to area coding, except that you merely change the height-to-width ratio. Again, the maximum number of sizes to be used should be six, with only three sizes recommended.

Example:

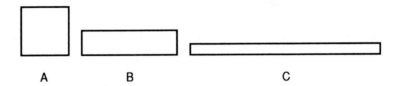

      A   B   C

5.   Size coding should be used only when displays are not crowded. It takes quite a bit of space to properly use size coding, and if your display is already crowded, size crowding will make the display harder to understand, increasing the probability of errors.

Example:

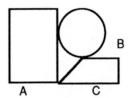

      A   C

6.   When size coding is used, each next larger symbol should be at least 1.5 times the height of the one before it.

Example:

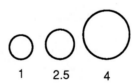

    1   2.5   4

Mimic Displays

1.   A mimic should contain just the minimum amount of detail required to yield a meaningful pictorial representation.

2.   Abstract symbols should conform to common electrical and mechanical symbol conventions whenever possible.

3.   Differential line widths should be used to code flowpaths.

4.   Mimic lines should not overlap.

5.   Flow directions should be clearly indicated by distinctive arrowheads.

6.   All mimic origin points should be labeled or begin at labeled components.

7.   All mimic destination or terminal points should be labeled or end at labeled components.

8.   Components representations on mimic lines should be identified.

9.   Identification of components should be consistent throughout the display.

Brightness

1.   No more than three levels of brightness coding should be used, with two levels preferred. For example, a data form might combine dim data with bright labels to facilitate display scanning.

2.   Brightness coding can be used to differentiate between an item of information and information next to it.

3.   High brightness levels should be used to signify information of primary importance, and lower levels should be used to signify information of secondary interest or to further describe the information at a higher contrast.

   Example:

   IMPORTANT: Extreme caution should be used when operating this machine.

4.   Brightness coding should not be used in with shape or size coding. This could cause confusion and could increase the probability   of error.

<u>**Wrong**</u>   <u>**Correct**</u>

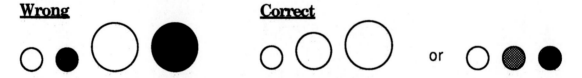

5.   When an operation is to be performed on a single item or a display, the item should be highlighted, as well as the option chosen.

6.   When graphical symbols or icons are close together on the screen, icons
      should be displayed in reverse video when selected.

Blink

1.   Blink coding should be limited to small areas on the display screen. The area
      should be large enough to attract the attention of the user, but not so large
      that it becomes annoying.

2.   The blink rate should be in the range of 0.1 Hz (once every 10 seconds) to 5 Hz
      (five times per second), with 2 to 3 Hz preferred. A blink rate of less than 0.1
      Hz will be unnoticeable, 8 to 12 Hz may cause nausea, and blink rates of
      approximately 12 to 20 Hz can induce seizures in people who suffer from
      photoepilepsy. Blink rates above 50 Hz will appear as a constant light rather
      than a blink.

3.   The minimum "on" time should be 50 milliseconds.

4.   If different blink rates are going to be used as a coding method, no more than
      two blink rates should be used.

5.   When two blink rates are used, the fast blink rate should approximate 4 Hz
      (four per second), and the slow rate should be 1 Hz (one per second).

6.   When two blink rates are used, the faster rate should apply to the most
      critical information.

7.   When two blink rates are used, the "on-off" ratio should be 50%.

8.   A means should be provided for suppressing the blink action once the coded
      data has been located.

9.   The "off" time on the blink rate should never be used to attract attention to a
      message.

10.   Blink coding should be reserved for emergency conditions or those situations
      requiring immediate action.

11.   When blink coding is used to mark a data item that needs to be read, an extra
      symbol (such as an asterisk) should be added as a blinking marker rather
      than blinking the item itself. This goes along with Guideline #1 under Blink
      Rates that says to keep blinking to small areas on the display screen.

12.   Blink coding should not be used with long-persistence phosphor displays.
      Long-persistence phosphor displays glow for a relatively long time before
      needing another charge of energy. This will cause the blinking to seem
      slower than it is, and thus defeat the purpose.

Reverse Video

1.   Reverse video (dark characters on a light background) should be used primarily for highlighting when the display screen has a lot of information on it.

> **See Sam.   See Sam run.**
> Run Sam run. Sam ran into the
> street, but forgot to look for any
> passing cars. Now Sam is as flat as
> a pancake, as any other roadkill is.

2.   Reverse video can be used to code display panel information that requires immediate response.

3.   Reverse video is the best way of getting maximum contrast between highlighted and nonhighlighted items.

AUDITORY DISPLAYS

Auditory displays should be used when,

1.   the information requires immediate attention or signals an emergency, situation.

2.   the usual visual display is overloaded,

3.   there are limitations on the lighting conditions of the room,

4.   during natural disasters such as earthquakes and tornadoes,

5.   the user is away from the terminal and cannot see the display screen.

Audio System Reliability and Testing

1.   Audio display devices and circuits should prevent false alarms.

2.   Audio displays should be able to run self-testing on their operability.

3.   Audio displays should be compatible with the surrounding conditions in which they are used.

4.   Audio displays should be distinct from sounds in the surrounding in which they are used.

Criteria for Audio Signal Selection

1.   If a signal type is commonly associated with a certain type of activity, it should not be used for other purposes. The auditory display should be similar to alarms the user has experience with.

2.   Only those errors that require rapid decision-making and intervention should activate the alarms.

3.   Early signs of a minor problem in the system should be identified by a low-level alarm since response time is not as critical.

4.   In some operations, it may be desirable to preprogram a hierarchy of alarms that could be altered if changes were to be made in the future.

5.   Each time one of the major system failures is detected and triggers an alarm, it should be possible to program the computer to display specific information concerning the problem areas.

6.   Quantity of alarms may be reduced by functional grouping.

Feedback

1.   Once the user has responded to an alarm by use of a control, such as a reset button, feedback should be indicated on the screen to acknowledge that action has been taken.

Audio Signal Integration with Visual Displays

1.   When used in conjunction with visual displays, audio warning devices should be used to alert and direct the user's attention to the visual display that is affected by the problem.

Criteria for Audio/Visual Signal Selection

1.   The frequency range of audio warning signals should be between 200 and 5000 Hz and, if possible, between 500 and 3000 Hz.

2.   If the user will be performing tasks at a considerable distance from the visual display, the auditory signal should be loud but of low frequency (less than 1000 Hz).

3.   If the user goes into another room or behind partitions, the signal should be of low frequency (below 500 Hz).

4.   The signal should be of a frequency that will not be masked by background noise.

5. If an auditory signal must attract attention and the previously mentioned guidelines are inadequate, the signal should be modulated.

6. The intensity, duration, and location of audio alarms and signals should be compatible with the location of the user and the situation.

7. Audio warning signals should not be of such intensity as to cause discomfort or ringing in the ears as an aftereffect.

Control

1. Controls for response to an alarm system should include silence, reset, and test modes.

2. The alarm should cease only after the user turns it off.

3. In the primary work area, the user should be able to turn off an auditory signal.

4. When acknowledged, the alarm control should terminate any blinking lights or warning signs. However, a steady illumination of warning signs should be maintained until the alarm is completely cleared.

5. Individual acknowledgment control should be assigned to each workstation to avoid any confusion as to where the alarm originated.

6. The reset control should silence any auditory signal indicating clearance and should extinguish the illumination of warning signs.

7. The reset control should be effective only at the workstation for the annunciator panel where the alarm initiated.

8. The test control should activate the auditory signal and flashing illumination of all tiles/windows in a panel. This will ensure that the working condition of each individual tile/window is being examined.

9. Periodic testing of annunciators should be required and controlled by administrative procedure.

Screen Formatting

Borders

1. Borders can be used to improve the readability of a blocks of numbers or letters.

2. If several labels or messages are clustered in the same area, distinctive borders should be placed around the critical ones only.

Spacing

1.   When a special symbol is used to mark a word, it should be separated by a space from the beginning of the word.

Dynamic Display of Information

Display Motion

1.   The speed of a graphic showing fluid flow in a pipe should be greater than 7.28 mm/s (0.29 in./s) but less than 295 mm/s (11.8 in./s).

2.   Changing values that identify rate of change or gross values should not be updated faster than 5 seconds nor slower than 2 seconds when the display is to be considered as real time.

3.   A display freeze mode should be provided to allow close scrutiny of any selected screen.

Appendix B: Training Assessment

This appendix provides software and system managers with a checklist for assessing the validity of any training program in their facility. The checklist can also be used by software course developers and evaluators for determining whether critical components needed for a successful and valid training program are adequately addressed. Training is an extremely important aspect of systems effectiveness since the behavior of people may have a dramatic impact on the performance of any particular system. Most training programs are never formally or statistically validated, hence many training development efforts may not do what they were intended. The cost to perform a validation assessment is quite small, particularly in the context of the total expense to develop and present a training effort.

Content Validity

Content validity refers to the comprehensiveness of the training program. This includes the topics presented and the degree to which all critical concepts and behaviors, necessary for the job to be performed acceptably and safely, are covered in the developed course.

To insure that a particular training program has a "high" value of content validity, one must first execute a training requirements analysis, based on an in-depth task analysis and an in-depth user profile analysis (Chapter 2). After the desired key tasks are identified, one must form a ratio: (the number of tasks addressed in the training program) divided by (the number of key task identified in the task analysis):

$$C.V. = \sum T_i / \sum A_k$$

where:

T_i = the number of key tasks identified in the task analysis
A_k = the number of tasks addressed in the training program

The equation should produce a value which approaches 1.0. In essence, a derived value of 1.0 means that all of the critical tasks identified and have been included into the training program. Most training programs do not address this very basic consideration, simply assuming that their training activities have an adequate level of content validity. Figure B-1 illustrates that there must be a one to one match between the task analyses items and the training course content.

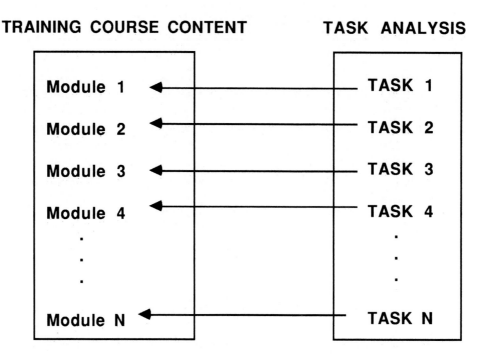

Figure B-1: One to One Mapping of Task Analysis to Training Content

Predictive Validity

Predictive validity is a reflects the degree of relationship between a student's class room score and the student's measured performance on the job. In theory, one would expect that people who perform well in a training program would do well when placed on the job. Predictive validity is not estimated, it is measured and assessed using a correlation coefficient. Predictive validity can be calculated using the following equation:

where:

$$r = \sum XY/Ns_x s_y$$

X = an individual's score on a training test
Y = the same person's rated or measured job performance after training
s_x = the standard deviation of the mean of x
s_y = the standard deviation of the mean of y
N = the total number of paired x and y scores.

Thus, r_{xy} reflects the relationship (i.e., correlation) between training achievement (X) and job performance (Y). In practice, a correlation of .85 or higher is considered an adequate degree of predictive validity.

Learning

Learning can be defined as the difference between an individual's pretest (PRE) score and their posttest score (POST). For a group of students, the degree or magnitude of learning is defined as the sum of students' pretest scores subtracted from the sum of their posttest scores. Typically, the mean for each test is calculated. The pretest mean is then subtracted from the posttest mean. This mean difference reflects the degree of learning imparted. In most cases, you would normalize the students PRE and POST scores, since there is more likely more variability inherent in the PRE score data. Statistically stated:

$$L = (\sum X_{Post}/N) - (\sum X_{Pre}/N)$$

where

> L = the degree of learning measured in relative units
> N = the number of students
> X_{Post} = the sum of all posttest scores
> X_{Pre} = the sum of all pretest scores.

Before the class begins the students are all pretested to determine how much they already know. The group mean of this pretest distribution is reflected in $\mu 1$. After the course, they are tested again to obtain the posttest group mean $\mu 2$. By simply subtracting $\mu 1$ from $\mu 2$, we are able to determine the difference in learning which has occurred as a result of the training. We can also use a t-test (Pagano, 1981; pgs. 315-341) to determine whether the difference observed between the two means is statistically significant/reliable.

Another definition of learning is the measured decrease in the variability of response to a particular stimulus. In essence, if a group of individuals is asked to perform some task without specific training, a rather large degree of response variability relative to a group who has received training will be observed. The relative reduction in the variability of scores or behavior is an indication of how much "learning" has taken place.

Training Efficiency

Training efficiency refers to the ratio of "number of people trained" to the cost of providing the training. As the dollar cost per training session is reduced, or as the time required to perform the training is reduced, relative efficiency increases. Training efficiency can be computed using the following formula:

$$E = \sum N / \sum C$$

where:

E   =   efficiency
ΣN =   the sum of all people trained
ΣC =   the sum of costs and/or time connected with the training.

Training Effectiveness

Training effectiveness (**T_e**)is the product of efficiency and validity. For example, if the efficiency of a particular training effort was 0.5, and the predictive validity of a training program was found to be .61, then the effectiveness would be (0.61 * 0.5) = 0.30. Assuming the same efficiency for a new course, which has a predictive validity of 0.94 , the increased training effectiveness score is: 0.94 * 0.5 = .47   Hence, we observe a 55% increase in effectiveness : 0.47 - 0.305 = .164/.304 = 55%! A perfect training effectiveness score would approach or exceed the value of 1.0. In practice, however, most **T_e** scores exceeding a value of 0.5 would be satisfactory.

The equation:

$$T_e = r \times E$$

reflects the degree to which a particular training program is effective. Where **r** is the validity coefficient, and **E** is the efficiency of training.

Note of Caution: Many managers feel that training, with its high cost and time requirements, is the most important aspect of their operation, in order to obtain high quality compliance or quality products. Unfortunately, this philosophy has generated a general deterioration of product quality and, in the case of DoE and DoD, a failure to comply with federal rules and regulations. The most important aspect of any operation is the interaction of criterion selected people using well designed tools and equipment to execute clearly defined and well thought out tasks with a set of unambiguous, valid procedures that are readable and compatible with the people, tools, tasks, and the training program. See Figure B-2.

This simple figure illustrates that any level in the system may cause quality problems regardless of how good the training program might be. For example, if you have a perfect training program, with a training effectiveness score of 1.5, but the people were poorly selected, the tools are difficult to use, the tasks required of the workers were ill planned and thought out, the procedures are unreadable, and the management does not really care, training alone will not provide adequate product quality or compliance.

A "total-systems" approach must be taken to identify discrepancies that contribute to degraded performance. Then, and only then, you can attempt to upgrade each system element including training. If you attempt to improve training alone, you may end up spending much money and time to realize only a small increment in total system performance and/or safety.

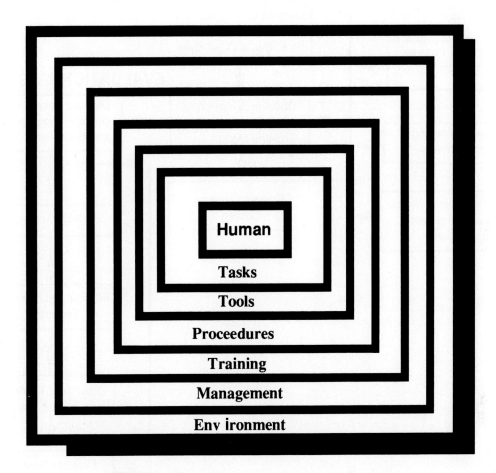

Figure B-2: Systems Concept of Training

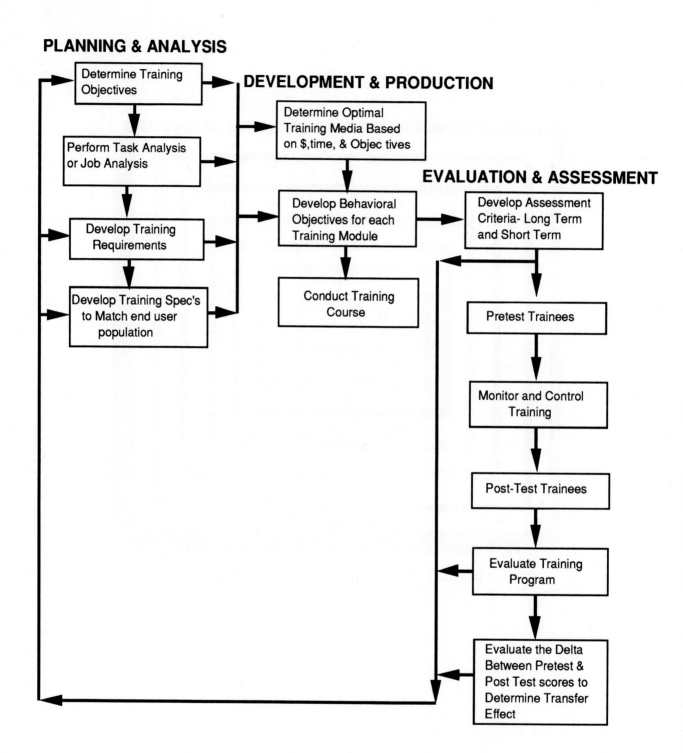

Figure B-3: Objectives-Driven Training Model

The Training Model

The most comprehensive literature available on the subject of training development and evaluation is written by Professor Irwin L. Goldstein . Another excellent book is the Training and Development Handbook edited by Robert L. Craig. However, this handbook is lengthy and would require considerable time to read.

Figure B-3 offers a training model that has various dimensional requirements and phases, which can be audited, assessed or implemented. The next section presents an easy to use checklist of items that are essential in the production of a high quality training program.

Checklist for Developing Training Programs

The checklist items which follow were chosen because they contribute to the goal of developing a training program that is observable, measurable, and testable" for quality. Emphasis is placed on items that would enhance the probability of a training program meeting the customer's needs (specifications and requirements). The checklist also addresses the issue of cost by identifying items that would lessen training program deficiencies or detect them early in the development phase when course modification is less expensive.

It is suggested that the checklist be reviewed before the start of each phase and checked off before moving to the next phase. The items listed in each phase may not be applicable to every situation. The evaluation team must decide which items are critical for the success of the training program.

1.0   DATA GATHERING PHASE

1.1   Identification of resources and target audience.

1.1.1   _ _ _   Managers of involved departments are identified.

1.1.2   _ _ _   Subject-matter experts are identified.

1.1.3   _ _ _   Target audience size is identified.

1.1.4   _ _ _   Target audience education level is identified.

1.1.5   _ _ _   Target audience experience level is identified.

1.1.6   _ _ _   Target audience job responsibilities are identified.

1.1.7   _ _ _   Target audience location and time constraints for training are identified.

1.1.8   _ _ _   Target audience members are identified.

1.1.9   _ _ _   An implementation plan has been developed containing a schedule, cost projection and milestones for review and delivery.

1.2   Gathering job-task and subject matter information.

1.2.1   _ _ _   Purpose, goal, and objectives of the job to be trained is identified.

1.2.2   _ _ _   Job is broken down into major functions.

1.2.3   _ _ _   Each function is broken down into tasks.

1.2.4   _ _ _   Each task can be measured or quantified during evaluation.

1.2.5   _ _ _   Frequency, difficulty and importance of each task are identified.

1.2.6   _ _ _   Aptitudes, skills, and knowledge necessary to perform the task are identified.

1.2.7   _ _ _   New concepts, skills or technologies are related to existing job functions and tasks.

1.2.8   _ _ _   Conceptual frameworks for tasks are identified.

1.2.9   Human factors aspects of the equipment and tasks are identified.

1.2.10   _ _ _   Existing procedures and documentation relating to the job has been reviewed.

1.2.11   _ _ _   Course developers have mastered the subject matter to be taught.

1.3   Determine the reasons and justification for a training program.

1.3.1   _ _ _   Knowledge or skill discrepancies are present and identified.

1.3.2   _ _ _   Knowledge or skill discrepancies are caused by knowledge or skill deficiencies.

1.3.3   _ _ _   Human errors in produced product can be reduced with training.

1.3.4   _ _ _   Student's personal safety will be enhanced with training.

1.3.5   _ _ _   Worker or systems productivity will be increased with training.

1.3.6   _ _ _   Litigation and law suits can be reduced with training.

1.3.7   ___   Employee turnover can be reduced with training.

1.3.8   ___   Satisfactory or good performance can be improved with training.

1.3.9   ___   Cost-benefit study shows that training will save the organization money.

1.3.10   ___   Training will make the employees job easier, more interesting and more rewarding.

1.3.11   ___   The organization will comply with existing laws, statues, or orders.

2.0   DATA ANALYSIS PHASE

2.1   Identification of tasks for training.

2.1.1   ___   Critical tasks for which training is required are identified.

2.1.2   ___   Prerequisite skills or knowledge required for training are identified.

2.1.3   ___   Tasks which will be taught and learned on the job are identified.

2.1.4   ___   Tasks are arranged into a sequential flow.

2.1.5   ___   Background information is integrated into the sequential flow.

2.1.6   ___   New and existing tasks and procedures are merged.

2.1.7   ___   Tasks are ranked according to frequency, difficulty, and importance.

2.1.8   ___   Risks (probability and consequences) associated with the job or tasks have been identified.

2.1.9   ___   Academic, administrative and systems specific knowledge requirements associated with each task have been identified and recorded.

2.2   Definition of goals and objectives.

2.2.1   ___   A general statement (goal) of what the training should achieve is developed and broken down into operationally defined terms of behavioral objectives.

2.2.2   ___   Training goals are linked to organizational objectives.

2.2.3   _ _ _   Performance objectives are defined for each goal (also called *terminal objectives*).

2.2.4   _ _ _   Performance objectives include a state of performance, the conditions under which performance is measured and the measurement criteria for acceptable performance.

2.2.5   _ _ _   Broad performance objectives have sublevel objectives of narrower scope (also called *enabling objectives*).

2.2.6   _ _ _   Method of measure or evaluate performance objectives is determined.

2.2.7   _ _ _   Objectives which will be covered in the training, but not measured are identified (also called *design objectives*).

2.3   Identification of instructional methods and media.

2.3.1   _ _ _   Knowledge objectives are presented in lecture or text format.

2.3.2   _ _ _   Knowledge objectives are reinforced by activities such as discussions, question and answer sessions, or role-playing workshops.

2.3.3   _ _ _   Skills objectives are presented in demonstration format (live or filmed).

2.3.4   _ _ _   Skills objectives are reinforced by hands-on workshops.

2.3.5   _ _ _   Large target audiences have procedures manuals and reference cards (job aids) to augment reduced personal attention.

2.3.6   _ _ _   Existing manuals and reference cards are used (or modified) if appropriate.

2.3.7   _ _ _   Training manuals are useful for on the job reference.

2.3.8   _ _ _   Simulators are used when real experience is not feasible.

2.4   Course outline development.

2.4.1   _ _ _   The first part of the outline is an introduction.

2.4.2   _ _ _   The introduction explains what the course is about.

2.4.3   _ _ _   The introduction describes the course objectives.

2.4.4   _ _ _   The introduction tells what the students' materials are and how the students are expected to use them.

2.4.5   _ _ _   The introduction gives any special information on facilities and equipment.

2.4.6   _ _ _   The second part is a conceptual overview of the subject matter.

2.4.7   _ _ _   The third part is the major topics and subtopics and associated instructional and evaluative methods.

2.4.8   _ _ _   The last part is the summary, review, and final evaluation.

2.4.9   _ _ _   Course is organized in a logical manner.

2.4.10   _ _ _   Course is organized around clearly defined objectives.

2.4.11   _ _ _   Course deals with what happens and why, not just with how.

3.0   SOLUTION DEVELOPMENT PHASE

3.1   Presentation material development (lecture, visual aids, technical manuals).

3.1.1   _ _ _   All sections of the outline that need presentation materials are identified.

3.1.2   _ _ _   Existing presentation materials are used if appropriate.

3.1.3   _ _ _   Oral presentations are complimented with visual aids.

3.1.4   _ _ _   Training aids are appropriate.

3.1.5   _ _ _   Training aids are simple.

3.1.6   _ _ _   Training aids are accurate.

3.1.7   _ _ _   Training aids are portable/durable.

3.1.8   _ _ _   Training aids are manageable.

3.1.9   _ _ _   Training aids are attractive.

3.1.10   _ _ _   Training aids are necessary.

3.1.11   _ _ _   Storyboards (small draft of each image with brief text to describe accompanying narration) are developed for each visual aid.

3.1.12   _ _ _   Each story board is limited to six sentences.

3.1.13   ___   Full size drafts of each story board were used to validate the visual aid.

3.1.14   ___   Final presentation materials is professional quality.

3.1.15   ___   Lettering on slides and transparencies are at least 1 inch tall for every 30 feet of room depth.

3.1.16   ___   Blank spaces between lines on slides and transparencies are 1-1/2 the letter height.

3.1.17   ___   Lettering on flip charts is 3 inches high using broad tip pen.

3.1.18   ___   Instructor's notes are prepared for each section of the outline.

3.1.19   ___   Instructor's notes include content of course covered in each section, broken down into steps.

3.1.20   ___   Instructor's notes include reference to presentation material, student materials, equipment, and supplies for each step.

3.2   Student material development (workbooks, simulation workshop materials, exercises, evaluation exams and questionnaires).

3.2.1   ___   Student materials are packed for ease of distribution.

3.2.2   ___   Handout type is varied.

3.2.3   ___   Outline is distributed prior to lecture.

3.2.4   ___   Material essential to discussion is distributed prior to discussion.

3.2.5   ___   Summaries are distributed after lecture.

3.2.6   ___   Supplementary material is distributed after lecture.

3.2.7   ___   Student evaluation material is prepared for each performance objective identified as needing evaluation.

3.2.8   ___   Test questions match the objectives and the instructions.

3.2.9   ___   Multiple choice questions are used to test recognition, recall, comprehension, application and analysis.

3.2.10   ___   Completion questions are used to test recall, comprehension, application, and analysis.

3.2.11   _ _ _   Essay questions are used to test recall, comprehension, application, and analysis.

3.2.12   _ _ _   Matching questions are used to test recognition, comprehension and application.

3.2.13   _ _ _   True-false questions are used to test recognition, comprehension, application and analysis.

3.2.14   _ _ _   Labeling questions are used to test recognition and recall.

3.2.15   _ _ _   Course evaluation form is prepared.

3.2.16   _ _ _   Students respond actively to the material in a way that is relevant to the training purpose.

3.2.17   _ _ _   Students receive immediate and unambiguous feedback as to the correctness of their responses.

3.2.18   _ _ _   Training process does not increase student's anxiety.

3.3   Administrative materials development (course schedules, student rosters, room reservations, equipment and facilities preparation).

3.3.1   _ _ _   Reservation system is set up for training rooms and equipment.

3.3.2   _ _ _   Student rosters and student profiles are prepared in advance.

3.3.3   _ _ _   Course schedules allow prerequisite courses to be taken first.

3.3.4   _ _ _   Instructor's guide enables a person with subject knowledge or skill to implement the course materials in the manner intended.

3.3.5   _ _ _   Self-paced material has a guide for administrator or student on how to use material.

3.4   Course material validation.

3.4.1   _ _ _   Course materials are accurate.

3.4.2   _ _ _   Course materials are clear.

3.4.3   _ _ _   Course materials are relevant.

3.4.4   _ _ _   Course materials are internally consistent.

3.4.5   _ _ _   Course objectives meet course goals.

3.4.6   ___   Enabling objectives match terminal objectives.

3.4.7   ___   Evaluation material matches objectives and instructional materials.

3.4.8   ___   Course materials are legible.

3.4.9   ___   Course materials are appealing.

3.4.10   ___   Course material is organized in a logical manner.

3.4.11   ___   Course material provides practice, reinforcement, and feedback.

4.0   CONDUCT TRAINING PHASE

4.1   Pilot test.

4.1.1   ___   Pilot group is representative of the target audience.

4.1.2   ___   Pilot group is informed that they are a pilot group to encourage candid comments.

4.1.3   ___   Pilot group includes technical and user experts.

4.1.4   ___   Pilot group includes users of different experience levels.

4.1.5   ___   Pilot group participates in rather than evaluates the training.

4.1.6   ___   Commitment to the pilot test is encouraged by telling the pilot group that the course was designed to meet their needs.

4.1.7   ___   The pilot group is prepared in advance with work that relates to the course.

4.1.8   ___   Invitation to participate in the pilot course is a form of positive recognition.

4.1.9   ___   Pilot test is not observed to prevent upsetting the group dynamics.

4.1.10   ___   Pilot is conducted in a manner as close to the intended final design as possible.

4.1.11   ___   Number of telephone assistance is provided for pilot self-paced classes.

4.1.12   ___   Objectives are clear.

4.1.13   ___   Student's performance is demonstrated.

4.1.14   ___   Instructor's performance is demonstrated.

4.1.15   ___   Time allocation is appropriate.

4.1.16   ___   Training strategies, material, and equipment are adequate.

4.1.17   ___   Facilities and logistics are adequate.

4.1.18   ___   Transportation is adequate.

4.1.19   ___   Administration and management is adequate.

4.2   Scheduling

4.2.1   ___   Course is not scheduled for Monday morning or Friday afternoon.

4.2.2   ___   Course session does not run longer than four hours.

4.2.3   ___   Six hour session is broken into 2 three-hour sessions.

4.2.4   ___   Half day session is scheduled in the morning.

4.2.5   ___   Sessions longer than 2 hours have 10-minute breaks every hour.

4.2.6   ___   Course date does not interfere with student's work responsibilities.

4.2.7   ___   Multiple sessions are not scheduled too far apart.

4.2.8   ___   Opening to break session is short, light, easy, motivates learning.

4.2.9   ___   Break to lunch session is heavy learning and input.

4.2.10   ___   Long breaks or lunches are avoided.

4.2.11   ___   After lunch to break session is short, heavy learning and
concentrated learning activity.

4.2.12   ___   Break to close session is very participative and active learning.

4.3   Environment.

4.3.1   ___   Desks or chairs are arranged in U shape or circle to facilitate
discussion.

4.3.2   ___   Group cohesiveness is developed.

4.3.3   ___   Coffee and light refreshments are provided.

4.3.4   _ _ _   Smoking is not permitted in class. Smoking area is provided during breaks.

4.3.5   _ _ _   Quiet cubicle is provided for self-paced courses with good access to needed equipment.

4.3.6   _ _ _   Comfortable chairs and tables are provided for courses over one hour.

4.3.7   _ _ _   Tables are provided when books or binders are used.

4.3.8   _ _ _   Lighting pattern provides at least 70 footcandles at table height when reading and writing are required.

4.3.9   _ _ _   Lighting pattern provides at lease 50 footcandles for note-taking.

4.3.10   _ _ _   Lighting is at comfortable levels.

4.3.11   _ _ _   Room temperature is comfortable.

4.3.12   _ _ _   Distracting lighting, noise, extraneous materials, traffic is avoided.

4.4   Media.

4.4.1   _ _ _   Media equipment is in good working order.

4.4.2   _ _ _   Media equipment does not block any student's view.

4.4.3   _ _ _   Screen or visual aid can be seen by all students.

4.4.4   _ _ _   Light are dimmed but not off during slide or film presentation (so that students can see to take notes).

4.5   Workshops and demonstrations.

4.5.1   _ _ _   Demonstration is separate from students attempts.

4.5.2   _ _ _   Everyone can see the demonstration.

4.5.3   _ _ _   Details that cannot be seen during demonstration are covered by another method.

4.5.4   _ _ _   Computer demonstrations are done with large screen data projectors, slides or networking to students terminals rather than clustering class around one terminal.

4.5.5   _ _ _   Workshop allows faster students to move on, while allowing slower students to take the time they need.

4.5.6   _ _ _   Materials needed for the workshop are prepared in advance.

4.6   Instructional style.

4.6.1   _ _ _   There is no hierarchical difference between trainer and students.

4.6.2   _ _ _   Instructor is relaxed, calm and natural.

4.6.3   _ _ _   Instructor displays his name and introduces himself to the class.

4.6.4   _ _ _   Instructor identifies and introduces topic to the class.

4.6.5   _ _ _   Instructor provides performance objectives to class (oral or written).

4.6.6   _ _ _   Instructor explains how the material is to be used.

4.6.7   _ _ _   Instructor explains why the material needs to be learned.

4.6.8   _ _ _   Instructor motivates and displays enthusiasm for the subject matter.

4.6.9   _ _ _   Instructor motivates interest and stimulates curiosity in the students.

4.6.10   _ _ _   Instructor displays adequate knowledge of subject matter.

4.6.11   _ _ _   Instructor demonstrates evidence of careful planning with comprehensive syllabus, handouts, schedule, and course requirements.

4.6.12   _ _ _   Instructor adapts material to the level of the class.

4.6.13   _ _ _   Instructor listens to individual student's questions and stated needs.

4.6.14   _ _ _   Instructor analyzes student errors and provides feedback.

4.6.15   _ _ _   Instructor corrects specific individual difficulties.

4.6.16   _ _ _   Instructor is patient, sympathetic, and friendly.

4.6.17   _ _ _   Instructor displays a sense of humor.

4.6.18   _ _ _   Instructor is at ease in social situations.

4.6.19 ___ Instructor is tactful.

4.6.20 ___ Instructor is cooperative, self-reliant, and confident.

4.6.21 ___ Instructor employs voice variance techniques.

4.6.22 ___ Instructor uses appropriate, body gestures and movements that facilitate the presentation and effect being demonstrated.

4.6.23 ___ Instructor maintains eye contact with class.

4.6.24 ___ Instructor maintains professional attitude.

4.6.25 ___ Instructor maintains class control.

4.6.26 ___ Instructor is prepared to use training aids.

4.6.27 ___ Instructor explains training aid to class.

4.6.28 ___ Instructor keeps teaching aid covered when not in use.

4.6.29 ___ Instructor displays material so that all students can see.

4.6.30 ___ Instructor talks directly to the class and not the aid or blackboard.

4.6.31 ___ Instructor does not pass around samples while talking.

4.6.32 ___ Instructor uses a pointer.

4.6.33 ___ Instructor follows instructor's guide.

4.6.34 ___ Instructor encourages questions.

4.6.35 ___ Instructor uses proper questioning technique (ask questions, pause, call on one student by name, emphasize correct answer).

4.6.36 ___ Instructor manages time efficiently.

4.6.37 ___ Instructor reviews lesson adequately.

4.6.38 ___ Instructor checks for student's comprehension.

5.0   EVALUATION AND REVISION PHASE

5.1   Analyze evaluation data.

5.1.1   _ _ _   Method exists to identify portions of the training materials that need revisions.

5.1.2   _ _ _   Importance and relevance of content is assessed.

5.1.3   _ _ _   Value of exercise is assessed.

5.1.4   _ _ _   Timing, pace and length of program is assessed.

5.1.5   _ _ _   Quality of materials is assessed.

5.1.6   _ _ _   Quality of instruction is assessed.

5.1.7   _ _ _   Levels of complexity is assessed.

5.1.8   _ _ _   Objectives are modified as needed.

5.1.9   _ _ _   Course material is modified as needed.

5.1.10   _ _ _   Instructional and evaluation methods are modified as needed.

5.1.11   _ _ _   Course outline is revised to reflect changes.

5.1.12   _ _ _   Instructor's guide is revised to reflect changes.

6.0   SUMMATIVE EVALUATION PHASE

6.1   Quantitative assessment

6.1.1   _ _ _   Improvement is measured by pretest/posttest delta.

6.1.2   _ _ _   Improvement is measured in prior performance discrepancies.

6.1.3   _ _ _   Improvement shown as perceived by employees and management.

6.1.4   _ _ _   Skill gained has been applied to job responsibilities.

6.1.5   _ _ _   Trainees retain the learning.

6.1.6   _ _ _   Training has positive organizational impact.

6.1.7   _ _ _   Trained group performs better than untrained control group.

6.1.8   _ _ _   Results are communicated to the pilot participants so they will know they were listened to.

Bibliography

Bernard, B. and Vaughan, J. (1966) *Training in Industry.* Belmont, CA: Wadsworth Publishing Co., Inc..

Caplette, M. (1988) Back to training basics. *Training and Development Journal.*

Connelly, S.M. (1988) Integrating evaluation, design, and implementation. *Training and Development Journal.*

Craig, R.C. (Ed.), *Training and Development Handbook.* Reading, MA: Addison-Wesley Publishing Co.

Fail safe pilot programs. (1989) *Training and Development Journal.*

Gane, C. (1972) *Managing the Training Function.* London: George Allen and Unwin Ltd.

Gardner, J E. (1981) *Training Interventions in Job Skill Development.* Menlo Park, CA: Addison-Wesley Publishing Co.

Goldstein, I. L. (1974) *Training Program Development and Evaluation.* Monterey, CA: Brooks Cole Publishing Company.

Group-Paced Instructor: Trainee Guide . (1986) (Director of Chief of Naval Technical Training, 1986).

King, D. (1965) *Training Within the Organization.* Chicago, IL: Educational Methods, Inc..

May, L. S., et al. (1987) *Evaluating Business and Industry Training.* Boston, MA.: Kluwer Academic Publishers.

Michalak, D. F. (1979) *Making the Training Process Work.* New York: Harper and Row.

Nadler, L. (1982) *Designing Training Programs.* Reading, MA: Addison-Wesley Publishing.

Pagano, R. R. (1981) *Understanding Statistics in the Behavioral Science.* New York: West Publishing.

Rogoff, R. L. (1987) *The Training Wheel.* New York: John Wiley and Sons.

Training 101. (1989) *Training and Development Journal.*

Appendix C: Display Format Summaries for 32 Representation Techniques

Arithmetic Line Chart (2D)

Description: Chart with two orthogonal axes. The horizontal axis (abscissa) usually indicates time, while the vertical axis (ordinate) indicates values that are a function of the abscissa. Successive data points are connected by a straight line.

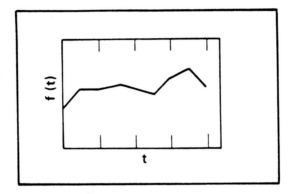

Input Data Type:

Unidimensional
Univariate
Series

Use Category:

Approximate value
Prediction
Pattern recognition

Specific Uses:

* Series with many successive values to be portrayed.
* Close reading and interpolation.
* Emphasis on movement rather than on actual amounts.

Not To Be Used:

* When there are relatively few plotted values in the series.
* When emphasis should be on changes in amounts rather than on movement.
* To emphasize differences between values or amounts on different data.
* When movement of data is extremely violent or irregular.
* When presentation is for popular appeal.

Comments:

* For 3D see Perspective Plot.
* See Schmid or Spear for detailed recommendations.

References:

C. F. Schmid and S. E. Schmid, *Handbook of Graphic Presentation*, 2nd Ed. (New York: John Wiley and Son, 1979), p. 32.
M. E. Spear, *Practical Charting Techniques* (New York: McGraw-Hill, 1969), p. 72.

Array Plots

Description: An $n \times n$ array of numbers shown by $n \times n$ cells. If an element $a(i,j) < y$, put a mark (color), if not leave blank. Rather than using a binary value system, the data can also be displayed with columns at the array intersections to give a 3D effect.

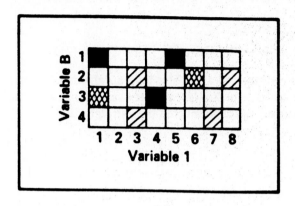

Input Data Type:

Multidimensional
Multivariate
Discrete

Use Category:

Deviation
Normal
Range
Status and warning
Pattern recognition

Specific Uses:

* Rapid assimilation of an array.

Comments:

* Similar to a 3D Column Chart that has been projected.

Reference:

G. H. Ball, *A Collection of Graphical Plots for Examining Multivariate Data*, Electric Power Research Institute, Palo Alto, California, AD 734 360, August 1967, p. 51.

Binary Indicator

Description: Simple indicator, such as a lamp, that lights when a certain limit of the variable has been exceeded, or vice versa.

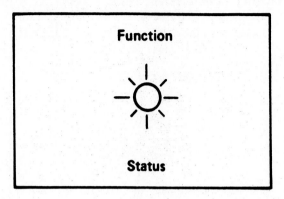

Input Data Type:

Unidimensional
Univariate
Discrete

Use Category:

Status and warning
Pattern recognition

Specific Uses:

* For annunciation of a limit violation.

Comments:

None.

References:

None.

Circular Profile

Description: Variation of the linear profile, in which the polygonal line connects points located on equally spaced rays, where the distance from the center represents the value for each variable. Each ray may have different units.

Input Data Type:

Multidimensional
Multivariate
Discrete

Use Category:

Approximate value
Deviation
Normal
Range
Pattern recognition

Specific Uses:

* To show the nature of a relationship between variables not having the same units.

Comments:

* Also called Polar Plots, Star Diagrams and Multivariate Polygons.
* Good mnemonic character.
* High dimensionality.

Reference:

J. H. Siegel, R. M. Goldwyn, and H. P. Friedman, "Pattern and Process in the Evolution of Human Septic Shock," *Surgery* 70(2), 232 (1971).

Appendix C

Color-Coded Matrix

Description: Grid with color used to indicate values for two independent but interacting variables. A matrix is established whose columns represent values of variable A by a series of colors. The matrix rows represent values of variable B, but use a different color series. The intersections of these colored rows and columns yield unique colors for those intersections.

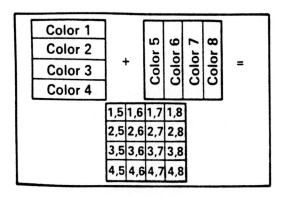

Input Data Type:

Duodimensional
Multivariate
Discrete

Use Category

Approximate value
Pattern recognition

Specific Uses:

* Cartographic statistical data.

Comments:

None.

Reference:

V. P. Barabba and A. L. Finker, "The Utilization of Primary Printing Colors in Displaying More Than One Variable," *Graphic Representation of Statistical Information*, Bureau of the Census, Technical Paper 43, 1978, p. 14.

Dendogram

Description: A node-link graph constrained NOT to be reentrant, i.e., a tree structure.

SEE REFERENCE

Input Data Type:

Multidimensional
Multivariate
Discrete

Use Category:

Status and warning

Specific Uses:

* To show the data relationships when a hierarchical clustering approach is used.

Comments:

* Limited to hierarchical structures.

Reference:

G. H. Ball, *A Collection of Graphical Plots for Examining Multivariate Data*, Electric Power Research Institute, Palo Alto, California, AD 734 360, August 1967, p. 59.

Deviation Bar Chart

Description: Chart with each item represented by a bar extending either to the right or left of a common vertical baseline to indicate the deviation from some "normal" value.

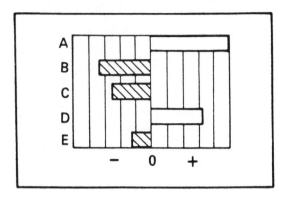

Input Data Type:

Unidimensional
Multivariate
Discrete

Use Category:

Deviation

Specific Uses:

* Presentation of positive/negative data for a number of items.

Comments:

None.

References:

C. F. Schmid and S. E. Schmid, *Handbook of Graphic Representation*, 2nd Ed. (New York: John Wiley and Sons, 1979), p. 71.

M. E. Spear, *Practical Charting Techniques* (New York: McGraw-Hill, 1969), p. 219.

Digital Readout

Description: Numeric display indicating the current value of the variable.

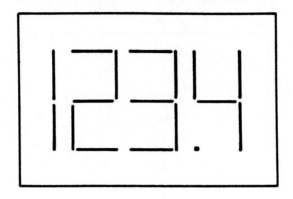

Input Data Type:

Unidimensional
Univariate
Discrete

Use Category:

Quantitative

Specific Uses:

* When very precise reading if a value is required.

Comments:

None.

References:

None.

Fourfold Circular Display

Description: Display with four quadrants used to represent different variables. The values of the
variables are indicated by the radius of the 90-degree arc associated with each variable.

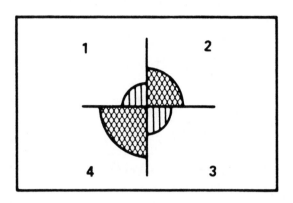

Input Data Type:

Multidimensional
Multivariate
Discrete

Use Category:

Approximate value
Status and warning
Pattern recognition

Specific Uses:

* Comparison tasks between different sets of four variable data.

Comments:

None.

Reference:

H. Wainer and M. Reisner, "Assessing the Efficacy of Visual Displays," *Graphical Representation of Statistical Information*, Bureau of the Census, Technical Paper 43, 1978, p. 83.

Frequency Polygon

Description: Display in which dependent variable is not necessarily time. The appropriate frequency of each class is located at the midpoint of the interval, and the plotting points are connected by straight lines. Similar to a Staircase or Step Chart.

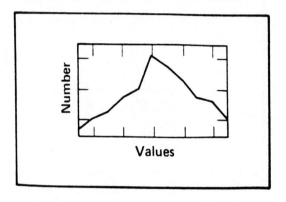

Input Data Type:

Unidimensional
Multivariate
Discrete

Use Category:

Approximate value
Pattern recognition

Specific Uses:

* Show continuous distribution.
* Recognize a "normal" distribution.

Comments:

None.

References:

C. F. Schmid and S. E. Schmid, *Handbook of Graphic Representation*, 2nd Ed. (New York: John Wiley and Sons, 1979), p. 119.
M. E. Spear, *Practical Charting Techniques* (New York: McGraw-Hill, 1969), p. 112.

Grouped Column Chart

Description: Chart with two or three columns representing different series or different classes in the same series. The related columns do not have spacing between them. Similar to a Simple Column Chart.

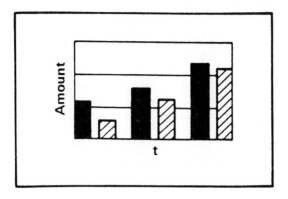

Input Data Type:

Unidimensional
Limited Multivariate
Limited series

Use Category:

Approximate value

Specific Uses:

* When comparing two or three independent series over a common period.

Comments:

None.

References:

C. F. Schmid and S. E. Schmid, *Handbook of Graphic Representation*, 2nd Ed. (New York: John Wiley and Sons, 1979), p. 85.

M. E. Spear, *Practical Charting Techniques* (New York: McGraw-Hill, 1969), p. 169.

Histogram

Description: Chart with vertical lines erected at the limits of the class intervals and with a series of contiguous rectangles or columns (interior lines may be deleted).

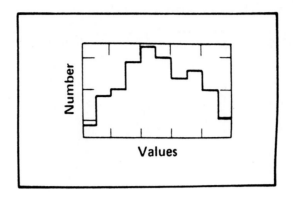

Input Data Type:

Unidimensional
Multivariate
Discrete

Use Category:

Approximate value
Pattern recognition

Specific Uses:

* Show the area of each rectangle that represents the respective class frequencies.
* Shows discrete series.
* Recognize a "normal" distribution.

Comments:

None.

References:

C. F. Schmid and S. E. Schmid, *Handbook of Graphic Representation*, 2nd Ed. (New York: John Wiley and Sons, 1979), p. 119.
M. E. Spear, *Practical Charting Techniques* (New York: McGraw-Hill, 1969), p. 115.

Linear Fourier Representation

Description: Display using a Fourier Series to generate a function of an angle *t* for each multidimensional point that is to be represented, i.e.,

$$F(t) = a/1.414 + b \cos t + c \sin t + d \cos 2t + ...,$$

where the coefficients of the trigonometric functions are the values of the variables.

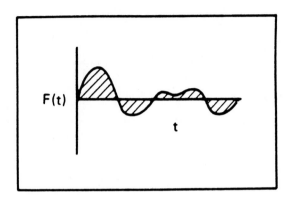

Input Data Type:

Multidimensional
Multivariate
Discrete

Use Category:

Status and warning
Pattern recognition

Specific Uses:

* To compare the interaction of several variables at the same time.

Comments:

* The first term determines the height of the function, *F(t)*, and the remaining terms determine its shape.
* Little emotional value.
* Low dimensionality.

Reference:

J. E. Mezzich and D. R. L. Worthington, "A Comparison of Graphical Representations of Multidimensional Psychiatric Diagnostic Data," in *Graphical Representation of Multivariate Data*, P. C. Wang, Ed. (New York: Academic Press, 1978), p. 123.

Linear Profile

Description: Chart with a polygonal line connecting the various heights corresponding to values of variables arranged along a baseline.

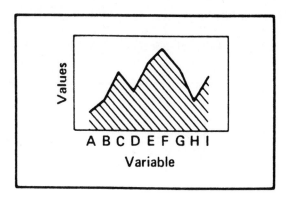

Input Data Type:

Multidimensional
Multivariate
Discrete

Use Category:

Approximate value
Pattern recognition

Specific Uses:

* To show the nature of a relationship between variables.

Comments:

* Better done with a Simple Bar Chart.

Reference:

J. E. Mezzich and D. L. Worthington, "A Comparison of Graphical Representations of Multidimensional Psychiatric Diagnostic Data," in *Graphic Representation of Multivariate Data*, P. C. Wang, Ed. (New York: Academic Press, 1978), p. 123.

Linkage Plots

Description: Plot with links established between nodes when a specified relationship exists. Each node and the center point of each link has a mnemonic label associated with it.

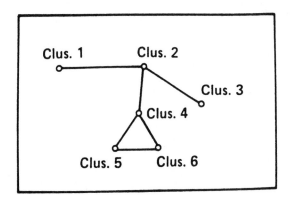

Input Data Type:

Multidimensional
Multivariate
Discrete

Use Category:

Status and warning

Specific Uses:

None

Comments:

None.

Reference:

G. H. Ball, *A Collection of Graphical Plots for Examining Multivariate Data*, Electric Power Research Institute, Palo Alto, California, AD 734 360, August, 1967, p. 53.

Lorenz Curve

Description: A special type of cumulative-frequency graph. Data are converted to percentages and arranged into "less than" types of cumulative-frequency distributions. The abscissa represents the percent cumulated from lowest to highest, and the ordinate shows the percent of the variable cumulated from lowest to highest.

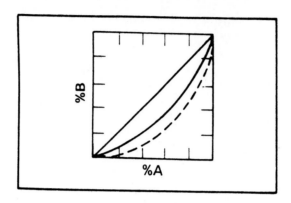

Input Data Type:

Unidimensional
Multivariate
Limited series

Use Category:

Status and warning

Specific Uses:

* Portray such data as the distribution of wealth and income in relation to certain segments of the population, the productivity of farms in terms of cumulative proportions of farms, distribution or retail sales as related to various groupings of stores, etc.

Comments:

None.

Reference:

C. F. Schmid and S. E. Schmid, *Handbook of Graphic Representation*, 2nd Ed. (New York: John Wiley and Sons, 1979), p. 136.

Mimic Diagram

Description: Diagram of alphanumeric and graphic representations of data related to a system in caricature form.

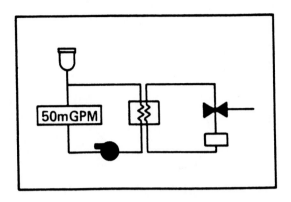

Input Data Type:

Multidimensional
Multivariate
Discrete

Use Category:

Quantitative

Specific Uses:

* When describing physical processes having variables with dissimilar units.

Comments:

* Used extensively in process control.
* A map is a mimic of a geographic entity.

References:

None.

Moving Pointer

Description: Display with a single moving line fixed at one end. The angle of inclination determines the current value.

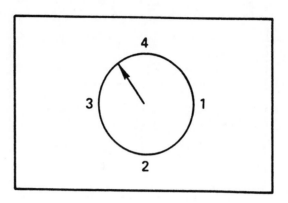

Input Data Type:

Unidimensional
Univariate
Discrete

Use Category:

Approximate value
Pattern recognition

Specific Uses:

* Historically used to indicate values, such as a time clock.

Comments:

* Good pattern recognition.

References:

None.

Multidimensional Scaling (MDSCAL)

Description: Display in which a multidimensional metric structure is inferred from nonmetric ordinal data, and is represented in a visualizable, geometric form, usually on a two-dimensional space. The points are arranged in the low-dimension vector space in such a way as to maximize the correspondence of the ranking of inter-point distances in that space to the ranking in the original, high-dimension vector space.

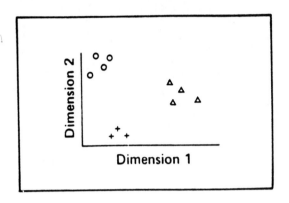

Input Data Type:

Multidimensional
Multivariate
Discrete

Use Category:

Status and warning
Pattern recognition

Specific Uses:

* For analysis of limited data types.

Comments:

* Washes out detail.

References:

J. E. Mezzich and D. R. L. Worthington, "A Comparison of Graphical Representations of Multidimensional Psychiatric Diagnostic Data," in *Graphical Representation of Multivariate Data*, P. C. Wang, Ed. (New York: Academic Press, 1978), p. 123.

J. B. Kruskal, "Multidimensional Scaling by Optimizing Goodness of Fit to a Nonmetric Hypothesis," *Psychometrika* **29**(1), 1 (1964).

Multiple Surface/Band Chart

Description: Chart with series of bands or strata depicting the components of a total series. Each band value is added to the previous value; the values are cumulative. The right side of the chart must be closed at the maximum abscissa value. Similar to a Simple Surface Chart.

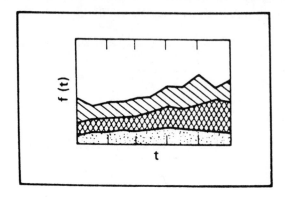

Input Data Type:

Unidimensional
Limited multivariate
Series

Use Category:

Approximate value
Prediction
Pattern recognition

Specific Uses:

* Same uses as Simple Surface Chart.
* When a general cumulative picture of components of a total series is to be shown.

Not to be Used:

* When changes in the movement of a series are abrupt.
* Where accurate reading of a component is of paramount importance.

Comments:

* Also called a subdivided surface chart.
* All the components must be related to the total.
* The sequence of bands should begin with the component of least movement.

References:

C. F. Schmid and S. F. Schmid, *Handbook of Graphic Representation*, 2nd Ed. (New York: John Wiley and Sons, 1979), p. 50.

M. E. Spear, *Practical Charting Techniques* (New York: McGraw-Hill, 1969), p. 141.

N-Axis Plot

Description: An extended 3D drawing where additional axes are added for each additional dimension.

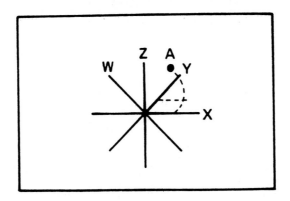

Input Data Type:

Multidimensional
Multivariate
Series

Use Category:

Status and warning

Specific Uses:

• Plotting points that are determined by a large number of coordinates.

Comments:

• Confusing due to the number of axes required.

Reference:

G. H. Ball, *A Collection of Graphical Plots for Examining Data*, Electric Power Research Institute, Palo Alto, California, AD 734 360, August, 1967, p. 36.

Net Deviation Column Chart

Description: Chart with the baseline is located above the bottom of the chart. The columns extend either above or below the baseline, but not in both directions. Similar to a Simple Column Chart.

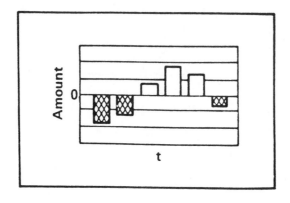

Input Data Type:

Unidimensional
Univariate
Limited series

Use Category:

Deviation

Specific Uses:

* When the emphasis is on increases/decreases, losses/gains, or deviation from a requirement or norm over a period of time.

Comments:

None.

References:

C. F. Schmid and S. E. Schmid, *Handbook of Graphic Representation,* 2nd Ed. (New York: John Wiley and Sons, 1979), p. 88.

M. E. Spear, *Practical Charting Techniques* (New York: McGraw-Hill, 1969), p. 180.

Paired Bar Chart

Description: Chart with each item represented by a bar emanating from both the left and the right of the same baseline. Different units and scales can be used for each set of bars.

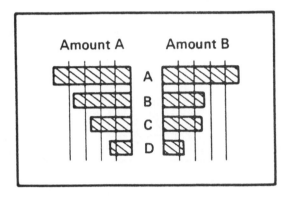

Input Data Type:

Duodimensional
Multivariate
Discrete

Use Category:

Approximate Value

Specific Uses:

* Two different horizontal scales may be used to compare a number of items in two respects.

Comments:

None.

References:

C. F. Schmid and S. E. Schmid, *Handbook of Graphic Representation,* 2nd Ed. (New York: John Wiley and Sons, 1979), p. 71.
M. E. Spear, *Practical Charting Techniques* (New York: McGraw-Hill, 1969), p. 213.

Perspective Plots

Description: Plot that induces the illusion of a third dimension by making size associated with a data point proportional to the slant range from the viewer's pseudo-position in data space to the position of the data point. A fourth variable can be added using tilt.

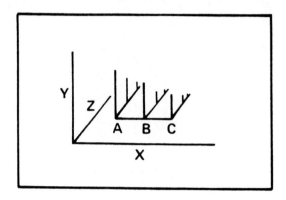

Input Data Type:

Duodimensional
Limited multivariate
Series

Use Category:

Approximate value
Deviation
Normal
Range
Prediction
Pattern recognition

Specific Uses:

* Realistic appearing display of 3D data.

Comments:

* Popular technique when used with Line Chart, Bar and Column Charts and Statistical Cartography.

Reference:

G. H. Ball, *A Collection of Graphical Plots for Examining Data,* Electric Power Research Institute, Palo Alto, California, AD 734 360, August, 1967, p. 31

Pie Chart

Description: Chart showing a circle whose interior is subdivided into wedges and shaded to represent portions of a total.

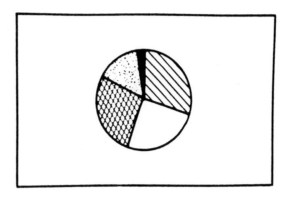

Input Data Type:

Unidimensional
Limited multivariate
Discrete

Use Category:

Approximate value

Specific Uses:

* Compares segments and shows their relation to the whole.
* Good for communication, but not analysis.

Comments:

* A Simple Bar Chart may be preferable, especially if analysis is involved.
* Usually has quantitative annotations.
* Also called a Sector Chart.

References:

C. F. Schmid and S. E. Schmid, *Handbook of Graphic Representation*, 2nd Ed. (New York: John Wiley and Sons, 1979), p. 146.

M. E. Spear, *Practical Charting Techniques* (New York: McGraw-Hill, 1969), p. 233.

Probability Plots of Ordered Distance

Description: See Reference below.

Input Data Type:	**Use Category:**
Multidimensional	Status and warning
Multivariate	
Discrete	

Specific Uses:

* Graphical plots of the statistical structure of multi-response data.

Comments:

* Limited to special cases.

References:

G. H. Ball, *A Collection of Graphical Plots for Examining Multivariate Data*, Electric Power Research Institute, Palo Alto, California, AD 734 360, August, 1967, p. 57.

M. B. Wilk and R. Gnanadesikan, "Graphical Methods for Internal Comparison in Multiresponse Experiments," *Annals of Mathematical Statistics* 35(2), 613 (1964).

Simple Column Chart

Description: Chart having an abscissa with a small number of values, while the ordinate has a greater number. Vertically oriented rectangles indicate the value of the independent variable by the length of the rectangle from a common horizontal baseline.

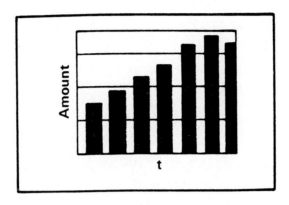

Input Data Type:

Unidimensional
Univariate
Limited series

Use Category:

Approximate value

Specific Uses:

* Depicting a small number of numerical values within a series, usually time. It can provide greater emphasis in portraying amounts in a single series.

Comments:

None.

References:

C. F. Schmid and S. E. Schmid, *Handbook of Graphic Representation*, 2nd Ed. (New York: John Wiley and Sons, 1979), p. 82.

M. E. Spear, *Practical Charting Techniques* (New York: McGraw-Hill, 1969), p. 163.

Simple Surface/Silhouette Chart (2D)

Description: Chart depicting a single series with shading, crosshatching, photographs or illustrations falling in the area between the data and the baseline. Similar to an Arithmetic Line Chart.

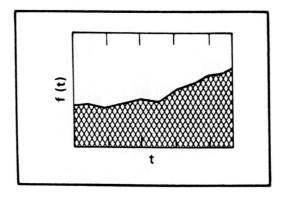

Input Data Type:
Unidimensional
Univariate
Series

Use Category:
Approximate value
Prediction
Pattern recognition

Specific Uses:

* When the magnitude of a series is to be emphasized.
* When some portion of a chart is to be accented for a specific purpose.

Comments:

* For 3D see Perspective Plot.

References:

C. F. Schmid and S. F. Schmid, *Handbook of Graphic Representation*, 2nd Ed. (New York: John Wiley and Sons, 1979), p. 50.

M. E. Spear, *Practical Charting Techniques* (New York: McGraw-Hill, 1969), p. 141.

Smoothed Frequency Curve

Description: Chart showing a smooth curve fitted to the sampled data. Similar to the Frequency Polygon.

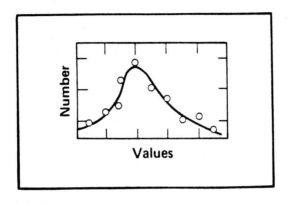

Input Data Type:

Unidimensional
Multivariate
Discrete

Use Category:

Approximate value
Pattern recognition

Specific Uses:

* Irons out or eliminates the accidental irregularities resulting from sampling errors.

Comments:

* Displayed data is not real but theoretical.

Reference:

C. F. Schmid and S. E. Schmid, *Handbook of Graphic Representation*, 2nd Ed. (New York: John Wiley and Sons, 1979), p. 121.

Spherical Projections

Description: Projection of three-dimensional data points onto a flattened sphere. Points with large residuals are indicated by an "x."

SEE REFERENCE

Input Data Type:

Duodimensional
Multivariate
Series

Use Category:

Status and warning

Specific Uses:

* Analysis in which data tends to fall on the surface of a hypersphere.

Comments:

None.

Reference:

G.H. Ball, *A Collection of Graphical Plots for Examining Data*, Electric Power Research Institute, Palo Alto, California, AD 734 360, August, 1967, p. 34.

Stereoscopic Plots

Description: Plot showing an axonometric projection of data onto two separate graphs, each with a slightly different viewpoint. When viewed with special equipment, a 3D impression is gained. Size and tilt could be used to add a fourth and fifth dimension.

SEE REFERENCE

Input Data Type:

Multidimensional
Limited multivariate
Discrete

Use Category:

Approximate value

Specific Uses:

* Display of 3D data.

Comments:

* Needs special viewing equipment.

References:

G. H. Ball, *A Collection of Graphical Plots for Examining Multivariate Data*, Electric Power Research Institute, Palo Alto, California, AD 734 360, August, 1967, p. 31.

J. R. Beniger and D. L. Robyn, "Quantitative Graphics in Statistics: A Brief History," *The American Statistician* **32**(1), 2 (1978).

Vector-Angle Plot

Description: Plot in which angles of a set of vectors are referenced to a common vector, given a particular data origin. The length of each vector can be indicated in the plot.

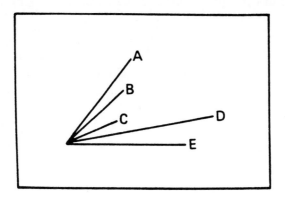

Input Data Type:

Duodimensional
Multivariate
Discrete

Use Category:

Approximate value

Specific Uses:

*   To display correlation measures of similarity.
*   For exploring the results of a principal component analysis or a factor analysis.

Comments:

*   Applicable mainly to analysis of data.

Reference:

G. H. Ball, *A Collection of Graphical Plots for Examining Multivariate Data*, Electric Power Research Institute, Palo Alto, California, AD 734 360, August, 1967, p. 61.